D1126647

PRISONS AND BEYOND

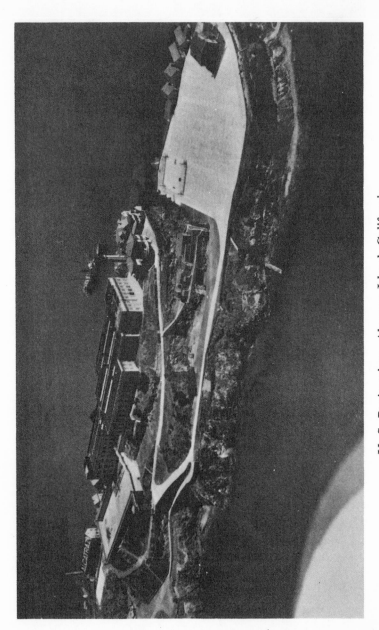

U. S. Penitentiary, Alcatraz Island, California.

PRISONS AND BEYOND

by

SANFORD BATES

BOOKS FOR LIBRARIES PRESS
FREEPORT, NEW YORK

First Published 1936
Reprinted 1971

INTERNATIONAL STANDARD BOOK NUMBER:
0-8369-5784-9

LIBRARY OF CONGRESS CATALOG CARD NUMBER:
72-157324

PRINTED IN THE UNITED STATES OF AMERICA

TO MY WIFE

ACKNOWLEDGMENTS

THE ACCOMPLISHMENTS described in this book of the Federal prison system are largely the result of the hard work and devotion of my associates: James V. Bennett, Esq.; W. T. Hammack, Esq.; Mr. Austin H. MacCormick; Dr. F. Lovell Bixby; Hon. Arthur D. Wood and the other Parole Board members, including Dr. Amy N. Stannard and Irvin B. Tucker, Esq., former members; Miss Nina Kinsella; Col. Joel R. Moore and Major Ray L. Huff. To them I desire to accord credit in the fullest manner.

I am grateful for the support of Attorneys General William D. Mitchell and Homer S. Cummings.

The suggestion for writing the book came from my friend Sheldon S. Glueck, to whom I am indebted for many valuable suggestions.

Especial thanks are due to Miss Isabel Smyth, for her intelligent and painstaking work with the manuscript.

CONTENTS

ix

ILLUSTRATIONS

PRISONS AND BEYOND

CHAPTER I

PROLOGUE

It was Armistice Day, November 11, 1918. The city of Boston, as did the rest of the world, breathed a huge sigh of relief and went off into orgies of patriotic frenzy. For a while to the accompaniment of the shrieking of the sirens I joined with the milling throng and participated in the "tumult and the shouting."

Of a sudden my mind reverted for some strange reason to the old Deer Island prison or house of correction. There were four hundred men confined on an island in the Boston Harbor who did not seem to be included in the celebration. They had no confetti to throw, and their noonday meal would consist of the good old Boston dish of baked beans—or possibly some chuck beef at two and one-half cents a pound (if it had been Friday they would inevitably have had fish chowder). I had had very little experience in the management of a penal institution up to that time, and no very clear idea as to the methods by which prisoners should be reformed, but the thought occurred to me, Why not let them in on the celebration? They were none of them very desperate individuals, and if they could partake of the exultation and inspiration so prevalent that day it might mark a turning point in their lives. I called up Judge Murray of the Municipal Court of Boston, an orator of no mean order, and informed him that he was going to have a chance to square himself with some of the men that he had sent "down duck." There had once been a little duck pond on Deer Island, from which rose the euphemism "to be sent down duck," meaning to be sent to Deer Island to serve any length of time from fifteen days to two years and a half.

The Judge, who was always ready to discharge a patriotic

or civic duty, said he would go. Dick Grant agreed to go down and lead the community singing. This boy could make anybody sing, and I had no doubt that he would be successful even with a bunch of jail inmates.

Somebody had to play the squeaking old piano. So my long-suffering wife agreed to go with us and perform this office. I say "long-suffering" advisedly at this time. You may think the prisoner suffers, or perhaps that the prisoner's family undergoes hardships, but the life of the wife of a prison warden or prison administrator is no bed of roses.

We contrived with the warden to have the prisoners assembled in the chapel at six o'clock. This arrangement was protested by some of the older officers. It had never been done before. It was one thing to let prisoners get together during the daytime, but at six o'clock it would be dark! Well, Armistice Day doesn't come very often, and we took the risk.

We were ferried in the lifeboat across Shirley Gut with its swift-running tides—the tradition was well circulated among the residents of Deer Island that these tides ran swiftly, and that a crossing could not be negotiated even by an expert swimmer. We found a somewhat surprised lot of men gathered in the chapel that night, the inmates no less so than the guards. Judge Murray made the best speech of his career. It is astonishing how an audience of prisoners often seems to challenge the best that is in the person who addresses it. Dick Grant said he had not heard such singing in all his experience—nor had any of us. After the first moment of embarrassment those men who had not sung for years furnished an exhibition of lung power which made the welkin ring. Mrs. Bates, who had never performed in public in her life, sang "The Americans Come," playing her own accompaniment on the twenty-five-dollar piano and, if I do say it, did a corking job. I have attended many patriotic meetings, but I have never seen a group more appreciative, more orderly, and more enthusiastic than this group of convicts.

I think that this performance was largely responsible for my intense interest in the prison problem which has kept me working at it ever since. I discovered that these prisoners were human beings after all. Perhaps they had families. If they had strayed into a recruiting station instead of a saloon, they might have been in France instead of Deer Island.

This was not the last assembly that I attended at the seventy-five-year-old House of Correction. I had been appointed Commissioner of Penal Institutions for the City of Boston by Honorable Andrew J. Peters six months before this. Mayor Peters served a four-year term as Mayor in between two of the recurring terms of the unquenchable James M. Curley. He seemed to think that I had helped him to get elected and rewarded me with the appointment as Street Commissioner. This was really what I wanted, but he didn't let me stay there and later appointed me Commissioner of Penal Institutions.

Let us hope that our reader will be gentle enough not to throw this up at me later on when we have something to say about the baneful effect of politics on the prison service. In my own defense let me also remind our reader that the Charter of the City of Boston requires that all appointments of heads of departments in the City of Boston shall receive the approval of the State Civil Service Commission. After due investigation and deliberation they found me properly "qualified by education, training and experience."

Nevertheless, my designation to such an office seemed rather absurd. While I had had much legal and legislative experience, I didn't know any more about prisons or jails than Mayor Peters did; but I promised to do the best I could until he found some one else. In a way this arrangement was advantageous. Some of the local politicians who were accustomed to demanding favors found that it made little difference to me when they threatened my removal if I did not acquiesce.

But the Armistice Day celebration was too much. It broke down my resistance. I reluctantly gave up the responsibility of taking care of the streets of Boston and with the help of Henry A. Higgins as Master of the Institution, and after further approval by the Civil Service Commission, tackled the job of administering Deer Island.

We established a school. We encouraged a debating society. We installed a system of partial self-government. We commenced to realize that prisoners were more than a series of numbers and that many of them had individual perplexities and questions to be solved. A temporary Naval prison had been occupying part of the Deer Island quarters, to the financial benefit of the city and the gastronomical advantage of the piggery. In the words of Tim Barrett, the genial pigman, "The garbage from the Navy barracks was swell swill." As a result we made a record-breaking success of the piggery. With the help of the reduction in our own population we turned back to the City Treasurer nearly $30,000 of the appropriation. This, as you may imagine, was a radical departure from accepted procedures in municipal departments.

Whether the latter circumstance attracted the attention of my frugal friend Calvin Coolidge, or whether he was actuated by the fact that I had occupied the next seat to him in the Senate of Massachusetts, I do not profess to know; but one evening as I sat at home the telephone rang. "Is this the Senator?" (To Calvin Coolidge any man who had ever served in the Senate with him was always a "Senator.") "This is the Governor. They tell me that you know something about the prison business."

"Well, I—"

"Come up and see me tomorrow."

And so, early in November of 1919, I dropped in to see the Governor. As usual he was unperturbed. No papers littered his desk. No secretaries raced in and out of his office. Nothing disturbed the peace and quiet of the surroundings. He told me that he had a number of appointments to make in the reorganization of some of the State departments, and that he would have to select a man for the State Department of Correction. He spoke to me about several mutual friends, including a colleague of ours in the Senate who then held the position of Commissioner. I mentioned several possibilities to him. He told me that he had offered the position to Charlie Davenport, an estimable lawyer in town. I couldn't think of any more competent man and offered to go to see Davenport and urge him to take the position. The Governor said I might do that, and added as I rose to go:

"Well, you had better do your best, because if he doesn't take it, I may have to offer it to you."

Davenport did not accept. One morning a few weeks later the telephone rang in my office in the City Hall, and over it came the Governor's nasal, Yankee voice. He recalled to me the conversation in his office, and then said:

"I am sending in your name to the Council for appointment as Commissioner of Correction this afternoon."

Whereupon, I said, "Why, Governor, I don't know what to say."

And the reply came back, "Don't say anything."

For nine years under Governors Coolidge, Cox, Fuller, and Allen I carried on as Commissioner of the Department of Correction for the State of Massachusetts. It was lucky for me that my predecessors had brought the penal institutions of Massachusetts to a high standard of efficiency and had provided an extremely progressive statutory framework for their administration. Likewise, was I fortunate in having the continued coöperation within the department of Senator E. C. R. ("Eddie" to almost every one) Bagley, Henry A. Higgins, and Seymour H. Stone, who were devoted to the difficult task of prison reform. There was plenty left to be done, but so closely was the administration of prisons regulated by statute that progress appeared extraordinarily slow. Between the Legislature and the Civil Service Commission and the Budget Bureau and the Commissioner of Administration and Finance, and the Governor's Council, it seemed as though one had to carry on a campaign of education before any innovations could be undertaken.

The prison industries of Massachusetts—thanks to the foresight of former Commissioner Pettigrove—were organized on an intelligent and progressive basis. The State-use system of prison labor largely obtained, but the inmates were paid no wages and had no incentive to work. For five years in succession the Department of Correction introduced a bill into the Legislature to permit the use of part of the surplus from the prison industries to pay wages to prisoners, and it was regularly rejected until it just naturally fell into the "hardy annual" class.

Only in 1928, with the help of the Massachusetts Civic League, did this carefully drawn Wages for Prisoners bill become a law. The Civic League rightly regarded the campaign for the Prisoners' Wage bill as a test of public sentiment on the whole question of the treatment of prisoners. Those in the Legislature who felt that punishment was the real end and aim of a prison commitment could see no reason for paying prisoners for their suffering. Those who perceived in a prison experience an opportunity to remake individuals or inspire them with a new feeling of self-reliance, and a new realization of their responsibilities to their families and to society, advocated the Prisoners' Wage bill with all of their energy and enthusiasm.

In 1928 there were seven roll-call votes in the Legislature on this question, most of them decided by a margin of one or a very few votes. I remember on one occasion meeting the redoubtable Martin Hays, a perennial member of the Legislature, a keen student and a resourceful debater with whom few of the more timid solons cared to clash swords. I asked Martin how he was going to vote on the Prisoners' Wage bill.

"Sanford, I won't listen to you. If you talk to me I might be convinced, and I don't want to be convinced." Thus frankly and somewhat jestingly, no doubt, Martin Hays expressed the attitude of many persons on the prison problem.

This time, however, there were just a few more legislators who were willing to take a chance, and the Prisoners' Wage bill finally prevailed and, to the surprise of the wise ones, was signed by Governor Fuller.

Mayor Peters had been a splendid boss. He had given me carte blanche at Deer Island and stood solidly behind me at every turn. So, indeed, had Governor Coolidge. On one occasion I had saved up several matters of unusual importance, involving general public policy, upon which I thought it necessary to obtain the counsel and advice of His Excellency. So I arranged a half-hour appointment with him. He was unhurried and imperturbable as usual. I took up the first matter. He listened carefully but vouchsafed no comment.

One by one, I unfolded the questions that had been bothering me; but on none of them did he commit himself. I finally told myself I was not getting anywhere, and as I arose to go the Governor dismissed me with this classic benediction: "Glad to have heard about your problems."

Even though I did get no advice, the solution of the problems became easier from having talked them over. In the last analysis we must solve our own problems, and on many occasions I found comfort in a saying of Dr. Guy G. Fernald, psychiatrist at the Concord Reformatory: "After all, there is only one right and one wrong. If you really want to find which is which, it is not so difficult."

During and after the War there was a slight reduction in the prison population, both in the State institutions and in the county jails, which were more properly known as houses of correction. This gave rise to a recurrence of agitation for the consolidation of the sixteen county institutions in the State under some kind of State supervision, and one of the bitterest battles ever fought in Massachusetts politics raged for several years between certain of the legislative leaders and the county politicians who were accustomed to being referred to in awed whispers as "the county rings."

Governor Channing Cox succeeded Calvin Coolidge, and he it was who plunged me into the middle of the contest with the county rings. I shall have something to say about the county jails of America later in this narrative. The houses of correction of Massachusetts were not so bad, but it was a foolish, expensive, and outmoded system which required every county to maintain its own penal system and its own jail. But try to get it away from them! The sheriffs and county commissioners will agree to coöperate just so long as it does not mean giving up any of the cherished perquisites of office.

The net result of the three years' battle for State control of county institutions was the passage of a law requiring the psychiatric examination of all prisoners in county jails. To this the county politicians agreed. "Let's find out who these men are whom we are taking care of before we undertake to do anything further with them."

For three years or more the Department of Mental Diseases, at an expense of $60,000 a year, tried to find out something definite about the misdemeanant prisoner—his mental condition, the social and environmental causes of his crime—and from a contemplation of these extremely valuable case histories came the conviction in my own mind that progress in the treatment of the criminal lay, first, in the adaptation of the penal administration to his individual needs, and, second, in the realization of the importance of crime prevention.

With the desire to utilize these case histories we formed the first official crime prevention commission in Massachusetts. Dr. Richard C. Cabot was chairman, and some public interest was roused in the whole matter of preventive activities. I have never changed my mind as to the importance of prevention.

In my early years of Massachusetts penal administration the outstanding problem grew out of the presence in the general prison population of so many prisoners of inferior mentalities. The feeble-minded, the psychotic, and psychopathic inferiors were just beginning to be recognized as a separate problem. Legislation defining the defective delinquent and suggesting special treatment and segregation for him had been passed in 1911, but nothing had been done. The establishment at Bridgewater of a separately managed colony for defective delinquents, divided into male and female sections, was accomplished by dint of great effort and had a distinctly favorable result, not only through providing special treatment for this group but through relieving the penal institutions of a number of individuals who were not susceptible to, nor indeed deserving, of the usual penal or reformatory treatment.

I have never lost sight of the importance of the proper application of psychiatry and the social sciences in the administration of prisons, and in a later chapter on "Science to the Rescue" I shall try to outline the significance of this relationship.

During the "reign" of Alvan T. Fuller, Packard automobile magnate, who came to national prominence at the time of the Sacco-Vanzetti trial, there occurred the periodical reaction against "coddling the prisoner." In my official connection with prison work I have seen the wheel of public opinion make two complete revolutions. During and just after the War the great heart of the public warmed towards the prisoner and ex-prisoner. He was a human being, after all. Give him a chance; put him on probation; don't degrade him by sending him to a damp, dark, dismal cell. About 1924 or 1925, however, there seemed to be an epidemic of serious crimes, hold-ups, robberies, murders. Whereupon the same prison régime which a decade before had been too severe now became too lenient. Prisoners must not be coddled, and investigations to determine whether prisoners were being brutally used were replaced by investigations to determine how much they were being indulged.

In the early days of the radio a profound impression was made upon the New England public by a concert which was broadcast from the Charlestown State Prison. Governor Fuller did not like the idea. He thought it was not quite fitting that men sent to the hoosegow for the commission of a crime should act as entertainers to the public. A great many of the public thought differently, however. We received five hundred and forty telegrams and eighteen hundred letters of a highly commendatory and extremely sympathetic nature. Several offers of marriage were received by the curly-headed colored boy whose marvelous voice thrilled his listeners when he sang "The Holy City." He had received his vocal training in a circus, and his education was probably about that of the first grade.

I felt that we had made a hit; that we had shown the great outside public that prisoners were not all bad, that they had traits and possibilities that could be cultivated, and that there was rather a poetic kind of justice in permitting these men who had wronged the public to return over the air some of the debt which they owed.

Governor Fuller was extremely alive to the importance of the prison problem. He wanted convicts to work. He wanted them to be treated fairly. A year after the radio concert, at his suggestion we designed an ornamental bookrack to be made by the men in prison just large enough to hold the six books that Lincoln read. (The Governor was a great admirer of Lincoln.) We determined that the following books would constitute the library: Weems's "Life of Washington"; "The Pilgrim's Progress"; the Holy Bible; Montgomery's "History of the American Republic"; "Aesop's Fables," and one other whose title has slipped my mind.

The racks were made. The books were purchased and were put on sale at twenty dollars a set, the proceeds to go to buy music for the prisoners. The Governor bought the first set. We immediately fished out the twenty-three hundred messages of appreciation that we had filed away at the time of the radio concert, and an announcement was sent to each of our admiring supporters. So quickly and completely had the wheel of public opinion turned in one year, however, that not one single set of books did we sell.

How difficult it is to analyze the public attitude towards this whole business of taking care of the prisoners and how unreasonable it sometimes seems!

I learned two important lessons from Governor Fuller. The first was that it was not enough merely to be kind to prisoners. I have always since been careful to defend the bestowal of privileges to prisoners as a whole on the basis that such privileges tend to improve the individual character of the prisoners and therefore ultimately to protect the community. Unless privileges can be so defended, they should not be bestowed.

In the second place I sensed the importance of equal treatment for all. As the years have gone by I have been more and more convinced that the greatest evil that can persist in a prison is to permit a preference of one individual or group over another. Any privilege or exemption in prison must be earned. However many exemptions and immunities the "big shot" may obtain on the outside through money or "pull," he must not be permitted to use either within the prison; and, as some of my later references may disclose, nothing is harder to enforce in the prison than this. I doubt if there is anything of greater consequence.

While admiring Governor Fuller I will say that he made it uncomfortable at times. He didn't seem to realize that accidents will happen, not only in the best regulated families, but in the best administered prisons. On one occasion a crazy Italian in some mysterious way obtained possession of a bootlegged revolver and shot and killed one of our best officers. Obviously the authorities at the prison could not have taken every precaution to prevent this. It is always easier to see where the administration has been lax after a thing of this kind happens than before.

We immediately plugged up every hole that we could. With the assistance of the State police we attempted to trace the source of the contraband firearm, and we tightened up on the rules and regulations. I left the Governor on a Friday afternoon about three o'clock, feeling that I had satisfied him that everything that could be done had been accomplished. I started off by automobile to attend the Harvard-Yale football game with Mrs. Bates. When I arrived at my brother's house near New Haven all was great excitement. The State police of Massachusetts and Connecticut had been combing the roads to find me, "on the Governor's orders." The next morning our children in Boston were alarmed by headlines across the whole front page to the effect that Governor Fuller had ordered the pursuit of the Commissioner of Correction by the State police in order that he might be interrogated on the recent killing at the State prison. I saw the Governor at the football game on the next afternoon, and he was his mild and genial self. That was "Allie" Fuller's style of operation.

But when we came to appointing a new warden later at

Charlestown he was the first to insist that no outside politician should be given the job, and that if it was possible to promote the deputy warden to the position, that should be done. He was more than glad to "hear about" my problems. He was only too anxious to help solve them.

It was during this era that the stormy petrel of Massachusetts politics, Frank A. Goodwin, from his position as Registrar of Motor Vehicles set out to help direct and manage the State and county penal institutions and to offer suggestions to the courts of the State whenever they made mistakes. On more than one occasion he decried the "coddling" of inmates at the Charlestown Prison. He it was who led the legions up to the State House in 1926 when the attempt was made to break down the parole and probation system and return to the era of old-fashioned punishment in our Massachusetts institutions. For two days the advocacy of the sterner system went forward; but later, when Herbert Parsons, myself, and others pointed out that there was less crime in Massachusetts rather than more, that Goodwin's own report was evidence of that fact, and that parole and probation not only did not increase crime but probably reduced it, the good old Commonwealth returned to normal and that particular billow in the crime wave was over.

My ardent interest in parole and its possibilities as a protective agency dates from this hearing. In a later chapter I shall point out how a misunderstanding of this much abused penal device has been disseminated throughout the country, and try to demonstrate what a simple and necessary piece of machinery it is and how unthinking any municipality would be to return from the modern device of parole to the older system of unsupervised release.

During my period of service in the Bay State I was brought into contact with many shining personalities. The wardens and superintendents of the institutions in the department were, with one or two exceptions, loyal and competent. But one of them stands out above the rest and should be long remembered by a grateful public for her pioneer work with women and girls. I refer to Mrs. Jessie D. Hodder, for twenty years Super-intendent of the Women's Reformatory at Framingham, for-merly Sherborn. Intelligent, courageous, kindly, and wise be-yond her generation, she built into the old brick and timbers of the Women's Reformatory much of her own charitable and Christian spirit. Her methods have been amply justified in the book which resulted from an invited analysis of the results of her methods.[1]

About this time I was happy to have had a hand in the compilation of data which later resulted in the publication of an epoch-making book on delinquency which should be read by every student.[2] Of what use is it to devote our time and energy to improving penal conditions unless we are willing to undertake a frank evaluation of our methods and practices? It is not particularly to the discredit of institution administra-tors that they have been apparently unwilling to do this. It is an extremely difficult task and probably they have not had competent assistants to undertake the project.

The notion that there might be certain established scientific criteria for the guidance of penal administrators intrigued me, and my interest in the prognostic table as a device for guiding the judgment of parole boards and prison administrators dated from this period. The superintendent and the staff at the Massachusetts Reformatory at Concord are entitled to high commendation for their participation in a very early, if not the first, attempt at scientific analysis of the reformatory problem. Not only the chapters on the prognostic device but the even more valuable parts of Dr. Glueck's book which establish the relationship between crime and social conditions have earned for it a permanent place in the literature on crime.

During my nine years at the head of the Department of Correction of Massachusetts many of the ideas which I shall try to set forth in this book, of course, became crystallized. I naturally acquired an interest in the situations in other States, and in 1925 attended my first International Prison Congress

---

[1] *500 Delinquent Women,* by Sheldon and Eleanor Glueck.
[2] *500 Criminal Careers,* by Sheldon and Eleanor Glueck.

at London. In 1926 the American Prison Association elected me its president. Inevitably I came to know most of the men and women who are carrying on institutional work in this country, and developed many highly prized contacts with workers in foreign nations.

Therefore, while occupation of this sort to many people may seem provincial or local in character, it naturally took on for me a national and international significance. When it was first suggested that I might transfer my activities from Boston to Washington, I declined with thanks, still not fully realizing the extent and importance of the Federal prison set-up.

The task of supervising the few Federal institutions then in existence was carried on by a Superintendent of Prisons who worked under an Assistant Attorney General in the Department of Justice. It so happened that this Assistant Attorney General was a dynamic and determined young woman by the name of Mrs. Mabel Walker Willebrandt. She obtained fame largely as a crusader for prohibition, her prowess as an advocate being such that she won almost every case in support of prohibition which the Department tried before the Supreme Court of the United States; meanwhile her work on behalf of the Federal prisons, though less spectacular, was an outstanding contribution.

The details of these accomplishments, carried out by Luther C. White, Superintendent of Prisons, and his successor Captain Albert H. Conner, formerly Attorney General of the State of Idaho, were all the more creditable in that there was little provided in the way of personnel or appropriations.

After the inauguration of President Hoover, Mrs. Willebrandt felt that there was every prospect that Congress would be disposed to carry out the recommendations of its committee and provide for the establishment of a prison bureau on a larger and more effective scale. At her request in April, I interviewed the Honorable William D. Mitchell, the new Attorney General and the only member of President Hoover's Cabinet known to be a Democrat.

I was at once impressed with Mr. Mitchell's quiet power of

concentration on the problem in hand, with his splendid legal training and uncanny memory for facts.

Presently the job in Washington came to take on the form of a challenge, and, if the truth were known, it was not too difficult to convince me that this invitation was an opportunity to attempt a really constructive piece of work.

However, this was a question that was going to be hard to decide. In my boyhood my sainted mother had helped to convince me that I was destined to be a lawyer. As long as I stayed in Massachusetts that was still possible. I had paid a high price for my legal education, working during the daytime from the age of fifteen and studying law in the night classes at the Young Men's Christian Association in Boston. To go to Washington meant to give up this hard-won prospect for the possibility of being connected with public service indefinitely. During 1917 and 1918 I had been a member of the Constitutional Convention in Massachusetts, and on one occasion a grizzled veteran of the law, Fred H. Williams of Brookline, had advised me in no uncertain terms on the folly of a public career. "Stick to the law" was his advice, thus preserving independence and amassing a fortune. And yet, once the virus is in the blood, once one has been inoculated with a desire for public service, it is hard to bring about a cure. How much Mr. Williams really believed in his own advice, I do not know; but I recall that later on his own son ignored parental counsel, by becoming county attorney, United States District Attorney, and Judge of the Superior Bench in Massachusetts. The emoluments that go with governmental positions may not be great, but there is nothing in private practice or business that can quite equal the satisfactions of public service.

And so, regretfully departing from my many and loyal friends in Massachusetts and after the customary embarrassment of a farewell banquet I came to Washington.

I was fortunate to find on the job an extremely able assistant in the person of William T. Hammack, and I soon induced Austin H. MacCormick, who is now Commissioner of Correction for the City of New York, and James V. Bennett of the Federal Bureau of Efficiency, who had shown an extraordinary grasp of the opportunities of prison work in his reports to Congress, to join me.

Without these men the work which we did, and which will be described in some of the following chapters, would have been entirely impossible. Their vision, their common sense, their utter honesty of purpose, their ability for endless, tireless work entitle them not only to my gratitude and appreciation but to that of the Government which they serve. Many a time and oft in the late watches of the night or at a lunch which lasted most of the afternoon, the four of us would argue, and debate, and differ, and eventually come to an agreement.

The first thing to be done, of course, was to adopt a policy. Both the Attorney General and the President had to be convinced that the course we proposed to follow was sound. The brief which we prepared in exposition of our policy was a justification of that kind of penal philosophy which looked beyond the date of a man's admission to a prison to the time of his discharge, and which justified the attempts which we proposed to make to improve, rehabilitate, and reëstablish Federal prisoners as a move in the direction of ultimate public protection.

The time eventually came when I was summoned to the White House. During that day the wires sang between the White House and the little Prison Bureau. Certain figures and statistics were wanted immediately—as to the number of prisoners in the Federal system, etc. Evidently the President was getting ready for the inquisition.

This was our first dinner at the White House (although I had broken bread with President Coolidge and his family, it was not at his Pennsylvania Avenue residence), and naturally we were somewhat agitated. My wife had one request to make of me, and that was that I refrain from breaking up crackers in my soup. As she sat at the round table in the main dining room between two elderly Senators, she eyed me rather apprehensively as the dishes of bright red potage were passed around the table. How relieved and vindicated I felt when I noticed the nonchalant way in which the President broke up crackers in his own dish of soup and ate it with evident relish!

After dinner the men mounted to the famous Lincoln room, and the President pointed out to us the very chairs—rescued from a cellar apartment—which appeared in the picture of the signing of the Emancipation Proclamation that hung on the wall.

After some desultory conversation, came the question which I had been expecting and which indicated the thought which the President had been giving to the problem.

"Mr. Bates, there are about 90,000 men in our State and Federal penitentiaries."

I had to admit this, because these were the figures we had given his office earlier in the day.

"Well, if you were provided with the utmost in the way of buildings, equipment, and intelligent help, how many of these 90,000 could be reformed?"

I tried to be conservative and said possibly two-thirds. Then came the question. It was the same question that had agitated Governor Fuller, and it was the question that had caused me many anxious moments:

"Which is the more important, to reform the 60,000 or to teach the 122,000,000 that crime does not pay? To which effort should we give most attention?"

I made the only answer possible:

"Why not do both, Mr. President? Why not so contrive the punishment of the 90,000 that it will be both deterrent and constructive? A prison need not be dirty, or lax in its discipline, or managed by grafting officials, or overrun with idle men, to exercise a deterrent effect. Men can be punished, and at the same time their bodies can be rid of disease and their minds cleansed of delusions. They can be subjected to a fair and equitable discipline. They can be kept busy at productive tasks, and they can be given opportunities for education and betterment without weakening the sanctions of the law."

This answer must have satisfied him, because a little later

Mr. Mitchell brought back word from the Rapidan fishing camp that our whole policy and program had received official approval by the President. We laid our plans to carry out this policy, and the legislation which was drafted during the summer of 1929 passed Congress [3] later in its entirety. Our organization of this Bureau under this mandate will be described in later chapters.

One thing we insisted upon, and in this matter we were supported not only during the Hoover Administration but with equal insistence during the Administration which followed—that if the work of prison administration was to be organized on a permanent and successful basis, it would have to be done by experienced career men and women and could not be subject to the control of party politics. Not only in the extensive field operations of the Bureau but in the Washington office this policy with very few exceptions has been adhered to.

We shall describe in Chapter X with some detail the methods employed to place upon a professional and secure basis the personnel of the Prison Bureau. It is enough to say now that this was the most important single accomplishment and will, it is hoped, have the most permanent results.

It was in the summer of 1930. I was spending a day or two in El Paso, Texas, in connection with the choice of a site for one of our new prisons, when the telephone rang. "Albany,

---

[3] H.R. 6807, Public No. 270, 71st Congress, to establish two new institutions; H.R. 7410, Public No. 201, 71st Congress, to establish a hospital for defective delinquents; H.R. 7412, Public No. 271, 71st Congress, to diversify employment of Federal prisoners; H.R. 7413, Public No. 202, 71st Congress, to create an independent parole board; H.R. 7832, Public No. 218, 71st Congress, to reorganize the Prison Bureau, to establish Federal jails, etc.; H.R. 3975, Public No. 310, to amend the probation law; H.R. 9235, Public No. 203, 71st Congress, to authorize the Public Health Service to provide medical service in the Federal Prisons; H.R. 9674, Public No. 777, 71st Congress, to make possible the more prompt deportation of alien criminals confined in the Federal penal institutions; H.R. 10598, Public No. 169, 72nd Congress, to provide for the transportation of certain juvenile offenders to states under the laws of which they have committed offenses or are delinquent; H.R. 10599, Public No. 210, 72nd Congress, to fix the date when sentence of imprisonment shall begin to run, provide when the allowance to a prisoner of time for good conduct shall begin to run and further to extend the provisions of the parole law.

New York, calling." Governor Franklin D. Roosevelt of New York was offering me the job of chairman of the newly created parole board of that State at a salary substantially in excess of the one I was receiving in the Federal Government.

The Federal job, however, was not half finished, and a few days later I regretfully declined this tempting offer.

In 1932 my opportunities for contacts with foreign penologists were increased when I was appointed by President Hoover to be the sole Commissioner on the part of the United States on the International Prison Commission. In a sense this rounded out the prison experience of nearly twenty years in city, State, national, and international relations.

In November, 1930, I received a telegram signed by Homer S. Cummings. The message inquired if I would be willing to help the sender of the telegram examine into the condition of affairs at the Connecticut State Prison and prepare material for a report. I remembered the name of Homer Cummings but I had not had the pleasure of meeting him and knew nothing of his interest in prison matters. It happened that I was soon to spend a week-end in Connecticut, and I arranged to visit the old Wethersfield Prison and later to spend three Sundays with Mr. Cummings and his committee. My respect and admiration for this tall distinguished Connecticut lawyer heightened and deepened as the investigation drew to a close, and I do not think this feeling was entirely on account of the fact that he seemed to think that my notions about prison administration were sound.

I could not accept the fee which he tendered me for the service, as Government employees on salaries are not supposed to work for a State or municipality, but I prize most highly among my souvenirs the letters of appreciation from this brilliant, progressive, and humane man. Little did I think at this time that Governor Roosevelt would be President, and that Mr. Cummings would be my immediate chief as head of the Department of Justice.

When the Administration changed in 1933, many of my

politically minded friends were anxious to write letters for me
or "to see the right people." But we all felt that, if we were
correct in assuming that the Prison Bureau had been built
upon a nonpartisan basis, we should have to continue in
operation on that same basis or not at all.

When I found that Mr. Cummings had been appointed
Governor General of the Philippines and the late Senator
Thomas J. Walsh of Montana had been selected to be Attorney General, I wrote a letter to the new Governor General
congratulating him on his appointment, and received a most
courteous and friendly reply, in which he said that, had he
been nominated Attorney General of the United States, it
would have been his intention to ask me to stay. Within five
days from the date of that letter he was, and he did.

A few days after Inauguration the new Attorney General tendered me a reappointment as Director of the Bureau of
Prisons. I am confident that this action on his part was based
upon a desire to put the prison work of the country on a plane
of business and professional permanence and forever remove it
from the domain of partisan politics. He has never swerved
from that determination.

For the patient and wise counsel and the continued support
of Attorney General Mitchell we had always been most grateful, and to no less extent are we indebted to Attorney General
Homer S. Cummings. Of an entirely different type of personality he has, nevertheless, on repeated occasions shown his complete understanding of the problems underlying prison work.
Placid but dynamic, urbane and farseeing, with a thorough
grounding in practical politics and the practice of the law, he
wanted the Prison Bureau expanded and enlarged to enable it
to fulfill its higher functions. The origin of the idea of a
penitentiary at Alcatraz Island was in his own mind, and the
fact that we have been able to carry out this project to his
complete satisfaction is cause for gratification.

Neither President Coolidge nor President Hoover was familiar with the details of prison administration, but President
Franklin D. Roosevelt not only is possessed of the requisite

sympathy and understanding but has a knowledge of details of prison administration, parole, and probation which is positively astonishing.

No less of an inspiration to our Bureau has been the sympathetic altruism towards the underprivileged and the unfortunate which is the outstanding characteristic of Mrs. Roosevelt. Whether the relations with other departments and bureaus are on the same friendly and understanding basis, we do not know. But there has been a certain security and satisfaction in the feeling that we have a man and woman at the helm of our national affairs who can be absolutely relied upon to judge every case from a humane viewpoint.

As evidence of the President's amazing versatility and his grasp of details let me cite one conference which I had. Our prison labor program had struck a snag. It was necessary every year to reappropriate the funds with which to carry on our industries in the various Federal institutions. Some of the representatives of industries affected (textile, boot and shoe, etc.) were of opinion that their business was being interfered with more than that of some other industries. They felt that perhaps the Attorney General wasn't quite able to see their side of the situation.

So a bill was proposed to turn over the control of the industries in the Federal institutions, at least as to the determination of the extent to which each industry should be permitted to compete with outside business, to a board on which labor, industry, the farmer, and the consumer should be represented. In return for this concession it was agreed that the annual appropriation of the funds should be eliminated and, in order that a continuous and uninterrupted policy might be developed by the representative board, the money would be handled on a corporate basis without reference to annual appropriation bills.

Perhaps without thoroughly understanding the importance of the legislation, officials of the Federation of Labor were led to oppose it; it seemed very doubtful if the bill could pass, and the future of the Federal prison industries, based as they were upon legislation calling for an exclusive state-use plan, was jeopardized.

One rainy morning I got a call from the White House. "The President would like to see you and Mr. William Green at 11 : 45."

My associate in charge of industries, James V. Bennett, and I spent one-half hour in the President's anteroom with the president of the American Federation of Labor and several of his advisers. On principle we were not very far apart to start with. The stand taken by the American Federation of Labor leaders has never been a destructive one so far as prison labor is concerned.

When we were ushered into the President's office, we were met by the invariably hearty greeting from this indomitable man.

"Hello, Bill," he said to Mr. Green. "We have a little problem here that we want you to solve for us."

I caught up my breath in amazement at this manner of approach.

"We all agree that prisoners must work at something, and we just want you to tell us what this work should be."

Mr. Green discussed what he considered the objectionable feature of the bill.

"Mr. President," he remonstrated, "this bill removes the matter from the annual appropriation bill."

(Now, I thought to myself, the President is stumped. He will turn to me and say, "What about that, Mr. Bates?" But not so. As a matter of fact, it was not necessary at any time during that interview for the President to ask me or any one else as to the details of the subject in hand.)

"Well, of course, it does. That is exactly what we want it to do. How can we develop a constant continuous program of prison industry if every member of Congress is to be permitted each year to amend an annual appropriation act?"

I made just one suggestion during that interview. At the appropriate time I suggested, "Well, perhaps the language of the bill is faulty, and I have no doubt that we can amend it to meet Mr. Green's objections," and the interview was over. We did amend it; Mr. Green withdrew his objections, and the bill became a law.

When has there been a First Lady in the White House who has personally inspected prisons and prison camps? I have had the rare privilege of being present on several occasions when Mrs. Roosevelt, driving her own blue roadster and with Mrs. Morgenthau or Miss Lorena Hickok as her sole companions, visited our institutions. The intelligent interest and unaffected manner in which she talked with inmates and informed herself at first hand of conditions not only were stimulating to us but make an occasion to be long remembered at these institutions.

As every one knows, Mrs. Roosevelt receives thousands of letters daily, and some of them find their way into the Prison Bureau, each with a little note of inquiry or a request that we do what we can for the unfortunate writer of the letter. All who have come in contact with this remarkable woman are astonished at the breadth and variety of her interest and marvel at the manner in which she finds time to accomplish all that she does. Her hospitality is unbounded. On several occasions we have enjoyed the rich but simple hospitality of President and Mrs. Roosevelt. Whether it is a formal dinner or scrambled eggs on Sunday evening, one is sure to find this remarkable couple interested in the guests and full of the joy of living.

While my years of striving to understand the crime problem and its many ramifications have, as might be expected, led me at times in ways that were dark and devious and full of doubt; they have likewise made possible a personal acquaintance with some of the outstanding figures of our times, both here and abroad. With their help the problem will not forever remain unsolved.

*   *   *   *

In the following pages after a brief introductory chapter I shall go more into detail as to the structure and administration of the Federal penal system; and in order to lay the proper background I will discuss, first, the administration of our county prisons on the theory that they are the most numerous, and that they are in the worst condition.

Second comes a consideration of what is wrong with the prison system. Why do we say prisons have failed, and why do prisoners riot? We describe how the Federal prison system recognizes the existing deficiencies, and with the aid of science has built what some day may become a model system.

Some of the practical problems in the administration of the prison and in the supervision of the system will then be discussed. Impressions will be given of what the prisoners think about at times, pointing out that their problem is not solely an individual one but involves their families and society. What happens when the prison door swings open leads us to an examination of the parole system, its weaknesses, and its possibilities. Can prisons be made to fulfill a useful function? What price can we afford to pay for good prisons? Is such an investment justified? What price will society pay if we do not improve conditions? What price prisons anyway? Will the prison of the future be on the present model? Shall we go back to the bastiles of the past? Shall we find some superior alternative to imprisonment in the form of probation, prison camps, or even prison colonies?

While the whole topic of crime and its repression cannot, of course, be adequately covered without stressing the fundamental importance of community efforts at prevention, that is not primarily the task of the prison administrator and will therefore merely be referred to herein as of paramount importance.

In short we shall endeavor to interpret to the public the function and purpose of a prison and prove our contention that a prison system so contrived as to aid in the reformation of its inmates offers ultimately the best protection to society.

CHAPTER II

WHY PRISONS

Our age and history, for these thousand years, has not been the history of kindness, but of selfishness. Our distrust is very expensive. The money we spend for courts and prisons is very ill laid out. We make, by distrust, the thief, and burglar, and incendiary, and by our court and jail we keep him so.

EMERSON—*Man the Reformer.*

IN the last two decades there has been an astonishing increase in the interest and concern which the general public has manifested in the conduct of our prisons. One can read the history of the growth and development of our American commonwealths during the whole of the nineteenth century and find no more than a few references to the prison problem. No one seemed to know very much about what went on inside these grim edifices, and the attitude of the warden was that the conduct of the penitentiary was his responsibility alone.

In the early part of the century, it is true, considerable agitation raged among those directly concerned as to the respective merits of the Pennsylvania and Auburn systems of penitentiaries. Industrialists occasionally protested against the exploitation of prison labor. The Friends Society in Pennsylvania, the Prison Discipline Society of Boston, and other altruistic organizations from time to time raised their voices in protest against what they considered to be prevalent abuses.

The American Prison Association was founded in 1870, and President Rutherford B. Hayes was one of the early leaders in that movement. No more farsighted set of standards has ever been enunciated than the Declaration of Principles adopted by the American Prison Association at its inception.[1]

[1] The American Prison Association still functions under the able leadership of E. R. Cass, General Secretary, with offices at 135 East Fifteenth Street, New York. The Declaration of Principles is set out in full as Appendix A.

25

So progressive and idealistic were these principles that they have, even after all these years, been scarcely realized in many States throughout the country.

But by and large the general public knew little and cared less about prisons.

Since the beginning of the twentieth century, however, the situation has materially changed. Ex-prisoners with a talent for journalism have written books in which they have unsparingly criticized the administration of the institutions in which they have been incarcerated. Crime commissions in the various States have called attention to the inadequacy of our penal systems. Moving pictures, such as "The Big House," "I Am a Fugitive from a Chain Gang," and "20,000 Years in Sing Sing," have been seen by millions of our fellow citizens. The large increase in the number of people who have been sent to prison since 1900 had no doubt broadened the general interest in the subject. The series of disastrous prison outbreaks during 1929 and 1930 focused public opinion on the prison problem to a significant degree.

The development of commercial racketeering in our great cities, and the increasing menace of organized crime, resulted when the criminal utilized swifter transportation, improved methods of defense and attack, and capitalized the fact that some of his criminal activities were not entirely obnoxious to many of his fellow citizens. One of the curious and shameful manifestations of American public life of the last two generations is the acclaim and admiration which have been accorded the successful gangster criminal.[2]

The heightened apprehension of our communities with reference to the growing menace of predatory crime inevitably carried with it a greater anxiety as to the security of our prisons and their general efficiency. The prisoner and the ex-prisoner have been thrust into the consciousness of our present generation to a greater degree than ever before.

I do not propose to discuss at any great length the general subject of crime, its cause, cost, and cure. Many admirable

[2] See e.g., *Mrs. Astor's Horse,* by Stanley Walker, p. 53.

books have been written on the subject of criminology, the titles of some of which appear in the Bibliography.

Generally speaking, the contributors to criminology fall into two classes: (1) writers who have seriously and intelligently studied the question, consulted the published statistics and who may be said to know something about the matter; and (2) prophets of disaster (all too numerous, I am afraid) who write articles or books based upon hunches or prejudices and do not hesitate at any exaggeration or distortion so long as the book or pamphlet makes a startling or scandalous statement of what they believe to be the situation.

Crime always we have with us. So far as recorded history goes, we have always had it with us; and that man is indeed an optimist who believes that any set of statutes or economic formula or political panacea will do away with it.

The belief most tenaciously held to by the large majority of people that there is a deterrent force in punishment has even been seriously questioned. We have defined a crime as an act committed against the expressed wish of the majority, either as inherited from the common law of England or as reflected in legislation, which carries with it the possibility of punishment.

By adopting this definition we could undoubtedly maintain the proposition that the United States of America is the most criminal nation on earth. Perhaps we have more crime because we have more crimes to commit. Perhaps we have carried the notion of personal liberty too far and have thrown safeguards around the criminal or potential criminal which are not in the interest of the general public. Perhaps our attempt to confer the rights and privileges of democratic citizenship upon people of so many cultural stocks has been more concerned with the granting of privileges and immunities than with the imposition of duties and obligations. Perhaps our educational systems have been faulty. Perhaps we have not yet discovered a valid substitute for the old-time religion.

Whatever the reason, we are harassed and perplexed by the vaulting numbers of lawless persons who seem to require some kind of public discipline which more often than not results in their incarceration in places which we call—with a somewhat naïve hopefulness—training schools, reformatories, and penitentiaries. It will do us little good to refer to the oft repeated comparison between this country and England and other foreign countries. Suffice it to say that such comparisons do not usually redound to our credit as a law-abiding nation.

Nor can I think of anything more futile than to guess at the cost of crime. Probably nowhere else in the treatment of contemporary crime problems has the imagination of the writers been permitted to such an extent to run riot. Those with imaginative brains and busy pencils have repeatedly given out to the country that crime costs fifteen billions of dollars a year. The fact that the total expense of government, Federal, State, county, and municipal, is around thirteen billions does not deter them. The National Commission on Law Observance and Enforcement (Wickersham Commission) filled one of their voluminous volumes with a discussion of this subject, and the following is the result of their investigation:

> It is wholly impossible to make an accurate estimate of the total economic cost of crime to the United States. This is true whether we look at the immediate cost of crime to the tax-paying and property-owning public and the individuals composing it, or whether we consider the net ultimate cost to the community as a whole. Many "estimates" of the total cost have been made, but they, in our opinion, have only been guesses; and we do not feel that any useful purpose would be served by still another guess.[3]

From tables which appear in the studies of the cost of crime by the National Commission on Law Observance and Enforcement, the nearest guess that I have been able to make as to the total estimated annual cost of crime in the United States is $1,070,836,331.77. I submit that this estimate is about as reliable as many others that have been made.

Just what good it does us to be told the sum total of all the money which some of us have stolen from the rest of us, plus what the criminals who are now in jail might have earned if

[3] National Commission on Law Observance and Enforcement, Report No. 12, *Cost of Crime*, p. 442.

they had been out of jail and able to get a job, plus the salaries of all those who are engaged in law enforcement work—plus a lot of other items, is hard to understand.

We can be satisfied with the statement that the energies and the productive capacity of altogether too many men are diverted not only into criminal activities but into efforts expended on the governmental control of these activities. It is easy to visualize the tremendous impetus that would be given to public education and cultural development if the amount of money used to combat crime could be employed in a more constructive effort.

Nor can one be dogmatic in these days as to the cause of criminal behavior. The Wickersham Commission after two years of deliberations and officially disposed of this phase of their inquiry in three paragraphs, one of which states:

We find it impossible comprehensively to discuss the causes of crime or factors in non-observance of law. Criminology is remaking, the social sciences are in transition, and the foundations of behavior are in dispute. It would serve no useful purpose to put forth theories as to criminality or non-observance of law, either generally or in America, on the basis of some one current psychology or social philosophy, with the certainty that it represents but one phase of the thought of the time and will not long hold the ground. For the same reasons, it would be quite as useless to develop the potentialities of each of the current theories.[4]

One of the best reports promulgated by the Wickersham Commission contains a critique of studies in criminal causation by Morris Ploscowe. In his concluding paragraph he states:

Crime is not one act but an aggregate of acts whose only essential common characteristic is that the State has deemed it necessary to prohibit them for the protection of individual interests or the furtherance of the general security. Crimes differ in nature, in seriousness, in apparent motivation, in the kinds of behavior they demand. They emanate from different types of personality and different kinds of social environmental situations. These variations in the elements that go to make up crime

[4] Report No. 13, *Causes of Crime*, p. vii.

lend support to the contention of the writers who state that there is no unit cause of crime.[5]

We can say, however, that the fact that we are unable to isolate any single cause of crime does not mean that we must not recognize certain tendencies or factors in our current civilization which seem to be the accompaniment, if not the motivation for, criminal activity.

The most convincing studies in the etiology of crime come, in my judgment, from the sociologists. After an experience of twenty years in the administration of institutions for the care and treatment of criminals and delinquent classes I have no hesitation in asserting that the progress of the coming generation in crime repression will be measured by the degree to which our communities succeed in improving social and economic conditions.

The temptation to discuss the breakdown of the family relation, the changing concepts of religious belief, the doubt of supernatural authority, the effect of bad housing conditions, the influence of the moving pictures, the radio, the tabloid and other modern instruments of culture, the indifference to the majesty and authority of the law engendered during the prohibition era, the worship of monetary success and affluence no matter how attained, the creaking wheels of our ancient machinery of criminal justice, the toleration by the people of certain kinds of lawlessness, must be resisted. They are among the subjects which the intelligent prison man of today often discusses; but these are not to be the subject of this book.

The greatly improved, and the constantly increasing number of reliable statistics being gathered by the Department of Justice, the Federal Bureau of Investigation, and the Bureau of the Census in Washington, together with the large number of private studies will throw more and more light upon these subjects and assist in their ultimate solution.

Some writers have maintained that we are all more or less antisocial by disposition, and have expressed the belief that

[5] *Op. cit.,* p. 138.

there is no living human being who has not at some time or other committed a crime. At least we will admit that many of us have been sorely tempted (relatively few, fortunately, ever get actually committed to a prison or jail). Others contend that it is not the threat of a prison sentence that keeps us from crime but our early training, our predilection toward self-respect and general aversion to criminal behavior. Few have gone so far, however, as to contend that prisons can be abolished.

What actual effect the conduct of our prisons and penal institutions has upon the problem of crime repression perhaps cannot be accurately stated, and yet to some extent the prison has become symbolical in the minds of many people of the retributive power of the government. This feeling, together with the increasing number of persons committed and an awakened interest in prison problems has led to a constantly strengthening demand for a newer kind of prison and a more intelligent and constructive type of prison administrator.

Viewed in the long light of history the use of the prison as a place of punishment is comparatively modern. The idea of the penitentiary as a place of penitence is new. The word "prison" is as old as the language. Lexicographers tell us that the word is derived from the Latin *prehendere,* meaning "to seize."

"I was in prison, and ye came unto me."

When the Scriptures referred to people in prison the writers had in mind those who had been seized and were awaiting their punishment. It was not until the latter half of the eighteenth century that the practice of incarcerating or segregating prisoners for extended periods in a closely built structure for the purpose of punishment was adopted. Before that time there were only isolated instances where certain monasteries were used for purposes akin to those of imprisonment.

Probably those who guided the destinies of the governments of the world one hundred and fifty years ago did not adopt imprisonment as a remedy for crime until they were forced to do so. There were plenty of other methods of punishment which had been practiced from early days—execution, exile, mutilation, disfranchisement, enslavement, attainder, the stocks, the pillory, and the ducking stool had all been tried. One has but to read the first half of Wines' book on "Punishment and Reformation," or "The Crime of Punishment" by Margaret Wilson, to realize and shudder over the extent to which the mind of man had gone in devising deterrent methods for the control of criminal conduct.

The humanitarian reversion against the awful and continuous slaughter of petty criminals in England at the end of the eighteenth century was followed by an era of deportation and penal colonization. And, in turn, it was no doubt the growth of commerce with the establishment of readier means of communication that finally put an end to the system of expatriation as a means of segregating and punishing criminals. We should have to search the seven seas today to find those unoccupied islands which held themselves so ready for this purpose one hundred and fifty years ago.

Perhaps, therefore, it may be said that our forefathers at the end of the eighteenth century built penitentiaries because there was nothing else to do with the criminals with whom they were confronted. Hitherto jails had existed and prisons had been built solely for the temporary retention of offenders.

Some years ago I had the privilege of visiting the old prison in Ghent, Belgium, erected in 1772 by that benevolent Austrian Princess, Maria Theresa, then temporarily exercising sovereignty over the Low Countries. This structure is said by some to be the oldest institution of its kind now in use. In many of its features it combines much that would meet the approbation of present-day penologists.

The "Panopticon" of Jeremy Bentham has been quoted by almost every writer on criminology as the forerunner of the modern prison. It had for its object the housing of large numbers of prisoners in such a way as to be always under observation. Here, again, it is interesting to note that the State of Illinois recently experimented at Statesville with the circular type of prison which was a modern replica of the old Panopticon. The trouble seemed to be that in spite of the suggestive name of this prison the one guard supposed to be stationed in the middle could not keep his optic on everybody at the same time.

Thus it was that the jail or prison as a place of detention became enlarged and developed into a place of punishment. Certainly, then, if it was to be a place of punishment, it must not be comfortable, and from all accounts it certainly was not.

It did not take many decades for pioneers like John Howard, Elizabeth Fry, and Charles Dickens to point out the inherent difficulties in such a system of punishment. The first and most obvious objection to the early prison was the fact that all classes had to be indiscriminately herded together. One conjures up a picture of the Black Hole of Calcutta, the Château d'If in Marseilles harbor, the Conciergerie and the Bastile in Paris, or the Marshalsea prison in England.

When men were put in prison merely to decide what other torture should be inflicted upon them, there was no particular reason for separating them, and when governments extended the use of prisons as substitutes for or to supplement other kinds of punishment, it never occurred to any one that there was any necessity for keeping individuals separated or even classified. But the dreadful results of such treatment were not long in being recognized.

It was easy to prove that the more impressionable and sensitive prisoner became contaminated by association with the vicious type, that tuberculosis was frequently contracted, that prisoners went insane and died by the score; and eventually the conscience of the community was aroused. It was perhaps inevitable when the change came that the handling of prisoners in England and many European countries should go almost to the other extreme of solitary confinement.

Following the French Revolution, therefore, both England and the countries of western Europe, being denied access to further penal colonization, had to give serious attention to the construction of new prisons. Somebody had told them that the recently settled country of the United States of America had erected some novel prison buildings.

De Beaumont and De Tocqueville of France and an intelligent barrister named Crawford from England came to America at different times, and strangely enough their glowing reports of our early cellular prisons did much to establish the type of prison construction which has remained almost unchanged in most of western Europe until the present time.

The attempt of our ancestors to house State prisoners more securely than could be done in the county jail resulted in the erection of the Eastern Penitentiary in Philadelphia, the Charlestown Prison in Boston and the ancient Auburn and Sing Sing prisons in New York State. All of these early American prisons were built with the idea of segregation and with the intention of avoiding the criticism which had been heaped upon the makeshift prisons and jails of the older countries.

The Pennsylvania System was somewhat different from the one proposed at Auburn. In the Eastern Penitentiary at Philadelphia the cells were larger. There was room for the occupant to do some work in each cell. He also had a private yard in which to exercise; but he had no communication with his fellows, and his reformation was to be accomplished through penitence and introspection.

In Auburn the cells were smaller and built upon an interior gallery, but the occupants were allowed to work in association during the day, provided they did not talk with one another.

These systems came to be known, therefore, as the separate system and the silent system. Charles Dickens in his "American Notes" was lavish in his praise of the interior cell-block system, but the other European investigators preferred the Pennsylvania or separate system.

Strangely enough, practically all of the cellular prisons built in this country during the nineteenth century followed the Auburn model, while England and western Europe followed the Pennsylvania plan. In visits to eleven countries of western Europe I have never seen anything resembling the menagerie, or galley cell-block, type of prison which was so generally adopted in this country.

The first era in the history of prisons as places of punishment may be said to have closed with the general acceptance of the cellular type of State prison or penitentiary. The second era ended with the recognition that something more than mere incarceration would be necessary if the prison was to fulfill its function.

Perhaps the first undertaking in the way of superimposed reformation of which we have record was by Pope Clement XI at Rome in 1704. Over the door of the hospital of St. Michael was inscribed, "For the correction and instruction of profligate youth, that they who when idle were injurious, may when taught become useful to the State." And in the hall where the boys were at work appeared the inscription, "It is of little advantage to restrain the bad by punishment unless you render them good by discipline." [6]

But generally speaking the third era began, in this country at least, with the development of the reformatory idea about 1875. During the last fifty years we have made spasmodic attempts at reformation. We have ameliorated much of the misery and degradation which had so long been tolerated in our penal institutions, but it has been only very recently that we have been willing to courageously face the growing importance of our impending prison problem.

We have not been satisfied with sending men to prison *as* punishment. We have clung to the idea that men have been sent there *for* punishment.

We are commencing to wonder whether civilized communities can justify the continuation of the southern chain gang; whether our toleration of the filthy county-jail systems in many of our States can be viewed with complacency, and whether the type of prison described in "Ann Vickers" does not do infinitely more harm than good. One thing is true— we cannot longer continue to close the doors of our prisons and forget the human problems that are locked inside.

[6] Wines, *Punishment and Reformation*, p. 122.

Some people have been courteous enough to refer to the business of punishing lawbreakers as a science and to label it with the high-sounding name of "penology," and a growing demand for persons trained in such a scientific attitude has been heard. There has, however, been in the past little attempt to treat the prison as a social or scientific problem, except in connection with a general study of criminology.

It is a source of satisfaction, therefore, to note how many young college men there are anxious to take up prison work as a profession at this time. This is but one of the symptoms of increasing public regard for a hitherto neglected subject. Perhaps some day they can help us answer the conundrum: Why Prisons?

CHAPTER III

FORGOTTEN MEN [1]

Jail: An unbelievably filthy institution in which are confined men and women serving sentence for misdemeanors and crimes, and *men and women not under sentence who are simply awaiting trial.* With few exceptions, having no segregation of the unconvicted from the convicted, the well from the diseased, the youngest and most impressionable from the most degraded and hardened. Usually swarming with bedbugs, roaches, lice, and other vermin; has an odor of disinfectant and filth which is appalling; supports in complete idleness countless thousands of able-bodied men and women, and generally affords ample time and opportunity to assure inmates a complete course in every kind of viciousness and crime. A melting pot in which the worst elements of the raw material in the criminal world are brought forth blended and turned out in absolute perfection.

JOSEPH F. FISHMAN—*Crucibles of Crime.*

I asked to see the meat box. Instead of a refrigerator I find they keep the meat in a sort of wooden chest. They feed no meat except salt side pork. Two or three pieces of salt side pork in the meat box were literally covered with ants and cockroaches. A big Spanish cockroach two inches long had been caught and mashed under the lid. I do not know when, but it lay there flattened out when I opened the chest. The colored cook told me they had a brush with which to brush the insects off the meat when they wanted to cook it. In this kitchen in broad daylight cockroaches were scampering everywhere, across tables, chairs, up and down the walls, on the pantry shelves, on the metal plates, and everywhere about the kitchen. Three cats sat contentedly on the shelves of the pantry. A battered and greasy gas range was the only equipment for cooking for the forty or fifty men in the jail.[2]

[1] Mention should be made here of the valuable and efficient work being done in the Bureau of Prisons by Miss Nina Kinsella, Executive Assistant to the Director. Much of the material for this chapter has been contributed by her division, which has oversight of Federal jail inspections. Long service in this field has made her one of the most experienced and authoritative workers in the country today. See her article in *American Journal of Criminal Law and Criminology,* Vol. XXIV, pp. 428–430.

[2] Excerpt from an actual report submitted by a Federal inspector during November, 1935, of a jail in a southern State.

First in importance in our penal system is the institution unfortunately most consistently overlooked—the County Jail. It affects by far the largest number of people and has a tremendous influence on its tenants—the guilty and the innocent alike.

Although not often so considered, the plight of the county jail is of prime importance in any consideration of the penal systems of America. The average yearly intake of all of our State prisons and reformatories is less than 60,000. The last published report of the Bureau of the Census finds that there were 46,292 sentenced persons present in county jails on January 1, 1933, and during the six months immediately following 273,818 more were admitted.[3] When we add to this figure the number held waiting trial or disposition we obtain a total of 1,000,000 persons annually committed, usually for a very brief time, to one or another of the more than three thousand county jails in the country.

In the midst of our concern as to the conditions under which the convicted felon is treated, the really forgotten men, and women and children too, are those unfortunate legions who are committed to these local places of detention. Many of these men and women are innocent and are incarcerated because they are too poor to give bond. A considerable number of them are kept in jail a much longer time before they are tried than afterwards.

One of the outstanding riddles of our American penal system is why persons who commit minor offenses or who have not yet been convicted are so much more badly treated than all the inmates of our State prisons.

Fifteen years ago Mr. Joseph F. Fishman published a sensational exposé of conditions in many of the southern and western jails in his book called "Crucibles of Crime." Dr. Hastings H. Hart, a venerable and dynamic personality, was even at the age of seventy-five an invincible crusader for better jail conditions. Four years ago the Honorable Alexander Pat-

[3] *County and City Jails*, Bureau of the Census, Department of Commerce, p. 5.

erson, British Prison Commissioner, spent four months in America, and his condemnation of the county jail was in scathing and unmeasured terms. Said Mr. Paterson:

There remains the smaller unit, known in each State as the County, and to this authority is delegated the care of prisoners who are awaiting trial or deportation, or who are sentenced to a short period of imprisonment. These County Gaols, scattered throughout the States, are with some remarkable exceptions, e.g., New York State and Massachusetts, the scandal and disgrace of a great community. Hard words about prisons were written by Charles Dickens eighty years ago; more bitter still were the graphic notes of John Howard a hundred before. The vitriol of the former and the indignation of the latter are still not out of place today in trying to depict the horrors of an American County Gaol. Young and old, virtuous and depraved, innocent and double-dyed, are thrown into the closest association by night and day. For the most part, they spend the whole day in idleness, reading tattered newspapers or playing cards, herded in cages, devoid of proper sanitation, with little chance of exercise or occupation. The smell of these places is foul, their whole suggestion is infamous; their effect on the young or innocent can only be deplorable. There they sit and lounge and lie this day, rotting in the foetid air, and though all agree that these things are unspeakably evil, yet they continue from year to year, and the public conscience is not sufficiently aroused to demand a cleansing of the stable.

But these were voices crying in the wilderness. Nearly twenty years ago Stuart A. Queen in a book of that name predicted the Passing of the County Jail. But it has not passed. It flourishes as the green bay tree, and, if it were not so tragic, the devotion of the county politicians to their dirty, evil-smelling jails would be laughable.

The jails of Massachusetts, known as houses of correction, are among the best in the country. Generally speaking, they are clean, well managed, and under proper discipline. But, as already intimated, the county rings in Massachusetts have for fifty years resented every move in the direction of State supervision or control.

What there is about a full jail that contributes toward the

dignity and prestige of a county has always been difficult for me to understand. A New England newspaper, during the heat of one of the recurring campaigns in Massachusetts to bring the jails under some measure of unified control, remarked, "The county jail as a symbol of local democracy is, to say the least, an anachronism."

Outside of a few States where efficient inspection systems are maintained and except for the sporadic activities of the committee on jails of the American Prison Association, about the only effort to improve conditions in the county jail is that undertaken by the Federal Bureau of Prisons.

From early times it has been necessary for the Federal Government to board its prisoners in local institutions. President Washington negotiated with the State authorities for the care of some early Federal miscreants in an old copper mine at Simsbury, Connecticut; and from that time to the beginning of the twentieth century the Federal Government had no prisons or jails of its own.

Early in the nineteenth century the States of the Union passed statutes authorizing the detention of Federal prisoners on the same terms as State prisoners. The sheriffs were authorized to contract with the Federal Government for their reception. The Federal Government has not, and never has had, any direct control over these institutions.

Apart from village and police lock-ups there are about thirty-one hundred so-called county jails and city workhouses throughout the country.

By the Act of 1930 the newly created Federal Bureau of Prisons was given control over all Federal prisoners, either convicted or charged with a Federal offense. This, of course, included prisoners who were awaiting trial and those who from the nature of their offenses and the short duration of their sentences were not eligible for confinement in a penitentiary or reformatory. During the peak of the prohibition era the best estimate that could be given was that there was an average of 12,000 Federal prisoners serving short terms or awaiting trial in more than one thousand county jails.

"There they sit and lounge and lie this day."

TABLE B

FEDERAL INSPECTION OF JAILS AND WORKHOUSES*

July 1, 1930, to June 30, 1935

STATE	LATEST INSPECTION RATINGS						TOTAL INSP.	COUNTIES IN STATE	YEAR ENDING JUNE 30, 1935	
	90–100 %	80–89 %	70–79 %	60–69 %	50–59 %	Under 50%			Jails Used	Da.Aver. Fed.Pop.
Alabama	—	—	—	—	26	42	68	67	18	96
Arizona	—	—	—	—	8	11	19	14	16	95
Arkansas	—	—	—	1	12	65	78	75	14	77
California	1	—	1	8	32	27	69	58	44	255
Colorado	—	1	1	1	20	39	62	63	5	68
Connecticut	—	—	1	3	4	2	10	8	6	25
Delaware	—	1	—	—	1	1	3	3	1	16
Florida	—	—	—	—	19	47	66	67	19	121
Georgia	—	—	—	1	31	125	157	161	28	132
Idaho	1	1	—	—	10	26	38	44	14	24
Illinois	—	1	3	6	41	52	103	102	24	239
Indiana	—	—	—	2	46	43	91	92	9	72
Iowa	—	1	2	—	57	42	102	99	14	26
Kansas	—	—	—	—	33	31	64	105	8	59
Kentucky	—	—	1	2	35	86	124	120	41	201
Louisiana	—	—	1	—	17	49	67	64	13	98
Maine	—	—	—	—	10	4	14	16	6	44
Maryland	—	—	—	1	7	17	25	24	11	41
Massachusetts	—	1	4	7	2	—	14	14	11	40
Michigan	—	1	—	4	49	28	82	83	22	36
Minnesota	1	3	2	5	40	26	77	87	20	110
Mississippi	—	—	—	—	10	67	77	82	12	201
Missouri	—	—	—	3	23	72	98	115	33	250
Montana	—	—	—	—	14	40	54	56	32	54
Nebraska	—	—	1	—	29	40	70	93	9	30
Nevada	—	—	—	—	5	14	19	17	9	55
NewHampshire	—	—	—	5	2	1	8	10	2	18
New Jersey	—	—	—	—	—	—	—	21	8	55
New Mexico	—	—	1	—	9	21	31	31	21	60
New York	—	2	2	1	—	—	5	62	48	74
North Carolina	—	—	—	—	22	78	100	100	49	92
North Dakota	—	—	—	3	20	29	52	53	15	18
Ohio	—	—	3	5	54	32	94	88	25	146
Oklahoma	—	—	1	—	25	58	83	77	39	333
Oregon	—	—	1	—	12	26	39	36	8	41
Pennsylvania	—	—	2	18	33	13	66	67	34	129
Rhode Island	—	—	1	—	1	3	5	5	2	8
South Carolina	—	—	—	—	11	36	47	46	26	100
South Dakota	—	—	—	—	20	40	60	69	13	53
Tennessee	—	—	2	—	20	73	95	95	32	162
Texas	—	—	—	2	56	155	213	254	37	481
Utah	—	1	—	—	4	21	26	29	4	19
Vermont	—	—	1	—	7	7	15	14	6	23
Virginia	—	—	—	8	32	70	110	121	24	42
Washington	—	—	—	1	17	25	43	39	20	102
West Virginia	—	—	—	—	12	45	57	55	36	182
Wisconsin	—	—	3	1	41	27	72	71	16	63
Wyoming	—	—	—	—	6	16	22	24	14	30
Totals	3	13	33	88	985	1772	2894	3096	918	4696

* This table includes a few State reformatories and training schools which have been inspected; and also a few county and city institutions other than jails and workhouses. A number of the above jails have had more than one inspection, but each jail is counted only once in this table. Inspections made by inspectors of the Bureau of Prisons, Washington, D.C.

The Federal Bureau of Prisons increased the number of inspectors from two to seven and set up a statistical report system whereby an accurate analysis of county-jail prisoners could be had. From July, 1930, to June 30, 1935, in the 3,096 counties of the country 2,894 jails were inspected.

An attempt was made to classify these institutions on the basis of security, discipline, cleanliness, food, administration, etc. The table on page 41 indicates that only 137 of these jails rated 60 per cent or over. Most of them were definitely rejected, because they were fire traps, were structurally unsafe, inadequately guarded, or hopelessly dirty, or had a record for permitting escapes or encouraging laxity.

The table on page 41 attempts to rate the jails according to the percentage of each of the eleven factors which enter into the Federal inspection rating sheet. In 2,568 out of 2,894 jails there are no hospital facilities; 2,300 of them rate under 10 per cent as to employment and industry and 2,709 rate under 10 per cent in the matter of offering any attempt at rehabilitation. In fact, not only do most of the jails make no attempt to rehabilitate or improve the prisoners, but many of them permit positively harmful and degrading practices.

It will be borne in mind that the Federal Government cannot compel any changes in personnel, nor can it provide any of the funds necessary for improvement,[4] except through the per diem rate which the Government allows for the subsistence of its prisoners.

A section of the Federal regulations contains a statement to the effect that Federal prisoners should be employed in accordance with the law, that the sentence of the court should be served in an impartial and dignified manner, and the prisoners given reasonably humane treatment. One sheriff, who obviously had not read the instructions very carefully, in his eagerness to impress the Bureau wrote that he would comply with all the regulations and finished his letter as follows:

[4] Except in special cases as under Federal Emergency Administration of Public Works.

There will be no employment for Federal prisoners, no sentences served in an impartial, proper and dignified manner, and no Federal prisoners will receive humane treatment!

To the credit of many of the sheriffs it can be said that when the shortcomings of their jails were called to their attention they made an earnest attempt at improvement. The only weapon in the hands of the Federal Government is to withdraw its prisoners, revoke its contract, and attempt to find more satisfactory quarters elsewhere. Often this results in inconvenience and expense—inconvenience to the court and District Attorney and expense for transportation. Many times this simple action on the part of the Federal Government, however, has the result of temporarily arousing the interest of the press and public in the local jail and the forgotten men and women who inhabit it.

1. *The County Jail Is Not Secure*

When I approached the jail, I was met at the front door by Mrs. ———, the wife of the jailor. She said she was in charge of the jail in the afternoon while her husband attended the ball game. Procuring the keys from an unlocked drawer, she went up to the second floor with me and attempted to unlock a room in which there were eight Federal prisoners. She had difficulty in operating the lock. Her little daughter, five or six years of age, asked her mother for the key, saying she knew how to make the lock operate. However, the mother did not give the key to the girl. A prisoner inside the barred door said he could operate the key and put his hand through the bars to do so.

The first count in the indictment against the average county jail is its lack of security. This is due sometimes to insufficient structural accommodations, to lack of personnel, or to the carelessness or venality of those in charge. The recent attempted escape of O. D. Stevens from a county jail in Texas resulted in the conviction of nine persons who received jail terms and fines for their complicity in the affair.

The escape of Dillinger from the Crown Point jail and of Harvey Bailey from the Dallas County jail are fresh in the public memory. Five members of the O'Malley gang shot their way out of the Muskogee city jail in November, 1935. The lives of three of them, together with that of a peace officer who attempted to stop their escape, were the toll which resulted. In this instance the insecure and inadequately guarded city jails brought about a tragic result, but it is doubtful if one-fourth of the county jails in the country today are capable of restraining desperate, resourceful men.

A jail in Oklahoma had one of its walls propped up only by the presence of the adjoining building. If that building had been removed, the jail would have fallen down.

In a jail in Missouri prisoners were housed in a low-studded wooden basement under a tinder-box wooden floor. A lighted cigarette dropped on a mattress would have caused them all to be burnt to cinders.

2. *The Personnel Is Untrained and Inefficient*

Here is another excerpt from a report of this same inspector:

The ———— jail is in the charge of a rather old one-armed man. He was locked inside with the prisoners. He carried the key to the outside door. The door between the jailer's office and the corridors and dormitories containing many prisoners was wide open. The jailer carried a revolver at his side, supported by the usual belt. Certainly it would be an easy matter for fifteen or twenty prisoners to gang the jailer, get the keys and the gun, and carry out a delivery almost any day they wished to do so.

In Illinois recently four Federal and one State prisoner escaped from a fairly modern and well constructed jail under rather extraordinary circumstances. In fact, the investigation which followed disclosed gross negligence on the part of the jail officials. For several days four of the prisoners had worked at removing rivets and had been creating considerable noise hammering on steel. The four conspirators on the day planned for the escape invited another prisoner to accompany them. When he declined they bound and gagged him and deposited him in an unused cell. Shortly before the jail delivery a turn-key brought in a newly committed prisoner and placed him in the cell block. But the turnkey was strangely oblivious to all that had been going on and saw nothing suspicious. Within twenty minutes, however, five of his prisoners, including—believe it or not—the one who had just been admitted by the turnkey, made good their escape. When at the appointed time, a few minutes later, the turnkey went to the cell block to lock the cells for the night, he took no notice of the prisoners, nor did he learn that any of them had departed. Some time later the prisoner who had been tied up managed to free his feet sufficiently to kick a garbage can around until he attracted the jailer's attention. He then reported the escape of the other prisoners.

A news clipping from an Arkansas paper reported that a bank robber "sang his way out of the local jail." It is stated that he took his place among a visiting religious group and walked to freedom directly past the jailer. Recaptured after a previous escape, he had been back in custody only one week when he joined in the psalm and hymn singing and, as the group departed, made himself one of them.

3. *The County Jails Are Unbelievably Dirty*

Take the case of a city jail in a State not far below the Mason and Dixon line. Three successive inspections by Federal men reported the jail as dirty, verminous, ill kept, and poorly disciplined. Following the last report in September, 1935, a letter was written to the official in charge, advising him that unless immediate improvements were made the Federal prisoners, few in number, would have to be moved to another jail. Five weeks elapsed without an answer. Another letter was dispatched. After two weeks more had passed the official replied, assailing the judgment of the inspector and denying that conditions were as stated. Shortly after this agents of the Federal Bureau of Investigation were in the institution checking up on an attempted jail break, and one of them sent to his Bureau this nauseating paragraph:

Upon entering the cell block, it was found so crowded that it was apparently necessary for several of the inmates to sleep on mattresses which were laid on the floor immediately in front of the cells, thereby making it necessary to actually have to step over some of the prisoners who were lying around on their mattresses. This cell block was found to contain old tin cans, decayed fruit, stale bread, contaminated food stuffs and an enormous miscellaneous collection of filthy clothing, blankets, pails, paper, etc. An iron water pipe extending into this cell block had been leaking and the floor of the entire block was damp and in certain places there were pools of water. Upon entering the cell occupied by two Federal prisoners, it was so dark that it was necessary to use flashlights. There were found in the cell decayed fruit, old spoons, knives, stale bread, a pound of decayed butter and in one corner of this cell was a toilet which could not be used without raising the lower bunk. This toilet apparently had not been in operation for some time as there was found on the floor and at the base of the toilet a pile of human excrement and another pile of used toilet paper. From all appearances this cell block had not been cleaned for weeks, or probably months, and apparently no inspection of the jail is made by the jailer who is a Deputy City Sergeant or by the City Sergeant.

The Bureau of Prisons felt justified in this instance in publicly announcing that it had discontinued the use of the local jail on account of "its filthy condition and the apparent indifference of the officials."

After the usual number of explanations, denials, and alibis by local and State officials real demands for improvement began to be voiced; the whole system of housing prisoners in jails was questioned, and eventually the leading newspaper of the State publicly commended the Bureau of Prisons for calling attention to the admitted evils.

One cannot dismiss this problem in the way that some good citizens are occasionally wont to do: "Well, who cares whether the jail is good or bad? Are we going to make these bums and vagrants and sneak thieves so comfortable that they will want to stay there all their lives? If these folks do not like the jail, they do not have to go there."

It is largely true that only the poor and uninfluential are required to visit jails nowadays, but it cannot be any justification for the continued toleration of such dens of misery and degradation. Many of the residents are innocent. Some are aliens waiting deportation, some are witnesses, unfortunate persons who happened to be at the scene of a crime, some have been held as long as six months or a year waiting for the term of court which may eventually result in their being put on probation. Little use it would be to put a first offender on probation after six months in the average county jail.

4. *Disintegrating Idleness Is the Rule*

Beyond the question of dirt, lack of sanitation and ventilation, insecurity, and lax discipline, the two outstanding evils of the average county jail are idleness and lack of segregation. The idle mind is the devil's workshop, and the devil has plenty of work in the average county jail. In fact, he is about the only one who does any work.

Even those jails which are clean, and in which discipline is well and evenly maintained, are faced with the almost insoluble question of how to keep the inmates suitably occupied. Idleness—constant, deteriorating, devastating idleness—is the rule. Look inside any county jail in the country, and you will see men sitting, sprawling, pacing up and down, dragging themselves through the long hours of the day as best they may. Occasionally a prisoner will be writing a letter, or perhaps preparing his own defense. One in a hundred may be reading a book, probably of the dime-novel variety. The keeper of a California jail was questioned by a lady as to why he did not furnish books to the inmates of his institution. His reply was: "Lady, this is a jail. This ain't no Sunday school."

Even the administrators of our State penitentiaries and reformatories are now at their wits' end to provide work for the prisoners. To do this to any extent requires the investment of money in shops and machines, instructors and overseers, and a place to sell the products. Except in some of our large cities, county jails have given up any attempt whatever to do this. Once in a great while a public-spirited sheriff will provide instruction in the three R's for some of the men in his institution who show interest in self-improvement. But it may be said generally that no effort whatever is made at education or rehabilitation in the average county jail. If some Gideon's band would place a few books in the county jails, as a Bible has been placed in every hotel room, they might save many souls from uncounted hours of despair.

What do people do when they have nothing to do? They nurse grievances. They find it very easy to convince themselves that the world is against them. They plot revenge. They listen to the voices of those more unscrupulous and more callous than themselves. And thus a jail becomes not only a place of physical contamination but a veritable source and inspiration of moral degeneration.

It is easy to admit that little can be done in the way of employment, education, and moral uplift during the short time spent in jail by most prisoners. The average term is a little less than sixty days, but many stay for months, and a few, for years.

There are a number of simple trades requiring individual effort that could be provided in every institution of this kind. The jailer would simply have to appeal to the local Rotary Club, or branch library, or other public-spirited group, to be furnished with ample reading matter.

5. *Rarely Is There Any Segregation*

The inspections of the Federal Bureau of Prisons show that any attempt at segregation, except of the sexes, is almost unheard of, and in many instances even this segregation is far from adequate. Young and old, sick and well, are housed in the same run-around, and in many places occupy adjoining bunks in the same cell. In a hoosegow in Missouri I saw a group of double-decked bunks placed on top of a cell block, one containing a pallid boy of fifteen suffering from a racking cough and another containing a drug-addict prisoner, who recognized me as his former landlord at the Fort Leavenworth Annex prison. The boy, I was told, could not be moved to the house of detention across the street because they only took boys of sixteen and upwards.

An inspector's report on a jail in a southern State discloses that the matron in charge of the women's section would permit male prisoners to enter the female section on the payment of a dollar fee. It was through the interception of a letter from this same matron to her private bootlegger asking where her supply of liquor had gone that evidence was obtained sufficient to justify the removal of all of the Federal prisoners from this ennobling institution.

In an Oklahoma jail, on top of a block containing three cells in which were eleven inmates, two mattresses had been placed; and sprawled on each, with not room enough under the ceiling to stand upright, were two boys, one holding out a tin cup that it might be filled with the noon meal. I remarked to the jailer that the place seemed to be overcrowded. He said no, he had often had more prisoners than he had then. Whereupon I inquired why the two boys were on top of the little cell block. With some pride in his penological progressiveness, shall we say, he answered, "Oh, these are juveniles, and we segregate our juveniles."

6. *The County Jail Is No Place for a Juvenile*

Although the Federal inspection reports show that no juveniles were kept in 1,100 jails, they also disclosed the appalling fact that in 611 jails juveniles are housed with adults and in only 8 per cent of these has any provision been made for separate quarters for the juveniles.

I entered jail an amateur in crime and stayed there a little over three months. In that time I learned more of the devious methods which crooks use against society than I had ever dreamed of knowing. . . . I mingled daily with men grown old in the underworld; I assimilated just as much of their vices as my immature nature would hold. I learned the language of the crooks. The tales told were strong with the flavor of adventure. They fascinated me and I looked up to the old crooks as men to be envied. . . . They came to be heroes, as it were, out of the great book of adventure.[5]

7. *Health Conditions Are Appalling*

You might think that the community, for its own protection, would be interested in the elimination of the disease hazard of the county jail. But 2,204 of these local jails have never been visited or inspected by local boards of health or any other health organization. Can any community look with complacency upon this kind of situation, as disclosed from an inspector's report:

> The sewage system has been out of commission for some time. The septic tank overflows not far from the jail kitchen, causing bad odors and great menace to health; also, causing most of the sanitary facilities to be stopped up. Since the windows have neither heavy screens nor fly screens, great swarms of flies today were seen all over the food which the prisoners were eating, and they had direct access to this awful cesspool.

On a certain occasion a smallpox epidemic was reported in a county jail in a southern State. An inspection report reflected the fact that prisoners had been using the water in the toilets for washing purposes and one prisoner, at least, appeared to have been drinking it.

We do not need to have any particular sympathy for those human beings who find themselves prisoners in our county jails to recognize, nevertheless, that such places may easily become foci of infection and as such should evoke a keener appreciation of the community responsibility therefor. The contaminations of the county jail cannot be confined within its filth-covered walls.

8. *The Kangaroo Court Thrives in the County Jail*

Thomas Mott Osborne, the great New York prison reformer, will perhaps be most remembered for his advocacy of

[5] *Seventeen Years in the Underworld,* quoted by Sutherland, *Principles of Criminology,* p. 235.

self-government in prisons. His mutual welfare leagues at Auburn and Sing Sing were designed to develop initiative and responsibility among the prisoners, and, as will later be shown, many a wise prison man today makes his task easier with the help and coöperation of inmate organizations.

Like many other schemes for prison improvement, these cannot succeed without courageous and skillful leadership. The kangaroo court,[6] as practiced in many southern and midwestern jails, has neither and therefore it constitutes one of the outstanding scandals in American jail administration. Charles R. Henderson, one of the most devoted of the prison reformers that America has known, in reporting to the American Prison Association for the Committee on Jails, at the annual meeting of the Association in Chicago in September, 1907, refers to these unique institutions in the following terms:

> We find explicit mention of self-government among prisoners, with some degree of control by the jail authorities, in several jails of the Western and Southern States. This self-government is sometimes called the "Kangaroo Court"; whether it was imported from the British South Pacific colonies, along with other strange marsupial animals, we have not discovered information. It seems to be an American revival of a vicious old English custom; its persistence is thought, by experts, to be a proof of the incapacity of the authorities to govern as their duty requires and as one more evidence that the crowding of offenders and suspects, of all grades, in one hall, gives power of tyranny to the basest bullies of the herd. This singular and dangerous institution must be discussed by itself with further facts.

In many cases the activities of the kangaroo court have grown beyond the control of the sheriff. He is not able, or does not dare, to discontinue it.

[6] The Haskin Information Service gives us the following as to the origin of the kangaroo courts:

"They started originally in Kansas and were an inferior court held by mayors and presided over by the mayor and justices of the peace; they had jurisdiction over prohibition violations and automobile traffic accidents. They had no fee except where the accused was convicted. They had no regular place of meeting and met on the spot of the accident or whatever caused the proceeding. They evidently got the nickname because they jumped about from place to place."

In brief, the organization known as the kangaroo court [7] is a combination of blackmail, terrorization, and privilege. Through some process of election or assumption of power one of the influential inmates becomes a judge. There are an assistant, a marshal, sergeant at arms or treasurer. On his arrival at the jail each inmate is importuned to pay either the admission fee or, as it is sometimes put, the fine for breaking into jail. If he cannot or will not pay, he is subjected to corporal punishment on the "sentence of the judge."

The money so extorted from inmates is used to purchase tobacco, to bribe the jailer, to get favored assignments in the jail or for other illicit purposes. Many times the control of the jail interior is taken over by the kangaroo court. A few years ago an Oklahoma jail keeper confessed that he did not dare go inside the confines of his jail for the purpose of disciplining the members of the court who had badly beaten up one of the inmates. In a recent case $2,500 damages were awarded by a court against the sheriff for permanent injuries received at the hands of a kangaroo court by a recalcitrant prisoner.

Some sheriffs defend the institution known as the kangaroo court. In certain other places it has been euphemistically called "sanitary court." One sheriff confessed that he could not keep the place clean or well disciplined without the help of this inmate tribunal.

The Federal Bureau of Prisons has repeatedly announced its unswerving opposition to the presence of the kangaroo court in any jail and has attempted in each instance to secure its abolition by the sheriff.

[7] An interesting forerunner of the kangaroo court is described in Burton's *New View of London*, p. 468, quoted in John Howard's book, *The State of the Prisons in England and Wales* (p. 13), first published in 1777:

"In the year 1730, Nicholas Bennet, Joseph Robinson, John Head and George Taverner, were indicted at the Old Bailey for robbing John Berrisford of two half-guineas, two sixpences, and two halfpence, in New Prison under the pretence of garnish, which fact being plainly proved, they were all found guilty of an assault and robbery; and to deter others from the infamous and inhuman practice of taking the money, and if they had none, of stripping poor prisoners that were upon any account committed to prison, so that often-times they have perished for want of cloathing and necessaries, they received sentence of death."

BREAKING. IN JAIL $2.00 FINE or 100 LICKS

TAKE BATH IMERDIATELY AFTER COURT 25¢ or 10 LKS

3. MAKE BED EVERY MORNING   20 or 20 "

4 SWEEP FLOOR AFTER EACH MEAL.   15 or 15 "

5. DONT SIT ON DRAG   20 or 20 "

6 DONT USE TOILET OR BREAK WIND DURING MEALS 25 or 25

7 EACH MAN MUST BE FULLY DRESSED ON SUNDAY.

FROM 9.45 AM TO 4. PM -   20 or 20 LKS

8 DONT THROW ANY KIND OF TRASH ON FLOOR
                                   20 or 20
OR IN BOLL RING OR PUT CIG, BUTTS ON BARS

9 DONT COME FORWARD OF NO 2 CELL DURING

VISTING HRS, OR STAY IN NO 1 CELL UNLESS YOU

ARE CALLED FORWARD   25 or 25

10. NO MAN WILL BE ALLOWED TO BUY FROM

STORE OR ORDER MONEY FROM OFFICE UNTIL

FINE IS PAID -

11 NO LOUD TALKING DURING VISTING OR

CHURCH HRS.   -   20 or 20

12. DONT SIT ON OTHER MANS BUNK OR

USE HIS PERSONAL PROPERTY WITHOUT HIS

PERMISSION -   20 or 20

Specimen of Kangaroo Court rules from a Southern jail.

9. *The Laxity of Discipline Is Notorious*

Occasionally an irate judge, learning of a particular fla-grant piece of lax administration has ordered the sheriff or keeper into court on a charge of contempt. Judge Wilkerson of Chicago found a sheriff guilty of contempt of court for permitting undue privileges, and in an opinion bristling with indignation Federal Judge McClintic of West Virginia sen-tenced a sheriff to four months for negligence in permitting the escape of a Federal prisoner.

In a Texas jail facts were disclosed which induced a right-eous Federal judge to order a Federal grand-jury investigation of the whole jail system. That particular jailer had established a schedule of prices for favors to be rendered—50 cents for a deck of cards; $2 for a drink of liquor and $5 for a shot of dope.

The Federal records disclose further instances of unbeliev-able carelessness—unauthorized absence of prisoners to attend baseball games, to visit race tracks, and to attend to private business concerns. It was on one of these occasions that an-other Federal judge lashed out at this evil. The language of the court in the case of *Hallanan* v. *H. H. Cyrus, Sheriff*, 83 W. Va. 30:

> The Sheriff must keep the prisoner confined in jail and grant him no privileges or indulgence inconsistent with his status as a prisoner and permit no relaxation of the confinement of his per-son, not only that he may at all times be within the control of the sheriff, but also, that the imprisonment may be actual, irk-some, and a service of discomfort, so far as confinement in the jail may produce such results.

Important from the point of view of adequate law enforce-ment as is the insecurity and lack of discipline in the average county institution, of far greater importance in the social sig-nificance. The influence exerted by these miserable places upon so large a number of our fellow citizens cannot be minimized.

In many cases the sheriff or jailer is a man possessing a con-siderable amount of sympathy for the unfortunate people temporarily under his control. He realizes the damage which is being done them through being obliged to remain in dirty, ill ventilated debilitating surroundings, and on occasions, perhaps, to compensate them somewhat for the indignities which the jail heaps upon them, he permits them special privileges and immunities. Rarely did the jailer's sympathy, however, lead him to distribute his largesse equally among all the prisoners. It more often was expended upon those who had a little extra money or who were influential in other ways. In many of the jails of a certain State on the Atlantic seaboard there were for a number of years two classes of prisoners, those who paid 75 cents a day in addition to what the State or Federal Government paid for their board, and those who did not. Those who did pay, ate in the sheriff's dining room and slept in comparative comfort in his house. Those who did not, were kept in the cell block at the rear of his residence.

The furnishing of liquor or "dope" to jail prisoners by a sympathetic sheriff (of which numerous instances have been recorded) has never been extended to the point where all the prisoners are permitted to participate in this bestowal, but has invariably been reserved for those who could pay for it.

Thus many times the sheriff's sympathies have but resulted in other outstanding abuses, and we find that the twin evils of degradation and favoritism go hand in hand.

10. *The Iniquitous Fee System Must Be Abolished*

Related to the difficulties incident to the manner of financing many of these smaller institutions is the stubborn persistence of the iniquitous fee system in many of the southern and southwestern States. The jailer or sheriff is dependent upon the fees which he collects for the board of his prisoners, not only to pay the expenses of the institution but to provide him the necessary profit from the job. In one southern State, at least, the job of sheriff or jailer is highly prized because of the fact that the Federal Government boards large numbers of prisoners there; and the more prisoners boarded, the larger the financial return to the sheriff.

One does not have to accuse the county officers of willful neglect or cupidity in this matter to come to the conclusion that the fee system is vicious and should be immediately abolished. Any system which puts a premium upon the continued retention of a prisoner in jail and which gauges the amount of profit which the sheriff is to make by the extent to which he can economize on food and other living expenses is a pernicious system.

The first step in the reformation of the county jail situation must come through the abolition of the fee system.

11. *The Jail Is Too Often Dominated by Politics*

One may well ask what is the reason for this condition, and why the Chambers of Commerce, the Rotary Clubs, the Women's Clubs, etc., tolerate such conditions? There are several reasons that may be assigned, and not the least of them has to do with the historical development of the county as a governmental unit. In the horse-and-buggy era, or the stagecoach days, the county had a logical place in the sphere of governmental administration. It was brought over from England, where the "Shire Reeve" had become the "Sheriff" and had wielded considerable power as an officer of justice. It was natural for the county to become established in our New England States and throughout the country after the English model. It is recorded that it required five days for the news of Washington's second election to get from New York to Boston. But with the development of transportation and communication and with their consequent dwindling in size many, if not most, of the functions of the county have been taken over either by the municipalities or by the State. People were keenly interested in their local town meetings and in their State elections, but the county was neglected and grew into a sort of invisible government. Just why we continue to maintain county political organizations today is somewhat of a mystery. Judges are qualified by the State. The laws which they enforce by jail sentences are enacted by State legislatures. The State administers all of the major penal institutions and undertakes the care of the insane, whereas, the township generally provides for the poor and the needy.

It was sixty years ago that England abolished the county jail and substituted the scheme of uniform governmental control. The result was the permanent discontinuance of nearly two-thirds of these expensive local institutions.

But although in an automobile one can drive across the whole length of most of our States in a day and in doing so pass through a dozen counties, we still tenaciously cling to this form of control of our short-term prisoners.

Because the county is largely an invisible government it is the more easily dominated by politics. The following is an excerpt from the report on a county jail in Texas made by a Federal inspector:

> The sheriff was urged to change these practices and he freely admitted that it would cost him votes with the prisoners and their friends. . . . He also stated that he had to be reëlected and could not afford to offend anyone.

More often than not, the county is poor. It has too little money for improvements. It cannot even pay the salary of the jailer, much less give him the necessary assistants. There is a supreme indifference towards his troubles on the part of most citizens, and oftentimes sharp differences of opinion between himself and the county commissioners who control the purse strings. In some States a sheriff is not subject to reëlection, and the least of his troubles is the kind of a jail he operates. Occasionally he comes in for censure or blame from the righteous elements in the community, especially where there is a large city in the county, and sometimes his maladministration of the jail may affect his political future. But these instances are rare.

Many of the southern sheriffs and jailers have to deal with the color question. They openly state that they have no interest in providing clean, comfortable quarters to be "messed up" and quickly made filthy on the arrival of some prisoners for whom in comparison with their usual squalid surroundings the jail may seem a welcome asylum.

Again, the jail turn-over is large, and the population at any given time is small. Many men come in only for a night or for a few days. Little can be done, say the sheriffs, to improve or rehabilitate men under such conditions.

12. *What Can Be Done?*

All these things may be admitted, and yet there are a few outstanding examples where all these handicaps have been overcome. Some jails are models of cleanliness. Many have programs of work, religious instruction, and rehabilitation. The Cincinnati Workhouse, the Allegheny County Workhouse near Pittsburgh, the Philadelphia County Jail at Holmesburg, Pennsylvania, the House of Correction at North Milwaukee, the Detroit House of Correction at Plymouth, Michigan, the New Haven County Jail, and most of the Massachusetts and New York jails leave little to be desired. In almost every one of these institutions, however, there is a considerable number of prisoners to care for, thus justifing the expenditure of larger appropriations by the city or county which furnishes the funds for the institution.

And so, while we note progress from year to year in the administration of many of our penitentaries, the scandal of the county jail remains. There is serious reason to doubt whether under the present form of county government the evils herein enumerated can ever be eradicated. I am one of those who believe that the whole system must be uprooted, and that attempts will continue to be futile if we build new county jails which in six months become filthy or elect a new sheriff who, in turn, gives up the hopeless job.

Pending this more radical accomplishment, is there any present solution for the situation? The county jails of America are maintained for two purposes: first, to safely hold those who are arrested and charged with crime in order that they may be present on the day of trial; and second, to punish for brief periods only the misdemeanant prisoners whose crime has not been serious enough to warrant a prison sentence or who are not of the young reformable type eligible for admission to a reformatory.

I have the following to suggest, realizing full well the almost insurmountable obstacles to their adoption.

(1) *We should attempt to reduce materially the number of persons detained in jail.*

It does seem strange and somewhat unnecessary that the community is called upon to pay for the board and keep for weeks or months on end of a suspected criminal, merely so that we may be sure he will be in a given court room at the hour set. We secure his attendance in court in many cases by exacting a promise from him or by accepting his bond to so appear. No matter how vicious or dangerous he is or how badly we want him, if he can give bond, we take the risk. If he is poor or friendless, howsoever trivial the case, he must spend the days and nights in the noisome confines of the county jail until he can be tried.

Have we not ingenuity enough to devise a better system than this? There are many cities of Europe in which the police exercise such a strict supervision over the inhabitants that they know exactly whenever the man whom they are watching attempts to leave the city. The universal passport system now prevalent in Russia may not be democratic, but it helps the G.P.U. to keep close watch on all suspects. The Argentine Republic has a universal registration and fingerprint system.

We are so much concerned with the individual liberty of our citizens that we do not even permit the fingerprinting of any person until he has committed a crime. Enlightened communities are just beginning to realize that there is no disgrace in a fingerprint, as everybody has one, and there would seem to be no reason why every person should not give his fingerprint as readily as his name and address.[8]

[8] See further discussion in Chapter VII.

The adoption of a universal identification system and as close a surveillance by local police as the American traditions of liberty will permit would do much to make it unnecessary to jail hundreds of thousands of our fellow citizens.

Professor Beeley in his study of the bail system in Chicago calls attention to the necessity for more careful investigation into the status of the accused persons. Do they have property? Are they first offenders? Do they have family connections? Is there a reasonable probability of their innocence? Beeley finds that this latter group forms a substantial percentage of persons who are held in jail awaiting trial but for whom less drastic methods might be adopted.

(2) *We can attempt to reduce the amount of time spent by persons in jail detention.*

Most courts now profess to give right of way in the trial of criminal causes to jail cases over the cases of those defendants who have been admitted to bail. Even so, with the long lapse of time between terms of court and with the delay occasioned by the preparation of the case, engagements of counsel, and other circumstances, we find too much toleration by courts and prosecutors in this matter of the period of detention waiting trial.

Statistics are not available as to the period of detention of untried persons in State and county courts, but the Federal Prison Bureau furnishes tables which indicate that the average period of detention before trial for all Federal offenders is 28.1 days, ranging from an average of 12 days in the Northern District of Georgia to 56.6 days in Wyoming.

Uncle Sam boards the untried prisoners at an average expense of 75 cents per day from two to eight weeks in county jails. Even those who are released on bail or recognizance are held an average of nine days before such release is accomplished. The general average of all defendants who are later acquitted or whose cases are dismissed is 33.8 days. Of all of the Federal cases who are later placed on probation or whose sentences are suspended we have an average period of six weeks and four days before such release is consummated. Truly a poor preparation for successful probation.

I am confident that the situation with respect to Federal cases is vastly better than with regard to many State and county cases. Information such as the above is freely circulated among the Federal courts and their attention is constantly directed towards the need, both from an economical and from a sociological viewpoint, for shortening the period of detention.

Much more can be accomplished in bringing to the attention of all of our courts the humanitarian necessity of prompt trial for jail cases. Celerity of justice is infinitely more important than severity. Whatever is to be done should be done quickly and impartially. If we could only bring about a situation where judges and district attorneys could be haunted nightly by the thought of their responsibility for all untried persons in their districts who are languishing in jail, I am confident a noteworthy bit of progress in local law enforcement could be brought about.

(3) *The county jail should be used as little as possible for the serving of sentences.*

If we can eliminate or largely reduce the number of persons held awaiting trial, we can even more easily solve the question of the misdemeanant prisoners. Indiana, Massachusetts, Ohio, New Jersey, and other States through the establishment of the State penal farm for misdemeanants have done much to reduce the jail evil. Under State supervision and with larger numbers of prisoners to handle, the problem of work and rehabilitation becomes much easier to solve. The per capita cost of maintenance is less, and living conditions can be immeasurably improved.

Every State has the opportunity immediately to authorize the establishment of a State farm for misdemeanants and provide by law that all short-term prisoners eligible for county jails may be sent there. Under such auspices degrading idleness can be replaced by work in the open air or in some con-

JAIL AND WORKHOUSE INSPECTIONS

RATINGS OF PRINCIPAL FACTORS CLASSIFIED IN INST[ITUTION REPORTS]

JULY 1, 1930, TO NOVEMBER 30, 1934

Classifications of Factors	Under 10%	10-19%	20-29%	30-39%	40-49%	50-59%	60-69%	70-79%	80-89%	90-100%
Administration and Discipline	5	11	18	31	68	324	855	1,030	434	81
Building and Equipment	12	48	161	109	296	484	665	642	333	75
Cleanliness and Sanitation	16	30	101	94	225	414	683	707	486	7
Employment and Industries	2,300	256	152	32	24	27	10	15	8	42
Food	10	1	3	8	36	137	737	1,287	570	6
Hospital	2,568	103	74	20	6	21	11	13	9	16
Medical Service	73	347	715	911	176	378	68	116	31	130
Personal Hygiene	63	40	115	291	166	414	367	683	562	58
Personnel	9	9	11	21	47	607	1,000	760	309	3
Rehabilitation	2,709	61	24	7	6	14	1	5	1	5
Religious Instruction	1,657	355	583	75	41	41	14	59	1	0
All Factors †		9	40	318	1,214	1,078	132	32	8	

* Based on reports of latest inspections made, by Federal Inspectors, of 2,831 institutions.
† This rating represents a weighted average for each institution, of all factors considered.

structive activity, and the prisoner instead of deteriorating through inactivity can pay his debt to society by the sweat of his face.

The Federal Bureau of Prisons can continue to point out the rotten conditions and refuse to use those jails which do not meet its standards, and thus in sporadic cases bring about substantial, albeit temporary, improvement; but the extent to which we continue to tolerate this "scandal and disgrace of a great community" depends almost entirely upon the lethargy or energy of our legislative leaders in our various States.

CHAPTER IV

HAVE OUR PRISONS FAILED?

I would like to know clearly, explicitly, and finally, just what people expect of a prison. Is its purpose to reform? To punish? To frighten? To prevent? To rehabilitate? What? Does any one know? . . . I am bedevilled by a conviction that there is something very important concealed in this matter.
DAVID LAMSON—*We Who Are About to Die.*

THE county jails do not, however, hold a monopoly on all of the evils connected with penal treatment. The State prisons or penitentiaries have come in for ample criticism in recent years. Before we can plan an efficient and satisfactory prison system it would be well to know what is the matter with the present one. In the next two chapters we shall discuss to what extent our prisons have failed and the reason for the recent prison disturbances and shall commence a discussion of the remedies therefor.

We conclude that the present prison system is antiquated and inefficient. It does not reform the criminal. It fails to protect society. There is reason to believe that it contributes to the increase of crime by hardening the prisoner. We are convinced that a new type of penal institution must be developed, one that is new in spirit, in method and in objective.[1]

These are not the words of a prejudiced, irresponsible agitator. They represent the conclusions of a group of conservative and distinguished people who in 1931 formed the personnel of the National Commission on Law Observance and Enforcement, popularly known as the Wickersham Commission.

The more or less unanimous editorial agreement with this

[1] National Commission on Law Observance and Enforcement, Report No. 9, *Penal Institutions, Probation and Parole*, p. 170.

conclusion indicates the general opinion that our American prison systems have failed. "Prisons Take the Count," "Prison Reform Called For," "Our Prison Methods Indicted," "Condemned," "A Great American Failure," "The Prison's Guilt," "Prison a Failure," were typical of the headings over many of the newspaper editorials of the country. Occasionally a newspaper would rise to remark, as did the Syracuse *Post Standard:* "If one wants a target, he will hardly find an easier one than prison administration. It has always been so. And, at the risk of rousing the incurable optimists, one can readily hold that it will always be so. A prison that was really pleasant would be a prison no longer. It would be a reversal of the purpose of prisons." The attitude of the average newspaper, however, was expressed by the Los Angeles *Express:* "A blush of shame will come to the cheeks of Americans when they read what the Wickersham Commission tells President Hoover about the prisons of the country."

Before assuming that all the prisons of the country, collectively, have failed, we ought to have clearly in mind what is, or should be, the purpose of a prison. If we desire an institution designed to make men suffer for their misdeeds, to bring such misery and degradation upon their heads that they will not want to repeat the offense for which they stand convicted, then we have no right to criticize our prisons as failures, if they are designed with that end in view.

"The prison has failed as an educational institution," said the Wickersham report.[2]

Educational institutions are provided throughout the land for those who can benefit by education. Is it reasonable to expect that an institution designed for the purpose of punishment and having in its confines only those who have been unable to profit by the lessons of our school systems can succeed as an educational institution?

"The prison has failed as a business enterprise."

Would the business interests of the country, employers and employed alike, hail with delight the establishment of fully

[2] *Op. cit.,* p. 111.

equipped and efficient factories in all of our penal institutions?
The average prison workshop is administered by untrained
and low-salaried employees; its operatives are only those who
have broken the law, whose mentalities are enfeebled and
whose strength and skill have been impaired by the ravages of
dissipation and indulgence. There exists among those who
labor no incentive for better work, and no one can be discharged from the institution because his work is unsatisfactory.
Could an industry conducted under such auspices be anything
but a failure?

"The prison has failed as a disciplinary institution."

Before passing judgment on the correctness of such a statement one must have lived in the confines of the average State
penitentiary, in daily contact with large numbers of scheming,
conniving individuals who have been selected from the community for sequestration in an institution, not because they
can be easily disciplined, but because drastic measures have
already become necessary to prevent injury to the public.

No one can deny that stern discipline is inevitably required in the administration of a prison. But, generally speaking, there have been few escapes; the frontiers of our prisons
have been maintained, and, although it may have taken steel
and stone and bullets at times, the public has been protected in
that a prison disturbance has rarely extended beyond the
prison gates.

No, it is hardly fair to charge the prisons with failure on any
of these counts. Those who are sent there are failures indeed
and it may be candidly admitted that such men who have
demonstrated their utter incapacity to live at liberty and in
harmony with the laws of their community have not in the
past often been made better after a term in prison. They may
well have been made worse. It is natural that the high rate of
recidivism in American prisons (though inquiries lead me to
believe that the rate is equally high abroad) should be used as
proof of this. Estimates of the amount of recidivism prevailing range all the way from 25 to 80 per cent. Census Bureau
figures reveal that out of 60,073 prisoners received into penal

institutions in 1933 only 21,340 could be identified as not having had any previous institutional experience. Out of this total number there were 16,036 as to whose record no report could be obtained. A fair guess therefore is that from 55 to 60 per cent of our prison population are recidivists. But is this entirely the failure of the prison, or is it as well the failure of the social conditions which produce its inmates?

The findings of Prof. and Mrs. Sheldon Glueck [3] to the effect that 60 per cent of the graduates of a State reformatory in the East relapsed into crime were hailed as convincing evidence of the failure of the reformatory system. A close study of the facts presented in this remarkable scientific study demonstrates, however, that not only were all but four single individuals out of the five hundred cases selected for study failures when they entered the reformatory but many of them, in fact, most, had shown repeated inability to adjust themselves in the community. The fact that 20 per cent of the cases so studied eight years after their discharge from the reformatory had had no contact with the law and that 17 per cent more had committed only slight offenses, is not so discouraging a disclosure as at first blush appears.

In his book on "The Human Mind," Dr. Karl Menninger says that the rate of cures in insanity is about 20 per cent and considers it cause for gratification. Society has yet to find a cure for cancer, Bright's disease, meningitis, and many of the less serious forms of epidemic distempers which occasionally visit the human race to its great danger and dismay.

But in all these instances those charged with bringing about a cure have the active and anxious coöperation of the patient.

The outstanding and, at times, seemingly insuperable difficulty in the cure of conduct disorders is the continued presence of a stubborn volitional process in the individual. Physicians may diagnose, scientists may prescribe, and opportunities for reformation may be presented; but when conduct disorders are to be cured all of our social doctors, from the humblest

[3] The full failure rate reported in *500 Criminal Careers* (Knopf, 1930) was 79.9 per cent; however, 62.1 per cent were classified as "total failures," 16.8 per cent as "partial failures." *Op. cit.*, pp. 184, 187–191.

case worker to the warden of the penitentiary, are more or less powerless to control the volitional processes of the individual.

Many of us have an inevitably curious mixture of ideas as to the purpose of our penal institutions. Which makes the public more indignant, to be informed that prisoners are mistreated, locked in solitary cells, strung up by their thumbs, and denied contacts with the world outside, or to be told that, after all, the penitentiary is not so bad—one has his three meals a day (albeit at an average cost of seven or eight cents each, his moving pictures, his baseball games, his pipe and daily newspapers? The burlesque of a modern prison apartment which one sees in the Broadway revue with the lawbreaker enjoying all the benefits of a private telephone, a manicure, and his personal chef, may bring a laugh; but, underneath, such paradoxes provoke almost as much resentment as do the disclosures of even a Wickersham Commission.

I quote from a letter written by a United States District Judge, now deceased, of one of our island possessions sent to the Federal Bureau of Prisons:

Lately I have noticed many articles in the papers, magazines and reports of commissions in regard to the very bad condition of United States Prisons, and thought it might be . . . encouraging to learn that in my district many people consider the United States Penitentiary at Atlanta, Georgia, and the United States Industrial Reformatory at Chillicothe, Ohio, as health resorts and as places where the necessities and luxuries of life are given them free of charge, and where they can obtain an industrial education without expense.

. . . .

Many of them consider them as their only chance in life to obtain an industrial education, and speak in deep and lasting gratitude of our Government for providing them with this opportunity.

However, unfortunately, our institutions of higher learning like the Atlanta Penitentiary . . . are not open to the general public, but a person desiring a course in training in these institutions must commit a crime against the United States in order to be sent there.

After discussing the case of a young cripple who, in the Judge's opinion, committed the crime with the intent to receive a sentence, he ends:

I would suggest that in view of the high regard in which the United States Penitentiary . . . are held by many people and their strong desire to avail themselves of the advantages of these institutions of higher learning, that you change your entrance requirements, so that a person does not have to commit a crime to obtain admission thereto.

On another occasion a Board of Public Welfare in a North Carolina county complained as follows:

There have been a number of men from this county who have served terms in the Federal Penitentiary at Atlanta, Georgia . . . Upon their return they invariably report good treatment and better food than they ever had in their lives and dilate upon the baseball games, moving picture shows and other entertainments arranged at the penitentiary. . . . I feel that a term in the Federal penitentiary should be made less attractive to a class of men who are inclined to regard it as a vacation from family responsibilities.

Can it be that these two writers are talking about the same type of place which incurred the wrath of the Wickersham Commission's investigation? Perhaps they are and perhaps they are both partly correct.

Perhaps the same people who shudder with horror at the report of "cruelty" in some of our prisons would writhe with righteous indignation at any attempt to provide "the comforts of home" at Government expense for those of their brethren who have visited the fleshpots of an American urban community.

Lax and unintelligent discipline in many of our prisons not only results in the presence of degrading influences but also in many instances is accompanied by ill advised, though sometimes well intentioned leniency of treatment.

The perplexing problem confronting the prison administrator of today is how to devise a prison so as to preserve its rôle of a punitive agency and still reform the individuals who have been sent there. If the prison, as was originally conceived, is to stand as the last milestone on the road to depravity, if it is to represent that ultimate of punishment which must follow a refusal to obey the rules of society, and if, as has been so generally contended, its principal object is to deter others from committing depredations which would bring them within its shadow, why must it not be made as disagreeable as may be? If punishment is effective to deter, it would seem as though the more punitive the prison was, the greater would be the effect of deterring others. If we execute men for murder, then why do we hide them away in the gray dawn of the morning and allow only a handful of witnesses?

It may be that the prison of a century ago was designed with the sole thought of making its inmates unhappy. Certainly the architecture of many of them will give that impression. In the "Rules and Regulations for the Government of the Massachusetts State Prison, with a Description of the Edifice, An Act of Legislature on the Subject and Remarks on the Present State of the Institution," dated 1811,[4] we read:

> The Massachusetts State-Prison, or Penitentiary, stands on the westernmost point of the peninsular of Charlestown, at Lynde's point, a pleasant and healthful spot, commanding a rich, variegated and extensive prospect. . . . The foundation is composed of rocks, averaging two tons in weight, laid in mortar. On this foundation is laid a tier of hewn stone, nine feet long, and twenty inches thick, forming the first floor. The outer walls are four, and the partition walls two feet thick. . . . The second story is like the first, except that the outer wall is but three and one half feet thick, . . . with double glazed windows, double grated with iron bars two inches square. . . .
> Competent judges pronounce this to be among the strongest, and best built prisons in the world. It has these advantages, over other buildings of this kind, it can neither be set on fire by the prisoners nor be undermined. The walls are built of hard flint stone, from six to fourteen feet long.

When the sole purpose of a prison was to make men miserable there was nothing particular to be gained by beautify-

---

[4] I am indebted for a copy of this old book to George E. Cornwall, of Boston, worker with discharged prisoners for half a century.

ing the architecture, by attempting to cure any loathsome disease which the men might have, by educating them, or even by improving their personalities except, of course, in so far as the will to commit crime could be terrorized out of them.

Why has the public revolted against brutality in prison ever since the dynamic attack of John Howard one hundred and fifty years ago? Is it pity for those who have done wrong and the feeling that many of them may not have had a fair chance to succeed? Is it the recognition of the fact that enfeebled bodies, inadequate brains, and damaged souls are somehow community responsibilities? Or is it the repeated insistence of scientists that, after all, in the commission of crime, the human will has little opportunity for free and untrammeled action? Whatever may be the cause, our ideas as to penal treatment are being challenged. We still insist on punishing people—but within limitations. We must make them unhappy but must do it in a more kindly spirit. We are confronted with the almost impossible and quite anomalous task of at once making our inmates sorry they committed the crime but glad that they went to prison for it. Now we are assailed by the horrible doubt that in mitigating the terrors of the prison commitment we may have laid our communities open to danger. We may as well agree with the Wickersham Commission to the extent of admitting that it is still too early to let such doubts overcome us. We may say in Scriptural fashion, "O, Prison, where is thy sting?" but it is noticed that the inmates will walk out whenever the door is open—and sometimes when it is not. There are enough riots, escapes, intrigues, and solicitation of political pressure among prisoners to reassure us that many of the inmates, at least, are not being coddled into a state of complete satisfaction with their surroundings. It will be some time yet before we have any considerable waiting list of persons anxious to break into even our best penitentiaries. After all, the most precious possession of the normal man is his freedom to go and come. "Give me liberty, or give me death," said Patrick Henry, and so would many of us if we were offered the alternatives of an indefinite confinement in a small though sumptuous apartment and the liberty to choose our environment, however humble it might be.

Occasionally one hears of a miserable human being who expresses a willingness to go back to prison or who even gives as a reason for the commission of crime the fact that he desired to return to a penal institution. These cases are extremely rare, however, and in almost all of them there is such a physical or mental abnormality as to make it unwise even to permit such a person to live under free and normal environment.

Apart from one or two sporadic attempts, there has been no thorough and scientific evaluation of prison treatment, either as to its therapeutic results in the case of men who have experienced it, or as to the deterrent effect upon the men who have not. The general assumption has grown, however, and is now fairly well recognized that mere residence in a prison will not in and of itself improve the personalities of the inmates. Moreover, history seems to prove that a prison cannot be sufficiently horrible to deter *all* potential lawbreakers.

To what extent these newer ideas have impressed themselves on penologists may be indicated by a passage from the report made in the summer of 1931 to the Assembly of the League of Nations by the Fifth Committee on Penal and Penitentiary Questions:

A penalty can no longer in these days be regarded merely as the infliction of pain or the expiation of a crime. Apart from quite exceptional cases, when the criminal has to be *eliminated,* a penalty is to be looked on as means of *readapting the offender to social life*—as a means of reclamation. It is moreover this view of the nature of punishment which has contributed to the great development of penology.

. . . .

If, in the immense majority of cases, the penalty is regarded as a means of reclaiming the delinquent, and if it is intended to influence the whole character of the criminal, it must obviously not be executed in a barbarous spirit, as then it would fail in its real aim, which is to reform and humanize the delinquent.

It seems to me that the controlling cause which is changing and will still further alter our prisons from places of misery
to institutions of constructive discipline is not any of the causes
quoted above, but a growing conviction that inasmuch as the
first duty of our penal law is to protect society; that society is,
in fact, more fully protected through the restoration of prisoners to society as better men and that in order to accomplish
this certain mitigations in prison punishment must be made. I
shall attempt to amplify this thought later on.

Some of the critics of our prison and reformatory system
become impatient at the slow progress from day to day. We
have only to look back fifty to seventy-five years, however, to
discover what significant changes have already taken place.
Thousands of "prisoners" are today serving sentences in open
labor camps, restrained only by their own sense of honor. The
ball and chain, the iniquitous lease system, the shaved head,
the water cure, and in most instances the striped suit and the
dark solitary are things of the past.

Arthur Train in "Puritan's Progress" tells of a Massachusetts prison in which in 1837 a man was discovered "confined
in a dark room in a cellar where he had lived for seventeen
years. He had protected himself against cold by stuffing hay
through the cracks in the door, his food being passed to him
through a wicket." The daily menu of the prison of a hundred years ago would be insufficient for a stray dog to live on
today.

Compare with these the simple yet sustaining menus in most
of our present-day penitentiaries, the more humane system of
punishments and the growing disposition to use the deprivation of privileges instead of the enervating or debasing types
of punishment, the successful effort to get prisoners out of
their cells into shop or farm or into the yard each day for
certain hours, and the development of the road camp system.
The great increase in the use of probation and parole, the
attempt to employ prisoners in industries and vocational pursuits, the introduction of carefully managed libraries, the insistence upon medical prophylaxis, the success of many States

in classifying their prisoners into a variety of institutions, the recent development of new types of prison architecture, the belated discovery that prisoners are individuals and must be treated as such if any attempt at their cure is to be effected, are hopeful developments to the credit of the last two or three decades.

Our difficult task in the coming years is to secure the adoption of these improvements throughout the forty-eight States. The more progressive commonwealths must assume the burden of leadership and defend and interpret their prison policies to communities less favorably placed.

Notwithstanding the progress noted above we must not be too optimistic in contending that the prisons as a whole have succeeded in their larger mission. There remains enough to be accomplished to challenge the interest of public-spirited citizens of many future generations.

To establish a prison environment which will not be a welcome asylum to the man who has lived in squalor and degradation and still not be a place of continual torture and deprivation to a man of finer sensibilities, is a considerable undertaking in itself. While one must of necessity insist upon equal treatment for all offenders and resolutely reject the granting of special privileges to the influential or wealthy prisoner, nevertheless, the special needs of individual personalities must in some manner be discovered and supplied.

At this point the skeptic will again rise up to inquire what will be the result of new and more adequate buildings, decent living conditions, improved diet, better qualified prison guards, and efforts to educate the individual. Will it remove the fear of punishment? Can we improve our prisons and yet deter the potential criminal? I believe we can. While our new system is to be built around the concept that all its prisoners must be returned to society, and that society is not protected unless they are returned more efficient, more honest, and less criminal than when they went in, at the same time, as I have already pointed out, such punishment need not lose its deterrent value. If the experience of punishment makes possible an acquaintance for the first time with some of the higher things of life, it may still be very desirable disciplinary experience.

There is no wise prison man but admits that, even with all the improvements that may be instituted in the modern prison, it will still be better for the prisoner if he can safely be kept out. There comes a time, however, in the community treatment of many an offender when he becomes unmindful of precept, immune to good example, heedless of warnings and advice, and positively dangerous in his activities. Social work, psychiatric diagnosis, probation, and Christian sympathy alike are futile. The case for the prison is merely this, that a strict program of prophylaxis, hard manual labor, enforced education, daily regimen, and fair discipline with a modicum of constructive recreation and opportunity for solitary introspection will not induce people to commit depredations on society; the possibility exists that it may do what all else has failed to do.

Our hopes for prison betterment will not be difficult to define. The splendid set of ideals laid down by the American Prison Association in 1870 and heretofore referred to has been the goal towards which the conscientious prison warden has striven. Questions of education, physical rehabilitation, training, recreational possibilities, and mental and moral improvement of inmates take equal prominence in discussions at prison meetings nowadays with the more practical matters of prison management.

Critics of our prison administration must continually bear in mind that the control of the difficult and dangerous personalities which go to make up the average population in our penal institutions is not easy. This may constitute one reason why we have not had better men to manage our prisons.

A person that can withstand continual association with human depravity and be constantly assailed by the anxieties and hazards which beset the average prison warden must possess more than the usual amount of physical, mental, and moral stamina. In all the varied fields of human relations it would be difficult to imagine a task requiring a larger quota of intelligence, patience, and the will to serve than is required of the prison warden under the newer ideals. He will need the respect and support of the public.

Notwithtanding the provision for opportunities for improvements, with steady employment at productive labor, with a force of tactful and intelligent prison guards, with suitable surroundings, nourishing food, elevating literature and stimulating recreation, no permanent reformation can be expected until in some mysterious manner the will to reform can be instilled into the individual personality. There is no doubt much to criticize in the management of our prisons, and there will be until there is a deeper public recognition of the need for more money, more intelligence, and more toleration.

But even if we were not able to point out the many directions in which prisons have been materially improved through the last few decades, the situation would be encouraging in two important respects. First, it is quite evident that the time has gone by when the secrets of the prison can be kept from the public. Governors, legislatures, social workers, investigators, friends and relatives, and in many cases groups of sightseers have thronged our prisons both inside and out. The manner in which our prisoners are treated has become a public concern.

Secondly, the standards of prison management that are demanded by investigating commissions, by editorial writers, and by students of penology are not the old standards of prison management. If the main or only purpose of the prison of today were to punish, these newer demands would have no force whatever. A report such as that filed by the National Commission on Law Observance and Enforcement could not have received the public approbation which it did have, had it been written fifty years ago. The criticisms that are being made of our prisons today and the dark picture which they paint indicate a definite change of attitude by the public, and themselves constitute a general recognition that the ideals aimed at by the enlightened leaders in prison reform are sound and hopeful standards.

In short, the prison has three purposes: to protect, to deter, and to improve. It has succeeded in the first two: few men escape from prison, and most men fight not to go there and burst forth at the first opportunity. It is in the achievement of the third purpose that most prisons fall short of expectations.

When we have provided the necessary tools therefor we can only hope that there will be as much success in realizing the newer ideals as there was in carrying out the old.

CHAPTER V

WHEN CONVICTS RIOT

He who would sound the depths of power divine,
Should for a time in gloomy dungeon dwell,
Where grief corrodes and harrows up the soul.
Domestic care should prey upon his mind,
To sorrow and to crosses long inured,
By various troubles and by tempests toss'd.
Would you improve in virtue's rigid lore
By sad imprisonment?
                    —*Autobiography of Benvenuto Cellini.*

In the last chapter we discussed in a general way the purposes and the failures of our prisons, their difficulties and inconsistencies and our hopes for their improvement. Before undertaking to describe the efforts of the Federal Government to meet and solve the problems of prison management there are a few further general observations to be made.

There are two prominent ways in which public attention has been focused on the prisons in the last decade. One of them involves the right of prisoners to work, which will be discussed in the following chapter. The other concerns the number of recent outbreaks in American prisons, which has been large enough to warrant serious consideration as to their cause and cure. Many of the disturbances were not general enough to be classed under the head of riots; but in most instances damage was done, high feeling was engendered, and the cause of the progressive penology received a severe setback.

But it is hard to convince the average citizen that all is well with our prisons when such dramatic occurrences as the very recent riots force themselves on his attention.

In Columbus, Ohio, in April, 1930, an uprising was accompanied by a fire in which more than 300 convicts lost their lives. In a riot at Auburn, New York, in July, 1929, a few

77

desperadoes made their escape, and hell was let loose. In Canyon City on October 3, 1929, a small group of convicts took possession of a part of the institution, held some of the guards as hostages and at intervals murdered a guard and threw his body out of the window into the courtyard below.

In August of 1929 a disturbance at Leavenworth Penitentiary resulting in one death and several wounded grew out of the intolerable heat and too much Mexican rice on the menu.

To the credit of the men who govern our prisons it should be said, however, that in most cases the insurrection did not extend beyond the walls. Drastic measures may have been necessary, but in most cases escapes were prevented and outside depredations forestalled.

We expect trouble of this sort in some of our 3,000 county jails from time to time—and we are not disappointed. But many of the institutions where trouble occurred are well financed and supposedly have experienced guards and wardens in control.

In the fall of 1935 I saw thrown on the screen of a movie theater the astounding prediction, in connection with some astrological hokum that was being perpetrated, that December would be among other things the month of prison breaks. Who let the secret get out, and whether it was cause or effect, I don't know; but the prediction came true. In Massachusetts, in Tennessee, in South Dakota, in Oklahoma, and in other places "breaks," or disturbances involving loss of life or damage, took place.

If our prisons can do nothing in the way of reform, have we not, at least, the right to expect them to hold the prisoner and prevent such distressing outbreaks?

What is the cause of this condition?

Some say we have been too severe in the treatment of the criminal and we are reaping the natural harvest of resentment and reprisal. Some say we have coddled the prisoner and he is taking advantage of our lenient treatment. Some say prisoners are just naturally depraved, and we must be resigned to such outbreaks and prepared to quell them with an iron hand.

Now, it is important to determine which of these reasons is the true one if we are to improve the security of our penal institutions. In nearly every major prison disturbance—that is, where there is more than a single escape or where the demonstration is participated in by more than a few men— there are a remote cause and an immediate cause. For a con- flagration to assume dangerous proportions there must be both torch and tinder—some inflammable matter and a spark to ignite it.

The most commonly cited immediate causes of prison riots are: first, bad food; second, cases of individual injustice, real or supposed, to an inmate; third, quickly developed anger against an employee; fourth, the sudden imposition of a new rule or regulation. Let us consider these in the order in which they are listed:

Weevils in the oatmeal, a piece of tainted meat or a batch of soggy bread—such things might be only an incident in the lives of many poor people; but in a prison, where men are constantly on edge, where it is one of the favorite indoor sports to nurse a grievance against society in general, such irritations take on a paramount importance.

Prisoners usually are loyal to one another. Osborne and others have pointed out the existence of a prison fraternity. Whatever the degree of criminality, they all consider them- selves brothers in gray, and a real or imaginary injustice to one is an affront to all. The more determined or restless prisoners sometimes use such an incident as an excuse for a demonstra- tion.

Some of our conscientious prison guards, through lack of tact or through some personal defect of character, get "in bad" with the prison population. The problem of supporting the actions of an unpopular employee is a serious one.

Rules we must have to govern a prison; but many a dis- turbance has been caused by the arbitrary imposition of dis- ciplinary regulations that are not thoroughly understood by

the inmates. Many wardens are finding it of value to maintain an inmate committee elected by the prisoners for the very
purpose of interpreting these regulations to their fellows.[1]

Although the incidents I have just cited are often the immediate causes of trouble, it is quite probable that any of
them could occur in a well regulated prison without causing
any outbreak. For a revolt to be of more than momentary
duration there must be some underlying stratum of discontent.
In recent years many such factors in the administration of our
criminal law and the conduct of our prisons have been pointed
out.

Briefly stated, these more remote causes of prison demonstrations may be said to be:

Overcrowding, with its attendant evils—cramped quarters,
reduced privileges, less yard time, utter lack of privacy, hastily
prepared food, inability to give individual attention to prisoners.

How much longer can we remain indifferent to the overcrowded condition of our penitentiaries or unmindful of the
baneful results—San Quentin, California, with 5,700, Jefferson City, Missouri, 4,700, Jackson, Michigan, 6,200 and the
prisons of Texas, Oklahoma, Arkansas, West Virginia, all
crowded to suffocation with conditions we would not tolerate
if the inhabitants were cattle instead of human beings.

We can lavish money on roads, schools, hospitals, band concerts, warships, but it takes a riot to open our eyes to the need
of spending a dollar for new prisons.

Wormwood Scrubs, the most populous prison in England,
averaged 934 inmates for the year 1934.[2] In Canada, St.
Vincent de Paul near Montreal was the largest with a daily
average of 990.[3] I have seen but one prison in Europe outside
of Russia designed for more than 1,200 inmates.

Take the case of the Kentucky State "Reformatory" at

[1] See Chapter XI.
[2] Report of the Commissioner of Prisons and Director of Convict
Prisons for the year 1934.
[3] Annual Report of Superintendent of Penitentiary, for the fiscal year
ended March 31, 1935.

Frankfort. I select this one because the earnest effort of the present prison administration in Kentucky to remedy the situation makes the subject timely. Constructed to house 1,000, it now holds 3,000, of whom 2,000 are absolutely and permanently idle. Look at this pictured group on the opposite page and ask yourself the question, Are they being reformed? Three of these boys you are looking at are serving twelve years for the theft of a hog—four years apiece. One hundred of them are under seventeen years of age. How much majesty is there in the kind of law which requires such requitals?

Our niggardliness in permitting overcrowded prisons, the smug complacency with which we fill and refill them with minor offenders, is nothing short of a national disgrace.

Idleness is a potent cause of unrest. Except in a few of our state institutions, only a small percentage of inmates are kept productively and continuously busy. Petty tasks are undertaken. Three men are put on a one-man job. Most of our prison labor is purposeless—and an idle or poorly occupied mind literally becomes the devil's workshop.

The character of our prisoners is changing. Since the war life in both urban and rural communities has been freer, faster and less under restraint than ever in the history of mankind. The almost unlimited distribution of firearms, the possession of rapidly propelled motor vehicles, high living—these have started many along the road that leads only to disaster. Many adventurous youths turn to criminal activities for the thrill which so many of our restless generation crave. Not only does the presence of increasing numbers of this class complicate prison discipline, but the confinement itself is much more of a punishment to prisoners of the twentieth century than to those of former eras. Even if their cages were entirely gilded, many of these birds would not be content!

The very tempo of modern life outside still further emphasizes the monotony and regimentation of prison life. The necessary denial of normal outlets breeds a discontent and a restlessness which few of those outside can understand.

It is a mistake to suppose that prisoners can be completely

immured and isolated from the world. In most prisons they have magazines, daily papers, radio, and news reels. It is part of the newer penology not to remove them from the development of civilization (if it is developing) around and about them. No reasonable success at reëstablishing a convict can be attained if his mind has stood still for the one, five, ten, or fifteen years of his sentence. The prisoner, therefore, knows what is going on outside; he draws his own conclusions and forms his own (many times warped) judgments. He even reads and ponders over the discussions about himself and oftentimes is amused or irritated thereat. Even if he had no direct means of communication he would know just the same.

Again, I have no doubt that there rankles in the breasts of many convicts a feeling of personal injustice. I do not say that it is a just feeling; I merely say that many of them have it. One keen foreign observer recently commented upon the tremendously long sentences which our courts mete out to certain types of offenders. It has been said that we attempt to strike a balance by lengthening the sentences of those we catch to operate as a deterrent effect upon those whom we do not. In the last decade not only have our legislatures increased the quantum of punishment for certain crimes, but courts and parole boards have been led to impose longer sentences. In a recent series of articles by President Roosevelt, entitled "Crime and Criminals," appeared the following: [4]

"In Auburn prison there are two youths, ages twenty-one and twenty-five, who are serving sentences of forty-seven years and six months to life for robbery. One of these will be sixty-eight and the other seventy-two years of age when released. One man sixty-nine years of age is serving a sentence of from fifteen to thirty years for robbery. He will be eighty-four years of age when released."

Is it remarkable that these men do not always remain complacent?

A feeling of injustice sometimes is engendered because punishment is inflicted in this country for acts which do not

[4] Quoted from the late Walter N. Thayer, Jr., a distinguished Commissioner of Correction for the State of New York.

Men in yard of Kentucky Reformatory.

constitute crimes in other countries. Drunkenness, drug addiction, sex crimes, and other violations are in this category.

The average prisoner is keen to detect any discrimination against himself. He neglects no opportunity to point out that the rich and powerful escape punishment, while the man without influence is sent to prison. Here again I do not say that he is justified in his belief. Many influential gangsters and public enemies of high rank have been gathered in recently by our law enforcement agencies. Other people in high places are commencing to feel uncomfortable over the prospect. The jail-house chatter of the present day, however, always comes back to this never-failing topic of conversation.

A mystified negro came in before the warden the other day. His record showed, "Violation Internal Revenue Act, 4 years." "But, boss, Ah wan't at the still." "Well, but, Joe, look here, your record says you pleaded guilty." "Yassir, boss, Ah *pleaded guilty to not doing it.* Ah told the Gov'ment lawyer Ah wan't at the still, so he says: 'O.K., Joe. You plead guilty, and we will let you off easy.' So Ah jes' pleaded guilty to not bein' dar, but heah Ah is."

To add to the general dissatisfaction of the men in prison, there is the quite common feeling that society as a whole has never given them a chance, that they were forced into crime by press of circumstances, and that if they had had the "breaks" they would not be there. Thus envy and resentment against what they think is discriminatory treatment provides a ready soil for the sowing of the dragon's teeth of rebellion.

Lastly, there is the all-important factor of the personality of the prison officer. His job is not a pleasant one. In too many institutions it is filled by discouraged and unqualified men, many of them so badly underpaid that they occasionally fall prey to the temptations which beset them. We can provide tool-proof prisons with unscalable walls; we can offer adequate educational, recreational, and occupational opportunities; but the presence of one crooked guard in an institution will do much to impede the reform or proper discipline of an inmate population.

The important thing for us to determine is whether these causes can be eliminated and if they can be eliminated, whether we may hope for an improved prison administration.

Once more, I emphasize that most of the sensational riots in our American prisons have been actively participated in by few prisoners. In many riots it was the leadership of adventurous, desperate, and long-sentenced men which instigated the outbreak. Many of these have been killed in the attempt or received further punishment as a result. One would think that the futility of these demonstrations would be borne in upon the prisoners; the fact that this is not the case is evidence of the intensity of the motives behind them.

Some one has said that these outbreaks are traceable to the American mode of living. As a matter of fact, our English brethren attempted to apologize for the disorders at the Dartmoor Convict Prison a few years ago by saying that too many American motion pictures of prison riots had been shown in Great Britain. It is significant that the immediate and remote causes are strikingly similar to those attributed in our own country. A paragraph from the report of the distinguished barrister who investigated this English prison riot is illuminating:

I believe that the prisoners had no substantial grievance, and that such grievances as they had would not have led to any disorder unless a few of the dangerous prisoners, partly by their power of leadership, partly by intimidation, had played on the feelings and the fears of others. In my view the belief that Y. had been cruelly assaulted on Sunday morning made a great many men resentful who would otherwise have been loyal.

Another of the conclusions of this impartial observer will be reassuring to some of the Doubting Thomases of our generation and is worth quoting:

Nor do I think that the more humane and reformative treatment of prisoners which has been the aim of prison administration in this country [Great Britain] for many years conduces to disorder, or that there is any reason to suppose that harsher treatment of the convicts would have prevented what took place.

The responsibility for a disturbance at the Kingston penitentiary in Ontario, Canada, not long ago was at one time laid at the door of several alleged American convicts, but this has never been satisfactorily proved.

We cannot overlook the importance of the method of housing prisoners.

In practically all of our prisons men work together, eat in a large dining room, mill around the exercise yard by the hundreds, go to church and the "movies" en masse, and even sleep in dormitories or in a cell containing more than one bunk.

England and other European nations adopted the separate system as their model. I have visited prisons in eleven foreign countries, and I have seen but one cell block, as we know it in America, although England now permits congregate activities during the day. In France, Holland, Italy, and other countries of western Europe solitary or separate confinement is the rule. The prisoner lives alone, works alone, eats by himself, and even takes his exercise and his religion literally in solitude. In many a prison in Europe no convict ever sees the face of a single one of his fellow prisoners. On the rare occasions on which he does leave his cell he wears a mask or head covering.

I remember standing with the warden of a prison in Florence, Italy, looking out over the exercise yard, which was cut into small cubicles. When I explained to him that in an American prison 2,000 men would be permitted to congregate in the yard he showed a great surprise and said it would be considered dangerous to follow that system.

One of the most interesting institutions which I ever visited is the large prison at Fresnes, a few miles outside of Paris. Here the separate system is maintained in every detail. The moment that the door of the cell was opened by the governor, the inmate instinctively reached for the wall whereon hung a burlap bag of dimensions suitable to fit his head, and with a quick and furtive look at the visitors he pulled on the cap concealing his identity, while apparently permitting him to look out through the heavy mesh of the burlap.

His exercise was limited to a few minutes a day in an enclosed stall. If he went to chapel, he was encased in an upright, solitary pew with a small opening in front through which he could see the priest or minister.

I compared notes later with another American who visited this institution the same summer. He was enthusiastic over the merits of the system. Here, he claimed, was no chance for contamination, nor the hatching of plots; nor would it be possible for the prisoners to "gang up" after they were discharged from their terms. But I just could not see it that way. The terrible abnormality of such confinement seemed appalling. If it is true that man is a gregarious animal, then the greatest lesson which we can teach him is how to live with his fellow men. I tried to picture what would be the attitude and capacity of a man released into a changing world after being immured for five years in a living tomb. However, my mind was open. If this kind of treatment deterred the criminal and prevented his return to prison, then it must be accepted as effective. Certainly no man in his right mind would ever come back to this institution if he could possibly avoid it.

So in halting French I inquired of the governor, "How many of the men who are now here have been here before?" He replied, "Fifty-five per cent," which is almost exactly the recidivism rate in the prisons of America. I said to him, fearing that I had not understood, "Do you have many recidivists?" To which he replied, with a shrug of his shoulders, "*Beaucoup de récidivistes*—two, three, four, five times."

On the other hand, in the Prison de la Forêt, in Belgium, where they have abandoned the solitary system for a system of congregate effort in shops and dining room, the officer in charge contended that the discipline was better, more humane and more hopeful under the new system, and that he would never willingly go back to the old.

In spite of the difficulties we are having in adjustment, it is evident to the progressive penologist that the solution does not lie in the adoption of the solitary system. In the first place, we have not money enough to build a single cell of sufficient size for each man. In the second place, we must realize that a man kept five years or more in solitary imprisonment is an unfit and dangerous person to live again with other human beings —that unless we can make men respect the rights of one another and the rights of their government in prison we shall have little hope that they will do so in the freedom of the outside world.

Charles Dickens, speaking of solitary confinement, used these words:

I am persuaded that those who devised this system . . . do not know what it is that they are doing . . . that there is a depth of terrible endurance in it which none but the sufferers themselves can fathom, and which no man has a right to inflict upon his fellow-creature. I hold this slow and daily tampering with the mysteries of the brain, to be immeasurably worse than any torture of the body. . . . I hesitated once, debating with myself, whether, if I had the power of saying "Yes" or "No," I would allow it to be tried in certain cases, where the terms of imprisonment were short; but now, I solemnly declare, that with no rewards or honours could I walk a happy man beneath the open sky by day, or lie me down upon my bed at night, with the consciousness that one human creature, for any length of time, no matter what, lay suffering this unknown punishment in his silent cell, and I the cause, or I consenting to it in the least degree.

The remedy for prison riots is not the adoption of the greater evil of solitary confinement.

What can we do about it? The purpose of this book is to undertake a discussion of some of the fundamental questions which lie behind the recent disasters in prisons. At this point it will be sufficient to say that our defense must be along the following lines.

1. Adequate structural defense to be maintained at all times. The safe prison not only will be of ample size and surrounded with an adequate wall, but will be provided with all the modern mechanical protective devices.

2. We must be more concerned with our personal defense. While in some prison systems progress is being made in this re-

gard, and while there are countless brave, honest, and faithful guards carrying on under difficult circumstances, we shall never, I am confident, permanently eradicate the underlying cause of unrest in our prisons until we have improved the character of prison employees. The warden and his officers must be trained and developed as carefully as our school teachers.

If we really want to prevent prison riots in the future we can take no more effective step than to insist upon the professionalization of the prison service. This is no idle or perfunctory statement. The prisons of many of our States and the jails in most of them are at this moment in the grip of party politics, and until this condition is changed it will be difficult to bring about any improvement.[5]

3. As a further defense we must insist that the social necessity of keeping prisoners employed under fair competition on State-use projects is at least of equal importance with the relief of unemployment generally.[6]

4. Finally, to prevent prison riots we must build up a new morale and a new attitude by and toward the prisoners— an attitude of fair play, an equality of treatment which does not sacrifice discipline on the one hand nor fairness on the other. If we increase the certainty of apprehension and the speed of disposition, we shall be better able to distribute punishment more equally, deterrence will be more effective, and the sense of injustice of those who are caught will be reduced.

In some way the prisoners' impression that they have been wronged must be supplanted by the cleansing emotion of repentance and contrition as a prerequisite to reform. Their loyalty to one another must be broadened to include a loyalty to the government. No one can prophesy that our prisons can ever be made riot-proof, that desperate enemies of society will not rebel even at the risk of their lives. Prison guards will be called upon from time to time to hold such attempts in check.

But the prison most likely to be without riots will be the

[5] See Chapter X.   [6] See Chapter VI.

one in which there will be neither coddling nor brutality, neither idleness nor industrial slavery, neither rigidity nor vacillation, neither disdain nor fraternizing. In it scrupulous cleanliness will rule and productive work will be the part of all—inmates and officers. There must be impartiality of treatment, impeccable honesty, just treatment for the poor and lowly as well as for the rich and influential.

Many of our prisons, reformatories and training schools carry on from day to day with fidelity, with safety to our communities, with a devotion to their difficult task and a resulting benefit to the public. Such routine is not new. Many of our penitentiaries have never had a riot of any sort.

We are passing through a transition stage not only in our prison administration but in the administration of our criminal law. We need not be entirely discouraged. Our people are aroused to the importance of prompt, vigorous and condign treatment of the dangerous malefactor. The problem of accompanying this treatment with a fair, humane, and scientific effort at rehabilitation of those who can profit by it is difficult but not insoluble.

CHAPTER VI

SHOULD PRISONERS WORK WHEN OTHER MEN CANNOT?

. . . The organized labor movement has been in accord with the position that men, or rather human beings, deprived of their choice of action and of their liberty must not be kept in absolute idleness. In addition to the fact that it is natural for a man to work, work is also civilizing and developing and educational. All persons must have work of some kind. The only question is what kind of work. The only question that has developed in connection with convicts is, What kind of work shall they do and under what conditions shall that work be performed in order that the convicts may get the greatest advantage out of the work and at the same time that there shall be no injury done to free workers through the products of prison labor?

What the organized labor movement has concerned itself with has been the nature of the work done by convicts and safeguards to prevent the products of their labor from coming in competition with the products of free labor and in that way undermining the standards and conditions of work which the free workers have established for themselves. This position of the American Federation of Labor has been repeatedly indorsed.

—Samuel Gompers.

The Argument Stated

"In other words," said Congressman A to Congressman B, in a recent debate on this subject, "a man ought not to have to go to jail to get a job." Here, tersely and convincingly put, is the argument against convict labor which is so difficult to answer. Mr. Average Citizen says immediately, "By all means, the reduced number of industrial opportunities should be first of all made available for the virtuous and hard-working individual who has not run afoul of the criminal law," and Mr. Average Congressman nowadays is most anxious not only that his actions in Congress shall receive the approval of his constituents, but that he may sincerely and earnestly help in the solution of the baffling problem of unemployment.

Such an argument against prison labor is easy to compre-
hend. Many people see the issue of prison labor from a comparative viewpoint. They feel that, after all, the virtuous
must have some preference over the sinful, and that, if there
is not enough work for both, they must regretfully consign at
least that limited portion of the sinful who become inmates
of our penal institutions to the limbo of idleness and disin-
tegration.

It may be that they have not sufficiently realized the fact
that idleness in a penal institution must be regarded as part of
the larger social problem fraught with dangerous economic
and sociological reactions. Is it in the interest of society as a
whole that prisoners should work even though some free men
cannot? I think it is.

In the discussions on this subject, the attempt is usually
made to rivet our attention on the right of the manufacturer
to produce a certain article and the privileges which workmen
in certain trades and crafts should possess to labor at certain
tasks. Seldom, if ever, have we analyzed the interests of the
consuming public. Not often have we approached prison
labor in its bearing upon the good of the whole community.

What, on the other hand, are the claims so ardently advanced by prison reformers in favor of allowing prisoners to
labor, which, at least up to the point of his own competitive
interest in the subject, the average citizen approves?

Prison Labor Reduces Expense of Prisons. It costs money
to maintain prisons. It adds to the individual taxpayer's obligations. The prisoner must be fed and housed, cured and educated, if possible, and sent on his way with at least a few
dollars in his pocket. If, during the term of his incarceration,
the labor of his hands or brain can be utilized to produce
things of value for the Government, the sum total of the cost
of his keep may be reduced.

Work and Discipline. From the point of view of discipline
it is indisputably true that an industrious man makes less
trouble than an idle one. Inactivity is nowhere more disin-
tegrating than in a prison, and the warden's difficult task of

keeping order and discipline is inevitably complicated if a large proportion of his men are idle or only partly employed. We have pointed out that riots and disturbances are, as a matter of history, less likely to occur in institutions where a good industrial program is in operation.

The Training Argument Must Not Be Forgotten. Ninety-eight per cent of the men who are sent to prison come out after a term which averages about a year and a half in the Federal prisons, and somewhat longer in the State prisons. Very few men die in prison, even those who are sent there for life imprisonment. The ideal of modern prison management contemplates something more than merely the administration of punishment. We have tried to make it clear that those who become inmates of our penitentiaries must inevitably suffer the deprivations and hardships of having lost their liberty and being required to live for a time amid restricted and abnormal surroundings. The shame and disgrace of a prison commitment is the crowning punishment in the case of a respectable man. The cessation of his activities is a good deal of annoyance even to the habitual criminal. The greatest single obligation on a prison is to establish in its inmates the habit of diligence. All of our recent scientific inquiries into the causes of crime indicate with startling unanimity the industrial shiftlessness and unreliability of the men who go to prison. Fortunate is he who has a trade at which he can earn an honest living, and safe indeed is the community in which the number of skilled artisans and willing laborers predominates.

The Public Aspect of the Problem. It is indeed futile to subject men from whatever walk of life to a period of enforced and degrading idleness and then delude ourselves with the belief that through some miracle they have been shriven of their sins and will not offend again. It is certainly no particular benefit to the individual prisoner to compel him to work eight hours a day in preference to wasting his time playing cards or smoking a pipe. There is no evidence of coddling or leniency or consideration for the happiness of our prisoners in our demand that a rigorous and condign work program be inaugurated in each prison. The traditional sentence carried with it a promise that it be service at "hard labor." Shall this labor be of a treadmill and destructive type or constructive and socially valuable? It is rather with a more intelligent regard for the *safety of that community* to which these prisoners must be returned that we are insisting that they acquire habits of industry rather than indolence, self-reliance rather than dependence, and, if possible, be equipped with the skill and training necessary to fit them for resumption of economic life on the outside.

Prison Labor a Social Problem

Such are the arguments for keeping prisoners busy. Are we justified in giving heed to these contentions rather than to the pleadings of the unemployed who have not committed crime? Well, our first proposition is that the *prison problem* is a general, social problem and that the terrible effects of our failure to handle it are not and cannot be confined in the prison walls, that every laborer, employed and unemployed, and every employer, whether he pays dividends or uses up his surplus, is affected by the wisdom used in its solution. By the same token I insist that the problem of unemployment is a general problem, that while we would all speed the day when our economic adjustments can be so devised as to give every worker an opportunity to support himself and his dependents, we cannot postpone the time when prisoners shall be employed until every free laborer shall be taken care of and until every manufacturer shall have resumed his dividend payments. Where shall we draw the line? How long and to what extent must the employment of prisoners be deferred to await the full employment of all free citizens?

The reasons for our business depression are deep and fundamental. Even were every prisoner held in idleness there would not be any appreciable improvement in our unemployment situation. We must go through long and painful periods of adjustment. In the meantime, can we afford to say that the prosperity of the workers, whether organized into unions or otherwise, is to any extent dependent upon the number of them in prison or even upon whether they work or not?

If it is the commission of crime which disentitles men to the opportunity to labor, why should they be allowed to resume their position in industry upon their release? If the virtuous should labor and the sinful remain idle, for how long should they remain so? All their lives? Why should not all those who are on probation also be put at the bottom of the list until all the innocent ones have gotten jobs? Why should the line be drawn at those who have been caught and sentenced and committed to prison? If virtue and probity were to be prerequisites to the right to labor, many of us, I am afraid, would be sitting around doing nothing. No, it seems to me, we cannot conscientiously admit that the employment opportunities should be reserved for the innocent and denied to those who have offended against the laws. It is not in the interest of our communities that we should do so. Once we admit the wisdom of such a restriction it would be to the interest of labor to have as many people as possible in prison and keep them there as long as possible, in order to increase the number of jobs for those who manage to stay outside. The unemployment problem does not stop at the prison wall. It must not be forgotten that many prisoners were workmen, at least those who were willing to work and who could get jobs, before they became prisoners. Their labor in prison in this competitive aspect is therefore but a continuance of their free labor. They are not taking away jobs from free laborers. Nor are their numbers added to the entire number of workmen in society. A certain percentage of them are merely transferred from one employer to another.[1]

If the problem were not so deeply obscured by economic selfishness and political shortsightedness, one might readily argue that, just as persons with physical ailments require more care and watchfulness, so should persons with dangerous anti-

[1] See "American Prisons, Houses of Idleness," by James V. Bennett, *The Survey*, Vol. LXXI, No. 4, April, 1935.

social tendencies receive greater industrial consideration than those who find little difficulty in obeying the laws and supporting themselves. One does not need, however, to rely upon any such idealistic conception to find sufficient justification for employing prisoners from a practical standpoint.

Economic Aspects of the Problem

The existence of so much unemployment in our communities has focused public attention upon the importance of a regular job as a measure of individual security. We want work because it brings wages with it and wages purchase the necessities and comforts of life. If we could have three meals a day, good books to read, a comfortable house to live in, and stimulating leisure activities, should we be so insistent in demanding a job [2]—a job which is often a deadening routine of monotony? The point I am making is that in our great emphasis upon the needs for employment we may have failed to analyze completely our social needs and objects. We have confused work and jobs.

Consumers Argument

Again, one could put up quite an argument to the effect the consumers have certain interests to be considered as well as the workmen. The housewife might assert that she has the right to purchase necessary articles at the lowest prices obtainable, and until it is demonstrated that there is a taint to goods made in prison, she cannot be denied the opportunity to purchase them.

A few years ago, while walking along one of the streets of Nice, I noted a sign over a neat little shop reading "Lingerie de Prisons." I engaged the trim little shopkeeper in conversa-

---

[2] I realize the extent to which this argument can be reversed against the prison by asserting that prisoners likewise can be employed in healthful pursuits without indulging in competitive labor. I am suggesting no exemptions for the prisoner.

When it comes to earning their keep I see no reason for preferring either prisoners or free men. My contention is that a reëxamination of the end and aim of human labor would help to clarify our views as to both classes.

tion and found that white goods, underwear, ladies' dresses, etc., entirely made by the women inmates of French prisons were publicly on sale in this store. I asked her whether the other tradespeople did not object, and she replied in effect, with some surprise, What had that to do with the question? The people of France knew that they could buy these goods cheaper and better when made in the prisons and that she had no difficulty in selling all the goods that were so made. What right had the other shopkeepers to control the people's purchases?

But perhaps it will not be necessary to solve these economic problems in order to arrive at a suitable solution of the prison labor question.

Investigators and commissions have from time to time called attention [3] to the abuses inherent in the lease and contract labor system, and to the effect which the indiscriminate sale in the open market of convict-made goods has to depress prices. The inequitable competition with private industries and the unfairness to private enterprises in having the Government enter into business has also been pointed out.

Evils of System of Distribution

The focal point in the discussion of the problem of convict labor is of course the method of disposing of the product.

It cannot be gainsaid that many evils have grown up around the use of prison labor. It has been used for private profit. It has unfairly competed at times. It has led to the exploitation of the prisoner. It has interfered with the working out of the disciplinary and rehabilitation problems of the prison by subordinating everything else to the increase in production of goods.

From time to time employers' associations and labor organizations, very likely with a desire to secure increased markets for their own goods, have proposed one scheme or another to

[3] See, for instance, *Convict Labor in 1923,* Bulletin 372, U. S. Bureau of Labor Statistics; *Laws Relating to Prison Labor in the U. S. as of July 1, 1933,* by Charles Francis Sharkey, Bulletin 596, U. S. Bureau of Labor Statistics; *Prison Industries,* Domestic Commerce Series, No. 27, U. S. Bureau of Foreign and Domestic Commerce.

limit or prohibit the output of prison factories. Legislative measures have been proposed requiring the labeling of prison-made products. In a sense this move was justified, as in many cases false or misleading labels have been used. However, if prison goods have been made of good materials, in clean shops, and under Government auspices, why should they not be so labeled? What would a prison administrator who insisted on selling to the public have to fear? It is quite possible that prison factories might make such use of the label that it would in no way curtail the distribution of such products. In fact, it might have the effect of increased sales.

These labeling acts of course are inapplicable where the prison distributes its goods only to State or Government departments. The need of labeling therefore has been advanced to take effect only where there are sales in the open market. There is no doubt that it has been considered by free manufacturers as a method of fostering the prejudices of the purchasing public and resulting in diminished sales.

Restrictive Legislation

The accumulated efforts of the manufacturers and the labor unions crystallized in January, 1929, with the passage of the Hawes-Cooper Act. This legislation, which was not to take effect for five years, was intended to divest prison-made goods of their interstate character. It was opposed by prison administrators as being an unconstitutional measure and an unwarranted interference in State activities. Its proponents contended that the States were powerless to determine their own prison labor policies so long as other States were permitted to flood the home markets with articles produced by convicts under the lease or contract system, and thus unfairly depress commodity prices. The bill was undoubtedly a conscious attempt on the part of industry and labor to restrict the output of factories of prisons and penitentiaries which did an interstate business although, they pointed out, there was business enough to occupy the convicts in any State through the manufacture of goods for the public, or "State-use" market.

The Hawes-Cooper Act was held to be constitutional by

the United States Supreme Court in March, 1936,[4] and has had a considerable effect in eliminating contract labor from State institutions. The expectations of its proponents are being realized, and apart from those States which have been able to shift over to the "State-use" system there has been a notable increase in prison unemployment.

I firmly believe that the adoption of the State-use system for prison labor is the proper solution of this age-long issue.

State-Use Plan

This plan, in brief, presupposes that the labor of State wards, housed at public expense in Government institutions, should not be allowed to go unutilized but should be engaged in the manufacture of products for Government consumption and in the reduction of the Government's tax bill. Under the State-use system the Government makes and sells to itself. If the price is too high the taxpayer wins. If the price is too low, the Government purchasing agency will be that much better off. There can be no unreasonable or cutthroat competition. Whatever Government subsidy there is inures for the benefit of all. There can be no flooding of the market or price reduction, and no individual may profit at the public expense. The burden which comes from the slight competition with free labor is a common burden. Like the burden of taxation, the burden of unemployment, the burden of poor relief, and all the other common ills which flesh is heir to it must be borne through the combined efforts of all our citizens. Those who are well must cure those who are sick, the rich must provide for the poor, the employed must stake the unemployed, the law-abiding must reform the lawless.

With the proper development of the State-use system we not only abolish unfair competition and eliminate private profit but, through diversification of industries, provide that the burden of such competition as cannot be avoided is fairly distributed and does not fall disproportionately on any one class or group. This we can and should do.

[4] See *Whitfield* v. *Ohio,* 296 U.S. 561.

Since the time of Samuel Gompers, the American Federation of Labor, officially, has sponsored for the State-use system of prison labor. The Federation approved the existing Federal Prison Labor Act.[5] While they find it hard to keep their constituents in line, the leaders have consistently held to this position. We have nothing but praise for this attitude. As a matter of fact we have more opposition from the manufacturers, who are interested in profits, than from the unions, who are interested in saving the maximum number of employment opportunities for their constituents.

The general recognition of and in some instances the adoption of the State-use principle, while undoubtedly it reacted to the advantage of the manufacturers, has brought trouble and anxiety to the States which previously operated under the contract and public use systems. The contract system was easy of administration. It is difficult to provide the expert administration in prison which is necessary for the conduct of the State-use system, and it is expensive to acquire the necessary machinery. It is safe to assume, however, that the State-use system is well on its way to adoption by every State which desires to keep its prisoners employed.

Problem Not Yet Solved

There was reason to believe that a truce had been concluded on this basis, that the war raging over the marketing of prison-made goods was over. We had hoped that the American Federation of Labor, the employing interests, and all concerned had met on a common ground. If the prisons would forego production of the commodities for distribution to the private markets of the country, it was not unreasonable to expect that they might be given preference in the public or governmental market. Enough commodities are consumed by public departments to keep all prisoners in our penitentiaries busy eight hours a day manufacturing them.

A disturbing tendency, however, has been noted since the

[5] An act to provide for the diversification of employment of Federal prisoners, for their training and schooling in trades and occupations, and for other purposes (46 Stat. 391).

onset of the industrial depression, in that, while leaders in both manufacturing and labor fields still adhere by word of mouth to the State-use principle, individual trades and organizations do not hesitate to throw every possible obstacle in the way of its legitimate development. Factory trades advise putting prisoners to work on the public roads, and yet the American Contractors Association several years ago succeeded in inducing Congress to place a restriction on the Federal Aid Highway bill to the effect that none of the appropriations carried thereunder might be used to aid in the construction of roads on which prisoners were employed. Where is there a finer example of State-use than the construction of roads! Similarly with public buildings, even prison buildings. If any kind of work might be expected to be reserved for prisoners, it would be the erection of their own houses; and yet nowhere have State and Government departments been subjected to more pressure than by the building trades and labor organizations connected with them. Would you not think that, if laborers and contractors were unmolested in their construction of all the other buildings in the world, at least prisoners who have been temporarily removed from such activities, and many of whom may have previously been engaged in that very line of activity, would have the right to build the houses in which they themselves were to live?

Federal Prison Labor Program

The Federal Prison Labor Law passed in 1930, which has been referred to as one of the most progressive and liberal pieces of legislation on the subject, prohibits unfair competition, denies the private market to Federal prisons, gives preference to the prisons in the public market, provides for appropriate arbitration in disputes, and states that no prison labor shall be so devised as to reduce the number of persons employed in Government workshops. There can be little doubt as to the soundness of such procedure.

Notwithstanding the logic of such a position, however, the Federal Bureau of Prisons constantly recognizes the desirability of reducing to the lowest point the competition of convict labor with that of the free men.[6] It has never taken full advantage of the prison labor law. Not more than 25 per cent of Federal prisoners are at work on goods the manufacture of which by Government agencies might be said to take employment away from free laborers. The Bureau is continually attempting to find stimulating activities for prisoners which will not accentuate the problems of the depression but will have an economical value. Some of these prison labor projects have added materially to the wealth of the public.

Public Works and Ways

In addition to the activities of the Civilian Conservation Corps and the many Federal and State work relief projects there are hundreds of miles of roads on Government reservations as well as levees and dams and other public works which cannot be built because of insufficient funds.

The fact still remains that we have thousands of able-bodied idle laborers being fed at public expense in our prisons, and that there are also millions of dollars' worth of work in the enrichment of the public domain still waiting to be done, with no money to compensate free labor to do it.

We are gratified to report that we are making a start in the direction of using Federal prisoners on public works. At El Paso, for example, where we now have a Federal detention farm located on the dry land adjoining the Rio Grande, the 500 men therein housed are employed in the reclamation and irrigation of its 640 acres. Border jumpers, bootleggers, and other gentry who have lived in squalor and idleness, and who

---

[6] Since the diversification law of 1930 was passed the textile business has not been extended, the shoe output has been carefully controlled, and all new industrial activities have been in the following lines: foundry, garment making, brush making, broom manufacture, mat making, mattresses, metal transfer cases, salvage, road making, public works, farming, clothing.

As the work of the Board of Directors progresses it will, no doubt, be found advisable to still further diversify, and the following lines have been suggested: cannery, hand weaving, hand spinning, needle trades, manufacture of jute and burlap, manufacture of small metal articles, such as pails and barrels.

have been boarded over and over again at public expense, will have the pick and shovel placed in their hands and be told to go and earn their daily bread by the sweat of their brows, and in doing so they will not take a single job away from a free laborer.

At Fort Eustis, Virginia, a decadent Army post was taken over, and for three years thousands of dollars' worth of usable material was reclaimed from the junk pile. Vast stores of surplus Army materials were made over and reconditioned by prison labor into equipment for our new prisons and jails. We have now relinquished this area to the Federal Emergency Relief Administration, which has 3,500 transients employed there.

Thus, through the salvaging of land and the salvaging of property, we approach the more important task of the salvaging of men. No one of our new Federal prisons or jails has been built simply to house men. Our plans for such institutions have been influenced by the ever-present and all-important problem of prison labor.

Roads in National Forests are being constructed by Federal prison labor in Arizona and Idaho. Public improvements at Army encampments are in progress in Alabama and Washington. No reasonable complaint can be made or has been made against the convict labor activities of the Federal Bureau of Prisons.

The prisoners of the State of Tennessee have recently built a road for $100,000—the estimated cost of which at W.P.A. rates would have been $750,000. Is $650,000 worth saving in addition to the improved health of a few hundred men?

Additional Restrictions on State Prison Labor

Following the effective date of the Hawes-Cooper Act already referred to, early in 1934, the prison labor situation in the States, however, rapidly approached a crisis.

There were certain country-wide organizations which urged State legislatures to pass new laws restricting the importation of goods from prisons in other States. By virtue of the authority in the Hawes-Cooper Act some of these laws went so far as to restrict even the manufacture of goods made for the use of tax-supported institutions.

Realizing that without some concerted action prison industries would be greatly hampered if not prohibited, the administrators of State prisons throughout the country met to consider ways and means whereby reasonable legislation could be insisted upon.

Code Restrictions under N.R.A

In the meantime, in the summer of 1933, a new threat to prison labor appeared. The National Recovery Act had been passed, and codes were being adopted in all industries, designed to prevent unfair trade practices. The prison people were prepared to combat the propriety of inserting a provision against contract or State-account prison labor in the Textile Code, in the Cotton Garment Code, or in the Cordage Agreement, but they were not prepared for a prohibitory provision which suddenly appeared in a draft of the Retail Code.

If this code were to be adopted by all retail stores and approved by the President, no prison goods could be sold under any consideration to a private purchaser, and millions of dollars of investment in State prisons would necessarily be scrapped.

About this time, also, Alabama vigorously protested against restrictions contained in the fair practice codes which interfered with the business conducted by its State Prison.

The President of the United States asked the writer to see what could be done to reconcile these conflicting interests. When an interview was finally secured with the indefatigable General Johnson, it did not take long to convince him and the N.R.A. leaders that such codes should not be used to coerce or obstruct the operations of sovereign States. A neat solution was eventually evolved. The following proviso was inserted in the Retail Trade and other codes and was duly approved by President Roosevelt:

Section 3. *Prison-made goods.*—Pending the formulation of a compact or code between the several States of the United States to insure the manufacture and sale of prison-made goods on a fair competitive basis with goods not so produced, the following provisions of this Section will be stayed for ninety (90) days, or further at the discretion of the Administrator:

(a) Where any penal, reformatory, or correctional institution, either by subscribing to the code or compact hereinbefore referred to, or by a binding agreement of any other nature, satisfies the Administrator that merchandise produced in such institution or by the inmates thereof will not be sold except upon a fair competitive basis with similar merchandise not so produced, the provisions of paragraph (b) hereof shall not apply to any merchandise produced in such manner in the institutions covered by such agreement.

(b) Except as provided in the foregoing paragraph, no retailer shall knowingly buy or contract to buy any merchandise produced in whole or in part in a penal, reformatory, or correctional institution. After May 31, 1934, no retailer shall knowingly sell or offer for sale such merchandise. Nothing in this Section, however, shall affect contracts, which the retailer does not have the option to cancel, made with respect to such merchandise before the approval of this Code by the President of the United States.

(c) Nothing in this Section shall be construed to supersede or interfere with the operation of the Act of Congress approved January 19, 1929, being Public No. 669 of the 70th Congress and entitled "An Act to Divest Goods, Wares, and Merchandise Manufactured, Produced or Mined by Convicts or Prisoners of their Interstate Character in Certain Cases," which Act is known as the Hawes-Cooper Act, or the provisions of any State legislation enacted under, or effective upon, the effective date of the said Hawes-Cooper Act, the same effective date being January 19, 1934.

Thus, the State prisons were permitted to continue so long as in the conduct of their industries they lived up to the provisions of the applicable N.R.A. code. Thirty-six States of the Union signed a compact, as a result of which a Prison Labor Code was adopted.[7]

A Prison Labor Authority, appointed in accordance with the provisions of the Executive Order, assumed the duty of

[7] See Appendix B.

administering the Code, and it looked as though a satisfactory solution of the matter had been reached.

But not for long!

Somebody discovered that Blue Eagle labels were being placed upon prison-made goods which met the requirements of the Code. This was too much to bear, and a spirited hearing took place in Washington which resulted in a more distinctive type of label being authorized which would distinguish between prison-made goods and those made by free labor.

But still certain groups who had felt the competition of prison labor keenly in the past were not satisfied. The industrial situation was bad, and somebody had to be blamed for it. The Alabama Textile Products Company and other members of the cotton garment industry brought an injunction in the District of Columbia to relieve them of the necessity of complying with the Cotton Garment Code and assigned as reason therefor that prison competition was so keen that they could not do so. This argument did not appeal to the court, and when it was indicated that the amount of such prison competition was inconsequential the injunction was dismissed.

The garment-making trade nevertheless prevailed upon the N.R.A. to appoint a special committee to inquire as to the amount of competition existing throughout the country by reason of prison labor, with special reference to the garment trade.

Ulman Committee Plan

This commission consisted of Joseph N. Ulman, Judge of the Supreme Court of Baltimore, Maryland; Frank Tannenbaum, who had been a special investigator for the Wickersham Commission; and W. Jett Lauck, a progressively minded student of labor problems. The report which was promptly filed by these three gentlemen, known as the Ulman Report, while it is short and took but a brief time to compile, is one of the most sensible and satisfactory statements ever issued on the prison labor problem.

In brief, it proposed the adoption of the State-use system but recognized the difficulties in which the States found themselves and the expense which would be entailed in shifting over from one kind of industry to another. It suggested that, out of relief funds which had been appropriated in large amounts by Congress, the Government grant or loan sufficient sums to the States to set up new industries on condition that such industries would conform to the State-use principle.

The report was approved by industry and by most prison administrators, but it was not until the following spring that action was taken upon it. During the summer the report received the approval of the N.R.A., and on September 26, 1935, the President signed the Executive Order authorizing the use of relief money by the Works Progress Administration for this purpose.[8]

Prison Industries Reorganization Administration

A board known as the Prison Industries Reorganization Administration was appointed with Judge Ulman as chairman, whose duty it was to determine the amounts properly to be advanced to the various States and advise the President and the Works Progress Administration when a sufficient compliance with the terms of the order had been made by any individual State. In other words, whenever in the judgment of the Board a State has adopted the State-use prison labor principle to a sufficient extent, grants in aid of its fulfillment of this object might be made.

Future of Prison Labor in States

To what extent the States will be able to take advantage of this offer is still problematical. It is apparent at this writing, however, that something drastic must be done. The restrictive measures adopted by virtue of the Hawes-Cooper Act, the further conditions imposed under the N.R.A., and the prejudice against prison-made goods which has been developing in the last few years have reduced to the lowest point the

[8] Appendix C.

number of men in State penitentiaries employed in prison industries.

Supporters of the State-use theory still contend there is enough work in each State to employ productively the inmates of the penitentiaries, and assert that with the assistance of the Federal Government and with the exercise of a purposeful ingenuity on the part of prison administrators there is a brighter prospect for a permanent way out of this vexing social dilemma than ever before.

Possible Solution

One way out might be to combine work and educational programs, to shift the emphasis from the production of goods over to the manufacture of character. We shall all be faced in the coming years with the necessity for learning how to use constructively our increasing amount of leisure time. Whether the activities of inmates are to be directed toward the manufacture of commodities or toward education, or toward a combination of the two, the fact remains that character cannot be manufactured through idleness.

Recent Federal Developments

The Federal Government, as stated above, is entirely committed to the State-use system of prison labor. The Federal program has been still further safeguarded in the interest of labor and industry with the establishment in 1934 of the Federal Prison Industries, Incorporated. Pursuant to an Act of Congress, the entire management of industries in the Federal penitentiaries is assigned to a corporation with a board of five directors appointed by the President, including one representative of labor, one representative of agriculture, one representative of industry, one of the consuming public, and one representative of the Department of Justice.[9]

This board is specifically charged with the duty of still further diversifying the output of Federal prisons and determin-

[9] The Executive Order establishing Federal Prison Industries, Inc., will be found in Appendix D.

ing the extent to which each industry competing in any way with private industry shall be carried on, and has as its executive officer James V. Bennett, a man of insight, ability, and integrity, and a recognized authority on governmental problems.

The Prisoner's Family Has an Interest

No discussion of the problem of convict labor would be complete without a word as to the prisoner and his family. We cannot treat convicts as a species of the genus homo apart from the rest of the body politic. The man who is in prison today was on the street yesterday and will be on the street again tomorrow. Whether a man is temporarily in or out of prison, the real query is, Is he busy or idle? An idle man, in prison or out, is a public liability. He must be supported, and his family cared for. A busy man in or out of prison is an asset. He is contributing to the public wealth. He is maintaining his self-respect. He is fulfilling his responsibilities. He is taking care of his dependents. Prisoners, after all, are human beings. They disintegrate with idleness. They respond in a remarkable degree to the same stimuli as persons outside. They are part of the unemployment problem. To a normal man, his wife and children mean more than anything else in the world. Even though he neglects and abuses them, the prisoner is to a surprising extent likewise concerned with his dependents. Is it not enough that society should be burdened with the support of the prisoner, without adding to that burden the support of his dependent and helpless family?

If what we expect from a prison commitment is the imposition of legitimate disciplinary measures to bring a man more sharply into contact with his responsibilities, how can we do this by absolving him from all responsibility for the plight of his family? How can we contribute to any great extent to his rehabilitation and not say to him: "You have offended against the laws of society, you are going to prison not only to expiate your sin but to repay the debt you owe society. Your family are still dependent upon you, you have no right to ex-

Foundry and farm scenes at the U. S. Industrial Reformatory, Chillicothe, Ohio.

pect to be supported in idleness. You are going to work eight hours a day. You will have the privilege of learning a trade. You may be paid a small wage, and you will be expected to contribute to some slight degree to the support of your family?"

This is sound economics. This is good penology, and from the point of view of public safety it is essential to the public welfare.

The superintendent of the shoe factory at the Federal penitentiary at Leavenworth recently ascertained that sixty of the men released on parole during the year had worked in his factory. Up to the time of his follow-up there had not been a single failure on parole among this group.

Several letters have been received at the Bureau from men whose toil in the foundry at Chillicothe resulted in their obtaining good positions on the outside. One man was reported to have set up his own establishment based upon the knowledge he had received at the reformatory.

Summary

Should prisoners work when other people cannot? Should prisoners eat when others cannot? Should prisoners receive physical and mental training when other people cannot? Should the Prodigal Son have eaten of the fatted calf? From the point of view of the boy who stayed home, no. From the point of view of society, yes. Prisoners must work because only thereby can society be protected. No prison administrator should hope to have work opportunities provided for his prisoners in such a manner as to give him an *unfair* or *improper* advantage over free labor. Thus, out go the lease and contract system, exploitation, and unfair competition, and in come State use, public works, and vocational training. Neither should labor or manufacturing organizations expect that the opportunities to reform prisoners and protect society will be neglected until every free laborer is employed.

Prisoners should work because it is economically necessary, socially advisable, and because it represents the most important element in the general attempt to solve the problem of delinquency. My answer to the question propounded, "Should prisoners work when others cannot?" (provided you will allow me to define "work" as a stimulating and helpful activity and not merely as the holding of a job), will have to be, "All men should work." And I would go so far as to give this same answer even though the question had to be, "Should free men work when prisoners don't have to?"

CHAPTER VII

SCIENCE TO THE RESCUE

Anti-social conduct should not be met in kind but should be met by the automatic segregation of the offender in an adequately supervised institution by such methods as would make him feel that his conduct led naturally to such results, that as near as it is possible to so express it he shut himself up in the institution because of the way in which he conducted himself outside and was not shut up by somebody else in order to make him suffer; and that he can get out, back again into the world of free men, by modifying his conduct, and that his conduct can be modified if he is able and willing to coöperate with the plan looking to that end which the institution stands for and administers. During the period of his incarceration he is encouraged to be a productive member of that section of society to which he now belongs, and he is also taught that by virtue of his anti-social conduct he can not expect to escape the legitimate responsibilities which he has acquired during his lifetime. This is the direction, it seems to me, in which we can hope to advance not only in our ways of dealing with anti-social offenses and offenders but in our ways of thinking about the penological problems they present.

WILLIAM A. WHITE, A.M., M.D., Sc.D.—*Crimes and Criminals.*

WE are prone to take for granted the extent to which "science" has modified our daily existence and added to the ease and efficiency of everyday living.

Looking upward, the ancients saw the heavens only as an inverted bowl, punctured at night by holes through which the starlight filtered, and traversed by day by that fiery equipage which Phaëthon managed so disastrously on one memorable occasion. But now we are told that light travels at the rate of 186,000 miles a second, and man has constructed a telescope that will discover in the heavens a blazing sun 1,000 light years distant. So common place has it become, that we do not sufficiently marvel at the progress which science has made in annihilating time and space. Literally there is no limit to man's vision.

Improvements in transportation and the dissemination of intelligence have expanded our horizons to an unbounded degree. A floating palace as long as two city blocks crosses the ocean in four and one-half days. An automobile sustains a speed, for 500 miles, of 109 miles an hour. We sit enjoying the luxury of an automatically heated house on a dark snowy evening in January and hear the play-by-play description of the Rose Bowl football game played in the warm sun of southern California. We sink back in a comfortable chair and have a hot lunch served to us while traveling at the rate of 200 miles an hour 5,000 feet above the surface of the earth and are guided to safety through fog and storms by radio beams. We listen in on the conversation between a reporter in New York City and one of Admiral Byrd's barking penguins at the South Pole. We see in motion pictures the events of the world news reënacted soon after they occur.

One of the encouraging aspects of the present-day situation is the immediate possibility of adapting scientific discoveries in our campaigns against crime. There are some remarkably interesting new devices now coming into common use that are destined to be of tremendous assistance in the struggle against lawlessness. Are we content to let the predatory criminal reap the advantages which come from increased speed, power, and mobility, due to improvements in mechanical science, and not strive to outstrip him and control his depredations?

What would the practice of medicine be today without the thermometer, the stethoscope, the X-ray, and the use of anesthetics? How can we expect to make adequate progress in the control of crime unless and until we are prepared to use the contributions of science as in the field of medicine and the other professions? We are all accustomed to hearing about the fingerprint system, which has completely replaced the once acclaimed Bertillon system, and furnishes us with a reliable and indisputable means of personal identification. Every man, woman, and child carries on the thumb a unique and inescapable pattern of identification. The five and one-half million fingerprints on file at the Department of Justice in Washington have been of tremendous assistance in the apprehension of criminals. In many quarters it is strongly urged that this process be extended to require every person in the United States to be fingerprinted, not only to aid in the apprehension of the guilty, but so that the innocent may be protected.

Surely no innocent person objects to giving his name and address, when questioned. This information is purely for the purpose of identifying him. What further possible objection could Mr. John R. Citizen have to being obliged to furnish his fingerprints in addition thereto? If he is a potential criminal, he naturally would demur. But if he is a law-abiding citizen, he should be all the more anxious to establish beyond peradventure of a doubt his identity.

Nor should there be any disgrace connected with the fingerprint unless a criminal record is disclosed thereby. The Federal Bureau of Investigation has collected many thousands of fingerprints purely for identification purposes and keeps them in a separate index.

Consider for a moment the revolutionary changes in our police patrol system, brought about by the use of the automobile and the radio. Some of us can clearly remember the lonely vigil of the blue-coated policeman tramping the streets of our suburban districts. Effective, perhaps, in the "Gay Nineties," but a useless formality in the present day of universal automobile transportation. Most of our progressive communities now have a fleet of high-speed motor cars equipped with radio and prepared to report in a few seconds on receipt of notice at any part of the police district. The telephone, the gasoline engine, and the radio have conspired to immeasurably improve the efficiency of our police protection. "Calling all cars," only a few years ago a radio novelty, is now a commonplace method of communicating with an entire force.

Probably no feature of our American city police practices has come in for more censure than the so-called third degree.

Criticized in unmeasured terms by the Wickersham Commission as being the personification of "lawlessness in law enforcement," and yet defended by many police officials as being the only means at their command to force confessions and bring about the conviction of the criminal, it still remains a clumsy, cruel, and uncertain method of apprehension. What an opportunity is, therefore, presented by the so-called lie detector or polygraph used with such success by Leonarde Keeler of the Northwestern University at the Scientific Crime Detection Laboratory in Chicago!

The lie detector permits asking questions of the accused person and records three types of responses: the speed or delay with which the question is answered, the respiration of the subject, and his pulse. I do not recommend the use of the lie detector for those who have a guilty conscience. It does not, of course, prove facts. Its purpose is similar to that of the third degree. In the hands of a skillful operator it makes a person tell the truth or it brands him as guilty. A refinement of this device called the psychogalvanometer records by a moving picture film the rapidity with which perspiration exudes from the palm of the hand of the suspect on being interrogated. Curiously enough, in only a few of our cities has this device been adopted. Why do the great majority of police departments continue to use the medieval barbaric system of the third degree when science presents a simple, reliable, humane method of eliciting the truth?

Why should not likewise every prison in the country be equipped with this simple device? Prison wardens generally find it very difficult to obtain reliable information as to what goes on even inside their own prisons. Prisoners do not usually commit infractions of the rules in view of an officer, and in many cases prisoner testimony is all that the disciplinary officer has to rely on. The code of the prison, fear of retaliation, an unwillingness to be called a "rat" or "stool pigeon" has caused many a cutting scrape in prison to go unsolved. Science tenders the use of the polygraph to the prison administrator. Will he accept it?

The story was told recently of an up-to-date police chief in an Italian city who had before him several persons arrested on suspicion of having drilled a safe. He subjected each of them to the application of a powerful magnet, and on the floor around the guilty man appeared a small quantity of metal filings which had lodged in the man's clothing as he bored through the metal door of the vault.

Seldom has been seen a more dramatic example of the power and usefulness of scientific investigation than in the Hauptmann trial, where, by study of the grains of certain wood, the ladder of the criminal was identified.

The astonishing results brought about with the help of the modern study of ballistics are well known to many. Through the use of a double microscope the bullet found in the murdered man may be absolutely checked with a test bullet fired through the gun of the suspected person. The microscopic examination of typewriting; the use of chemicals; and the scientific handwriting tests are among the other modern contributions of science.

What a significant group of words is contained in the phrase, "scientific crime detection laboratory"! How much more hope of success is there in the use of such methods than can be realized by a continued reliance upon the old methods of brute force and bluff!

In the more immediate field of prison administration we find ourselves likewise tremendously encouraged by the new assistance which science has to offer. In our Federal penal institutions we have installed high-powered electric floodlights, automatic telephones with special cut-in emergency devices, radio communicators, automatic annunciators; toolproof or unsawable steel bars; harmless tear gas—an effective and humane substitute for the club and the pitchfork as a means of restoring order.

In some of our open institutions we have found an effective ally in the Swiss police dog, whose keener scent and unswerving devotion to his task are especially effective in the prevention of escapes and the tracking down of fugitives.

The dogs that chased Eliza to
The fierce Ohio ice
On posters thrilled my childish view,
And lent dull life a spice;
And news like this wakes memories from
The tragedy of "Uncle Tom."

The hunting dogs that hunted men
And women long ago
Stirred many a tongue and many a pen.
As all historians know—
But now, as mum as any clam
We watch like ways in Uncle Sam.

Behind the convict's doom is law.
Law cursed the fleeing slave;
The perfect parallel we draw
With this reflection grave:
Humanity is torn to shreds
When men are chased by quadrupeds.
                                        JOHN ALDEN.

But the dogs that chased Eliza were just plain bloodhounds. The Federal Prison Bureau feels justified in including those referred to as Swiss police prison dogs under the head of science. These dogs are carefully trained and have no vicious characteristics. They do their work in a conscientious, matter-of-fact manner, and they are at all times under the complete control of the guard to whom they are attached. H. L. Merry, superintendent at the Southwestern Reformatory, reports as follows:

You will be interested to know that the Lieutenant sends Prince to the Captain's office at stated intervals to get orders; Prince receives them in an envelope, and no one else but the Lieutenant can obtain possession of this envelope. The officer on the morning watch, in checking the count before breakfast, sends Prince to the Hospital and to the Cell House, the officers in each location giving the dog the count for his master. There are doubtless many other ways that these dogs could be used if our officers could think of them. They handle now just as well with the officer on the back of the horse as on foot, and the dogs apparently are much attached to the horse that they accompany.

One of our bad boys was heard to say the other day, "If it wasn't for them damned dogs I'd take that fence on a jump." We have, as you know, always felt the moral effect of the dogs was worth all they have cost.

Perhaps the most interesting and notable of these new inventions, so far as our prisons are concerned, is the instrument which we call the gun detector. The fear always uppermost in the warden's consciousness is that a gun or other weapon may be introduced into the institution.

We have installed at a few of our institutions, notably the prison at Alcatraz, an electrical magnetic device to prevent this happening. Such a mechanism has been installed at each entrance to the prison. When any person passes through the opening protected by this device, the presence of any piece of magnetizable metal on his person is immediately discovered and recorded by the machine. Recently, as a demonstration, the warden secreted a hack-saw blade in the sole of his shoe and walked through the opening; but he could not fool the machine, which promptly flashed the warning signal in three different places that a saw was on its way into the prison.

We are experimenting likewise with what is known as the body capacity ray. This is an invention which electrically charges a certain area about a building or wall or other place to be protected. Thousands of travelers have marveled at the door in the Pennsylvania Railroad station in New York City which automatically opens as you approach. That is a mechanism which operates as a body passes by a light ray. Traffic signals have been operated (we have them in the city of Washington) by means of a photoelectric cell. When an object, a horse for example, passes the range of the camera, the taking of his picture automatically sets the traffic signal. The body capacity ray differs from both of these. I have seen it demonstrated in cases where a small wire is placed around a desk on which are valuable papers. Any person approaching within several feet of the desk, or placing his hand over the same, immediately sets off an alarm. We are now working out a demonstration of the use of this device on a prison wall. It can be accompanied by an annunciator system.

Consider a midnight picture of the prison of the future! Instead of an institution bristling with firearms, with silent, lonely figures of guards passing up and down the wall, their salaries paid at great expense to the taxpayers, we shall have an institution protected entirely by science, and we shall be able to divert our pay-roll money to provide that type of personnel service which may guide and instruct the prisoners toward the day of their release. There will be a high surrounding wall protected by this invisible electrical zone. There will be rooms or cells out of which a prisoner cannot step without giving an alarm. There will be a force of guards asleep near by who can be readily roused in case of an emergency, and there will be a signal system so that in the event of any approach of trouble, either from the inside or from the outside, the whole place may be flooded with light, the guards aroused, the place of attack at once located, and a sufficient force of officers immediately recruited at that point. Science is providing us with a cheaper, more reliable and more humane prison control if we will but accept it.

And, by the way, what an unlimited amount of grief, sorrow, and public clamor could have been prevented had the Lindbergh baby's crib been surrounded with this invisible and implacable scientific protection! Is it not better for our millionaires to spend a few dollars in the adoption of this scientific preventive protection rather than hundreds and thousands of dollars in ransom money and the frantic pursuit of the kidnapers?

Have we not reason for being enthusiastic over the possibilities which the contributions of science may make towards the program of crime control? Those instances that I have given may be but samples of what can be done in the future.

You may well ask, Why hasn't more use been already made of these devices? And, indeed, this question should be asked

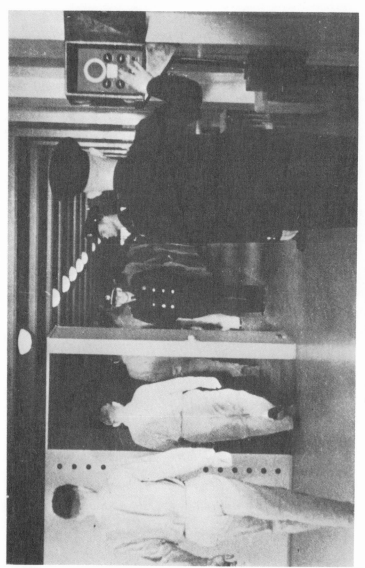

Inmates passing through gun detector.

of every police department and prison in the country. How long shall we continue to fight the modern menace of crime with medieval methods? The horse and buggy days are over. Our greatest hope and our greatest encouragement lie in our being willing to equip our crime-fighting agencies with modern ideas.

It was inevitable that we in the Federal Prison Bureau should receive many a letter unfolding a new and scientific solution of the crime problem. It is surprising the number of citizens who have given their attention to the question of what to do with offenders against the law. Sometimes it is not easy to tell whether the writer is just a plain "nut" or whether he has an idea which might even revolutionize the prison system. No doubt many of the discoverers and inventors of the past were originally looked on as partially insane.

One man proposed that we should encircle Alcatraz Island with a huge net and fill the intervening water with sharks. He would feed the sharks just enough to keep them alive but not sufficient to take the edge off their appetites; in case a prisoner should attempt to swim away from the island, the shark would be in an expectant frame of mind. The moving picture producers evidently thought there was more in this idea than we did.

Another man sent in sketches of a new variety of prison bar. He would make it of hollow metal and connect it with (a) water, (b) poisonous gases, or (c) scalding water which would be sprayed upon the venturesome inmate attempting to saw his way out, thus hoisting him with his own petard.

Another would tattoo all persons convicted of any violation of the law with the name of the city and date of conviction. A second offense would have another line of tattooing. Those persons who committed a third offense would be treated similarly and would be gathered up and shipped to some distant island where they would be isolated from the rest of mankind for the remainder of their lives.

One thing is surely evident, the inventive genius of humankind has not yet exhausted itself.

It will not be amiss in this chapter to refer to the great contribution that is being made to the science of penology by the expert statisticians through the use of sorting and computing machines like those at the Bureau of Investigation and the Bureau of Prisons in Washington. The gathering of current statistics is being made more easy, more thorough and more reliable.

The so-called Prognostic Tables when constructed from accurate statistics will be of tremendous assistance to courts, parole boards and prison administrators. Sam Bass Warner, Hornell Hart, Prof. and Mrs. Sheldon Glueck, G. B. Vold, and E. C. Burgess have made notable contributions in this new field. The Prognostic Table will never be a substitute for executive or judicial judgment but will be and is a logical means of applying the accumulated experience of the past, unaffected by political or other influence, to the important problems of the future.

No expert in any other profession attempts to speak with authority unless and until he has at his command the record of past experiments in his field. Too long have we worked in the darkness of absolute ignorance or depended upon empirical methods. The use of modern statistical analysis will shed light in many dark places in the fields of probation, parole, and prison administration.

Preventive medicine and sanitation are only just beginning to be utilized in the prisons of the country. It took 1,000 cases of "Athlete's Foot" to bring us to a realization of the importance of installing antiseptic thresholds at the entrance of all shower baths in our Federal prisons. Bubbler fountains were installed not only for the convenience of the inmates but because the old tin drinking cup with its inevitable rust was a prolific source of contagion for trench mouth and other communicable diseases. The importance of proper ventilation and heat distribution in the average cell block cannot be overemphasized.

The fact that men are in confinement and under restraint is all the weightier reason why special care should be taken in the scientific handling of milk, the frequent testing of the water supply, the prevention of disease carriers among the live stock and scrupulous care with the butchering or curing of the meat.

In the development of programs for sanitation and cleanliness in our Federal prisons the advice and assistance of medical and scientific men have been of great value to us.

*　　　*　　　*　　　*

We cannot close this brief consideration of the outstanding contributions which science is making to the solution of the problem of penology without some reference at this time to the so-called social sciences. Notwithstanding the fact that Lombroso and the criminal anthropologists received more or less of a body check at the hands of Dr. Goring and his English investigators—who pretty nearly wrecked the notion that there were physical stigmata of crime—nevertheless, the modern anthropologist has a contribution to be made. There are professors [1] at more than one eastern college who are eager to be turned loose in a penitentiary to study the dents and bumps on the heads of many of our notorious criminals.

Much more impressive to my way of thinking are the claims of the sociologists. They have demonstrated with remarkable success the effect on conduct of inadequate social conditions. We do not believe that we can thoroughly study the case of an individual criminal today without some knowledge of the social milieu from which he was evolved. [2]

The psychologists and the psychiatrists are becoming a valuable addition to the staff of every up-to-date penal institution. The psychiatrist had no place in a regime of mass punishment. He becomes indispensable, however, where the object is to know and treat the individual.

The science of psychiatry has suffered on account of some of its devotees. The definition by a certain legislator of a psychiatrist as "a nut who is employed to chase another nut" has occasionally been justified. Psychiatrists who are medically

[1] E.g., Ernest A. Hooten, of Harvard University.
[2] Clifford R. Shaw, Frederic M. Thrasher, Sheldon Glueck.

trained and scientifically qualified psychologists must not be confused with those folks who several decades ago posed as psychologists, nor with the quacks or soothsayers of any age. The professionally trained expert in the diseases of the brain and the vagaries of the mind, who has all the common sense and practical judgment of the ordinary physician, is an asset to any institution, and our prison wardens are today fast coming to realize his usefulness.

The acceptance of psychiatry as an aid in prison management could have no better demonstration than the thorough way in which it has been included in the general routine of our Federal prisons. Some time ago a meeting of all of the wardens, the chief medical officers, and the psychiatrists was held at the Federal Prison Medical Center. On that occasion F. Lovell Bixby, Ph.D., Assistant Director of the Bureau of Prisons at Washington, in charge of classification, education, and welfare in Federal institutions, said:

> The recent history of penology is characterized by the appearance, on the roster of institutional officials, of psychiatrists, psychologists, social workers, and other specialists from fields dealing with the understanding and control of human conduct. Too often, however, we find that these specialists have been superimposed upon the existing prison organization without actually being assimilated in it. It is not uncommon to find the professional staff sitting lightly upon the institution organization like the foam upon a glass of beer, adding considerably to its appearance but quickly blown aside whenever there is serious work to be done.
>
> The Bureau of Prisons has no intention of being content with lip service to the value of psychiatry and its allied fields. We believe that there is a great advantage to be gained in the way of more effective rehabilitation and in the way of more efficient administration from the practical application of psychiatric principles and methods. For that reason we are giving a great deal of thought and study to this question of coördinating professional services in the solution of administrative problems.

To a surprising degree the scientific and practical men found themselves in accord. In one instance the oldest warden in our service collaborated in a paper with the resident psychiatrist of the United States Public Health Service, entitled, "The Personality Factor in Prison Discipline." This veteran prison officer with forty years of actual contact with all kinds of prisoners read the paper, in which he stated:

In order properly to cope with infractions of the prison rules, it is necessary to have an understanding of the various personality types and to understand the motive or reason back of any disobedience of the rules. The types unable to adjust to prison life are the problem cases who give us the greatest concern. These constitute approximately 15 per cent of the prison population.

.   .   .   .

In the enforcement of discipline, it is not possible to apply mass methods if we are to achieve desirable results. Since the personality of one individual differs from that of another, so it is necessary to apply methods of discipline suitable to these different personalities. Unless and until such differences in personalities are recognized, the results achieved in the matter of enforcing discipline among the inmate body will be disappointing. Not only is it necessary that this fact be fully recognized, by the management of a penal or correctional institution, but it must be made a matter of instruction to the entire officer personnel. To the extent that such recognition and instructions are made effective, will an improved discipline become apparent, a discipline of good behavior which respects the rights of fellow beings. Such a discipline is a necessity in any institution if high results in reclamation are to be attained. It may be obtained with a minimum of friction or punishment, if, and when, full recognition is given to the fact that each inmate has a distinct personality of his own and that mass treatment as a class will not accomplish good results.

The head of another institution was of opinion:

The psychiatrist and psychologist should take a very active part in the everyday routine of the institution and should overlook no opportunity to contact the inmates. There should be absolute understanding and coöperation between the psychiatrist and psychologist on one hand, and the administrator and his associates on the other. This is highly essential. The chief source of contact with those who find themselves unable to conform to the institutional routine or those who do not desire to conform, is in the treatment of disciplinary infractions.

.   .   .   .

I feel it proper, however, to emphasize the importance, in our opinion, of the psychiatric service: for without this service it would not be possible to carry on a program of individualized treatment.

I believe it would help our wardens throughout the country to realize that psychiatry is not an occult science. As Walter Lippmann says so trenchantly in his "Preface to Morals":

Great progress has been made in scientific psychology within the last generation, enough progress, I think, to supplement in important ways our own unanalyzed and intuitive wisdom about life. But it would be idle to suppose that the science of psychology is in a stage where it can be used as a substitute for experienced and penetrating imaginative insight. We can be confident that on the whole a good meteorologist can tell us more about the weather than even the most weather-wise old sea captain. But we cannot have that kind of confidence in even the best of psychologists. Indeed, an acquaintance with psychologists will, I think, compel anyone to admit that, if they are good psychologists, they are almost certain to possess a gift of insight which is unaccounted for by their technical apparatus. Doubtless it is true that in all the sciences the difference between a good scientist and a poor one comes down at last, after all the technical and theoretical procedure has been learned, to some sort of residual flair for the realities of that subject. But in the study of human nature that residual flair, which seems to be composed of intuition, commonsense, and unconsciously deposited experience, plays a much greater rôle than it does in the more advanced sciences.

The uses of psychology to the moralist are, therefore, in confirming and correcting, in broadening and organizing, his insight into human nature.

A good psychiatrist is a wise student of human nature. He does not know it all—but neither does the warden. The warden and his deputy and the observant prison officer become psychologists in a way. They learn from experience many things that the psychiatrist does not learn from books. They do not call a man with a split personality a schizophrenic, but they are more than apt to remark that he is a "Dr. Jekyll and Mr. Hyde." They would be more likely to call one of their conduct problems "an ornery cuss" than a constitutional psychopath. But both the deputy and the psychiatrist know the men they are talking about nevertheless.

The point to make, of course, is that all our wardens should accept the services of the psychiatric fraternity. They permit the chief engineer to run their power plants, the electrician to repair the breaks in the transformer, and the bookkeeper to work out his trial balances. They can likewise trust the psychiatrist to advise them on many of the problems of personality defects. It is surprising the many points at which the psychiatrist becomes a useful assistant. He should be called in whenever punishment is to be inflicted. He should be a member of the classification committee. He should occasionally help the paid personnel with their problems of adjustment, and on many occasions, because he is a professional man, he may win the confidence of a recalcitrant inmate whose mentality is beclouded or whose emotions are in a turmoil. If by so doing he can forestall an incipient disturbance in the institution, even the most matter-of-fact warden will admit his usefulness.

There is nothing about the practice of psychiatry in a prison that savors of leniency. In fact, the experienced prison psychiatrist is the hardest man of all to deceive. It is not coddling prisoners to see through their malingering and expose their tricks and intrigues.

The psychiatrist, or character analyst, or mental therapist, or whatever he may be called, is in prison work to stay. No approach can be made to the solution of the problem of individual rehabilitation without his insight and assistance. He must not content himself, however, with diagnosis. He has been too prone in the past to tell us what was wrong with our offenders without going into the necessary details of what should be done to correct and cure these defects.

The social sciences, therefore, as well as the mechanical are becoming the warden's greatest allies. Together they may rescue the prisons of the country from the slough of despond of hit-or-miss, politically controlled, unintelligent stagnation in which they have been immersed and raise them to the level of intelligently conducted business enterprises.

We have "philosophized" to some extent about the prison problem in general as it concerns State and local activities as well as Federal, and commented on a few of its more prominent ramifications; we have paused to hail the advent of a new ally in the shape of science—mechanical and social. In the next few chapters we shall be referring to United States Government institutions and shall discuss the manner in which those in charge are contributing to the solution of the prison problem from a Federal standpoint.

CHAPTER VIII

FROM ATLANTA TO ALCATRAZ
OR BUILDING A PRISON SYSTEM

Is this beneficent influence of beautiful building upon the offender a thing to be lightly treated? So for his sake let us abandon the ill-considered prison plan and the ill-intentioned prison design. Let us have decent prison building for this reason if for no other. But there *is* another. The effect upon the personnel of the prison by creditable structure is immeasurable. The effect of environment is just as noticeable and far more important upon the prison official than it is upon the prisoner. Put the soldier in uniform, and he becomes a different and a better soldier. Put a man in charge of an institution graced by dignified architecture, and he becomes more alert to that moral responsibility which is the very soul of his control there. Can the crassest critic of things supernatural and eternal shout out his derision in a cathedral? Could Voltaire himself go into Chartres and laugh at the faith which built it there? The spirit of ennobling environment never fails to make its appeal whether it be expressed in the sheltering structure of college or cathedral, or within the high enclosure of prison walls. The design of the prison becomes one more influence for the regeneration of the prisoner; it becomes one more factor in building up the morale and widening the scope of those who, as the long years go by, will come to exert their influence upon him; an influence which modern penological thought has proved should be wise and tolerant. And it is in this tolerance of the normal inconsistencies and the frailties of our human kind that the architect as well as the warden himself should go about his task. They may both well remember that noble pronouncement of the poet and the prophet:
"God hath made man upright, but they have sought out many inventions."
ALFRED HOPKINS—*Prisons and Prison Building.*

That which is past and gone is irrevocable; wise men have enough to do with things present and to come.

THESE words from Bacon, engraved upon the proscenium arch of the chapel at the new Federal penitentiary at Lewisburg, Pennsylvania, may be said to be suggestive of the ideal underlying this new Federal prison program. It is not predicated on fear of a man's past so much as it is expressive of hope for his future. It suggests courage and opportunity rather than hate and vengeance.

Up to the close of the nineteenth century the Federal Government had no penal institutions of its own. In 1891 Congress passed an act establishing three penal institutions; but there was no appropriation for the purpose and nothing was done to provide for Federal housing of prisoners until July 1, 1895, when the Department of Justice took over the military prison at Fort Leavenworth, Kansas. In the next year Congress authorized the acquisition of 1,000 acres of the military reservation adjoining Fort Leavenworth and the erection thereon of a penitentiary with a capacity of 1,200 prisoners. Work began in 1897, and with the completion of this first penitentiary of its own the Department of Justice on February 1, 1906, returned control of the old military prison at Fort Leavenworth to the War Department.

The Atlanta Penitentiary, although authorized in 1899, two years after work began at Leavenworth, was virtually completed in January, 1902, on a 300-acre site at the southern limits of the city of Atlanta, with total accommodation for at least 1,200 prisoners.

These two penitentiaries with the small territorial jail located on Puget Sound, which was later destined to become the McNeil Island Penitentiary, constituted the entire investment of the Federal Government so far as penal institutions went until 1925.

On June 30, 1909, the Federal Government had 1,796 prisoners in its custody. The accompanying table which shows the increase of population year by year furnishes food for thought to the student of governmental problems, particularly as to the relationship between the Federal Government and the States. No more revealing words can be used to describe the course of the Federal prison population than the well known "leaps and bounds." The chart accompanying the table in-

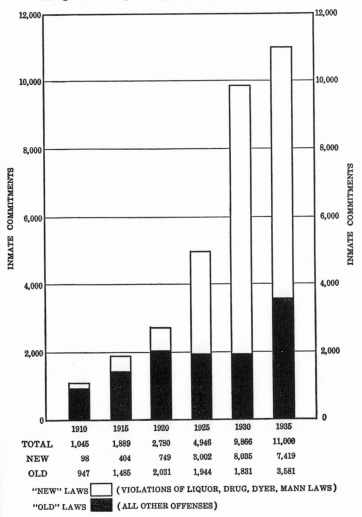

COMMITMENTS BY PRINCIPAL OFFENSE GROUPS
For Federal Penitentiaries, Reformatories, etc., (*)
During Years Ending June 30, 1910, 1915, 1920, 1925, 1930 and 1935

	1910	1915	1920	1925	1930	1935
TOTAL	1,045	1,889	2,780	4,946	9,866	11,000
NEW	98	404	749	3,002	8,035	7,419
OLD	947	1,485	2,031	1,944	1,831	3,581

"NEW" LAWS ☐ (VIOLATIONS OF LIQUOR, DRUG, DYER, MANN LAWS)
"OLD" LAWS ▓ (ALL OTHER OFFENSES)

(*) Includes Reformatories and Camps after 1925 and medical center in 1935

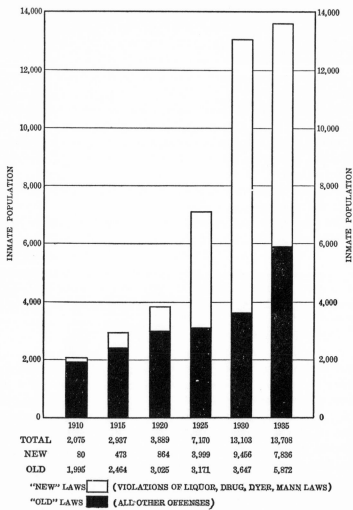

INMATE POPULATION BY PRINCIPAL OFFENSE GROUPS

For Federal Penitentiaries, Reformatories, etc., (∗)
as of June 30, 1910, 1915, 1920, 1925, 1930 and 1935

	1910	1915	1920	1925	1930	1935
TOTAL	2,075	2,937	3,889	7,170	13,103	13,708
NEW	80	473	864	3,999	9,456	7,836
OLD	1,995	2,464	3,025	3,171	3,647	5,872

"NEW" LAWS ☐ (VIOLATIONS OF LIQUOR, DRUG, DYER, MANN LAWS)
"OLD" LAWS ■ (ALL OTHER OFFENSES)

(∗) Includes Reformatories and Camps after 1925 and medical center in 1935 dicates graphically the source of this new increment. The additional crimes resulting from new types of legislation, such as interstate theft regulations—particularly as to automobiles —narcotic drug and liquor law violations, together with the steady increase in the old violations, such as counterfeiting and postal crimes, brought about this astonishing result. While there has been a rather steady growth in prison commitments throughout the State institutions from 1910 to 1930, the proportion of increase in the Federal Government has clearly outrun the general increase. Even when the prison population commenced to recede in 1932 in the State institutions the diminution in Federal commitments was but temporary. Prohibition commitments to Federal institutions, of course, sharply declined in 1932–33 only to increase as soon as the activities of the former prohibition unit were resumed by the revenue officers of the Treasury Department.

By 1925 the pressure upon the three existing institutions had become overwhelming, and with the necessity for new accommodations came the demand for different types of institutions. To meet the more modern requirements for group treatment of varying types of offenders, two reformatories, one for women at Alderson, one for men at Chillicothe, were sanctioned by Congress in 1925.

Upon the shoulders of Attorney General Harlan F. Stone (now Justice of the Supreme Court) and his progressively minded assistant, Mabel Walker Willebrandt, fell the responsibility of meeting this new and expanding situation. At that time the work of supervising Federal institutions, recommending the parole of inmates to the Attorney General, and inspection of jails was administered by a handful of people in the Department of Justice. The business of taking care of prisoners had never been a serious concern of the Department of Justice. Things went from bad to worse and that right quickly, so that in 1929 a committee of the House of Representatives, of which the late William J. Graham of Pennsylvania was chairman, made a thorough investigation and reported that the time had come for the establishment of a Bureau of Prisons, the construction of a group of new institutions and the passage of such legislation as would result in the organization of an integrated Federal penal system.

Upon the revelation of shocking conditions of overcrowding, both at Atlanta and at Leavenworth, and with the explanation of the need for the development of both parole and probation systems in the Federal Government, legislation was prepared and transmitted to Congress in December, 1929, with the active support of President Hoover and Attorney General William DeWitt Mitchell. Congress passed the legislation in May and June, 1930. Every recommendation of the Department of Justice was adopted, and the Federal Bureau of Prisons became a reality.[1]

By this legislation, the powers and duties of the Bureau were defined and the development of a complete prison system with classified institutions was envisaged. A separate Board of Parole was established. A new penitentiary and an additional reformatory were authorized. A hospital for the care of the insane and the sick became the subject of enabling legislation. The Federal Probation Law was clarified and expanded. The United States Public Health Service was instructed to furnish adequate medical and psychiatric services to Federal penal institutions; the construction of a limited number of Federal jails was provided for, and an act was passed calling for the installation of a diversified system of prison industries.

It is doubtful if any prison system in the world ever received such a plenary and liberal charter, or such abundant and understanding support. The new organization was given carte blanche to work out a modern prison system for the Federal Government.

With the authorization of the women's reformatory and the appointment of Dr. Mary B. Harris to be superintendent thereof, the problem of the female Federal offender was in a fair way to be solved. The number of women Federal prisoners has, comparatively speaking, never been large—the average being 4 per cent of the total of all Federal prisoners. The

[1] See footnote 3, Chapter I, p. 18.

work of Dr. Harris has been well described in her book [2] and will not be referred to here otherwise than to say that her administration of this unique institution has been one of the outstanding accomplishments of the Federal penal system.

The task of the proper disposition of the male prisoners, young and old, was much more difficult. Not only were we called upon to plan a permanent group of institutions, but of necessity the first and most vital activity had to be the immediate relief of the dangerously overcrowded penitentiaries. We could not wait for buildings to be constructed, nor even for the development of properly supervised parole and probation systems.

For help in meeting this emergency we are greatly indebted to the War Department. In September, 1929, they again turned over to us the splendidly administered Disciplinary Barracks at Fort Leavenworth, which the Department of Justice had returned after its temporary occupancy in 1906. We were not long in filling this institution to its capacity of 1,800. Several pieces of unused property were transferred to us by the War Department, and prison camps were speedily set up on reservations adjoining half a dozen existing army posts. During this transition period prisoners were quartered in War Department barracks at or near Fort Bragg in North Carolina, Fort Meade in Maryland, Camp Dix in New Jersey, Camp Wadsworth on Staten Island in New York, Fort Riley in Kansas, Camp Eustis in Virginia, Maxwell Field at Montgomery, Alabama, and Fort Lewis near Puget Sound in the State of Washington.

A large permanent camp was erected on the 3,000 acres formerly comprising the Camp Lee reservation near Petersburg, Virginia. A further description of the successful operation of the prison camps by the Federal Government will be given in a later chapter. It is enough now to say that the ready coöperation of the Army authorities gave the Prison Bureau sufficient time to properly plan its permanent reorgan-

[2] *I Knew Them in Prison* (Viking Press, 1936).

ization and undoubtedly saved serious trouble in our greatly overburdened penitentiaries.

Congress promptly appropriated money for building the new institutions, and the Bureau of Prisons set about their planning and construction with the full realization that the tender of nearly ten million dollars presented an unusual opportunity and likewise imposed upon us a grave responsibility.

United States Northeastern Penitentiary at Lewisburg, Pennsylvania

Since the historic conflict between the Auburn and the Pennsylvania style of prison architecture very few new ideas have been developed in this field, with the exception of the panopticon prison, elsewhere described. Through sheer necessity prison managers had been obliged to use corridors, schoolrooms, and shops as dormitories to take care of the increasing number of convicts. But the typical English or Continental prison cell had been very little used in this country. As a matter of fact, State prisons had been so strongly and permanently constructed on the conventional plan during the early part of the nineteenth century that most economically minded communities had been content to let them remain. Thus we still find dotted over our American landscape prisons of the bastile type, many of them over a century old and erected with but one thought in view; namely, to provide a place from which no prisoner could by any possibility escape.

If the architecture was so forbidding and the environment so disagreeable that a person would dread to go there, then so much the better!

It became increasingly evident that there was a fundamental inconsistency between the architecture of the old fortress prisons and the attempt at character rehabilitation of the men who lived in them. How could one have any hope of reaching the individual problem of the prisoner and applying the right measure of training or restraint, instruction or discipline in his case if all of them were treated exactly alike and each one put in a separate cage like the dangerous animals in a menagerie?

It requires considerable detachment of mind to read a book on the human soul, for example, where the light has to be filtered through the barred door of a cell.

The site for the Northeastern Penitentiary, as it was to be called, was chosen from 106 applications after a careful analysis of the relative merits of each, by means of which sixteen factors were considered. The highest rating (86 per cent) of all the localities which met the specifications laid down was secured by the town of Lewisburg in Union County, Pennsylvania, and therefore nine hundred and fifty rolling, fertile acres on hills overlooking the Susquehanna River were acquired.

In the construction of this first new prison building the Bureau was determined that, so far as possible, the architecture should be consistent with the new penology. If, as had so often been proclaimed, the older prison had failed, why was it not wise and prudent to try a different type? If we were endeavoring to rehabilitate men, why not have a structure that was compatible with such an effort?

There is no particular virtue in ugliness, and while the new prison at Lewisburg withstood any tendency towards over-ornamentation an edifice was erected which is dignified and pleasing in its aspect. Alfred Hopkins of New York was the architect. To some extent the whole spirit and purpose of the Lewisburg Penitentiary is contained in the closing pages of his book, "Prisons and Prison Building," a quotation from which is carried at the beginning of this chapter.

In brief, the design of Lewisburg calls for (1) security without depressing restraint; (2) ample space in which to develop farm activities outside the wall and the circulation of light and air within; (3) a greater diversity of housing facilities (for a possible population of 1,300 there are only 88 steel cells divided into small groups, 450 securely guarded rooms like any other small room but with an outside window, and dormitories of different sizes to house the rest of the population, affording opportunity for varying degrees of restraint); (4) adequate schoolroom facilities; (5) a library of pleasing design and ample proportions; (6) well lighted and ventilated hospital facilities; (7) a central control corridor to facilitate ready supervision; (8) a plain but stately mess hall so contrived that it may be divided into four parts; (9) a chapel, exhibiting a simple dignity consistent with the purpose to which it is to be put.

While no one can fail to be conscious of the fact that here is a building in which men are deprived of their liberty, the visitors to Lewisburg are struck with the fact that it introduces a novel feature into prison architecture; namely, an edifice designed to suit the aims of modern penal treatment. The whole plant was constructed economically and well within the appropriation,[3] and at a much lower cost than other recent State institutions in the East which were built along the same lines as the older prisons.

The new prison is secure. In four years of operation no convict has escaped from within the walls. It not only contains facilities for the close confinement of the recalcitrant prisoner but also offers opportunities for individual progress and improvement with increasing liberty and independence even to the time of discharge.

The prison was opened on Friday, November 11, 1932. The public was invited to inspect it, and on Friday, Saturday, and Sunday, 42,000 people came to see this experiment in penology, 27,480 of whom passed through on Sunday.

The United States Industrial Reformatory at Chillicothe, Ohio

The increasing number of younger men coming into the Federal prison system made imperative the establishment of an industrial reformatory similar in function and purpose to the historic Elmira institution in New York, founded by Brockway in 1873. The advisability of distinguishing in the treatment of the first offender and the recidivist is now of course universally recognized.

[3] Out of an original appropriation of $3,850,000, $250,000 was returned to the Treasury.

In the Act of January 7, 1925, establishing the United States Industrial Reformatory, Congress expressed the hope that by vocational and academic training novices in crime might be reclaimed for future useful citizenship. In January, 1926, the first group of young prisoners were established in the temporary barracks on the acreage formerly occupied by Camp Sherman at Chillicothe, Ohio, and in conformity with the policy of Congress, as announced in the enabling act, the construction of permanent quarters was begun by prison labor in the autumn of 1927.

No one could foresee the tremendous influx of young convicts, or that in 1930 there would be 1,800 of them still housed in temporary barracks. So acute became the situation that work was speeded up through the letting out at contract of some of the larger buildings, and on January 1, 1934, the permanent institution was substantially completed.

The plant includes cottages or dormitories of various types; a detention unit comprising 108 steel cells and 288 strong single rooms; a separate hospital, dining room, and kitchen building; warehouse; school building; auditorium; six vocational shops; administration and receiving building, and farm structures. The next chapter will tell of the educational and vocational program of this institution. It is enough to say here that the Government has provided for the younger or first offender at a cost of about $2,600,000 a complete, modern, fireproof reformatory institution which has few equals anywhere in the world.

United States Southwestern Reformatory at El Reno, Oklahoma.

It was the intention of the enabling legislation of 1930 that the Chillicothe reformatory be reproduced in the western part of this country. One thousand acres of land was secured by transfer from the always coöperative War Department at the El Reno Remount Depot in Oklahoma. The temporary drop in prison commitments during 1932 resulted in a material retrenchment in the plans, but there is now in operation an unwalled cottage institution of the reformatory type thirty

miles west of Oklahoma City, which aims to extend to young
or first offenders committed from the western States the same
facilities now afforded at the United States Industrial Reformatory at Chillicothe, Ohio. A cell block houses two hundred of
the more hazardous risks, and schoolrooms, hospital, shops,
and farm buildings complete the layout.

United States Penitentiary, McNeil Island, Washington

In the meantime, there were "gradually" erected on McNeil
Island the permanent buildings of the third of the original
units of the Federal penitentiary system. This institution has
evolved from a small primitive building used as a jail when
the State of Washington was in territorial status. Its population has grown from fewer than 100 at the beginning of the
century to an average of nearly 1,000 prisoners.

The Congress of 1935 authorized the acquisition of the
remaining half of the 4,400 acres on McNeil Island and the
development of a self-sustaining community. Attorney General Homer S. Cummings, the present farseeing chief of the
Department of Justice, has predicted an interesting and constructive future for this institution. It has already become
famous throughout the Northwest as the "Prison Without
Walls" and under the leadership of a particularly progressive
and experienced prison warden [4] is taking its place among the
best institutions of its kind.

Federal Reformatory Camp, Petersburg, Virginia

Not the least interesting of the Federal penal institutions
from the structural point of view is the reformatory camp at
Petersburg, Virginia. Four large dormitory buildings have
been erected of inexpensive but durable materials, the sides
being constructed of two thicknesses of corrugated metal en-
closing four inches of rock wool for insulation. These dormitories house 150 men each and form the sides of a large quadrangle at the front of which is a handome brick building

[4] Edward B. Swope.

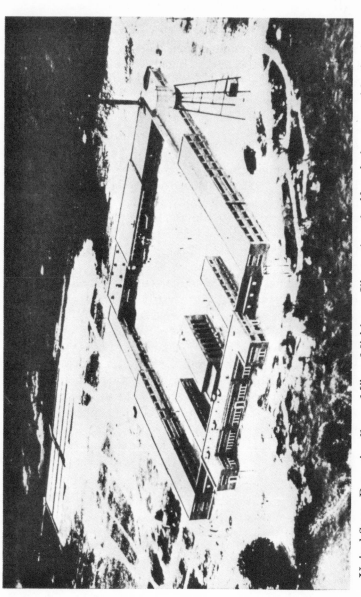

United States Detention Farm, Milan, Michigan. Illustrative of self-enclosing type of institution.

painted white which houses the offices, guards' quarters, hospital, receiving room, and twelve disciplinary cells. The rear end of the quadrangle is formed by the dining room, kitchen, laundry, and power plant buildings. An up-to-date brick storehouse and a chapel and school building made of the same material complete the equipment. The institution is located on a high bluff overlooking a bend in the Appomattox River and is surrounded by fertile land, on which garden crops are grown and a large acreage of timber has been scientifically cultivated.

In spite of the wide-open character of this camp, which has only twelve cells with a population of 600, escapes are extremely rare [4]—a real tribute to the care used in the selection of its inhabitants, and to the skill of its superintendent, C. O. Nicholson.

One of the great events in the history of the institution was the visit in 1934 of Mrs. Franklin D. Roosevelt, who expressed admiration for the scrupulous cleanliness and discipline that was maintained there.

Federal Jails

Under the authority granted by Congress in 1930, four regional jails or houses of detention have been constructed: one in New York City; one on the southern border at La Tuna, Texas, near El Paso; one at Milan, Michigan, near the international border at Detroit; and one in New Orleans, where the historic old Mint has been remodeled into a very satisfactory and economically administered detention headquarters for the Gulf District. [5]

The New York jail was acquired in a hurry and was remodeled from a warehouse property in the lower part of the city. The two detention farms at Milan and La Tuna, however, have been referred to as models of their kind, built for economical operation and ease of supervision (see picture),

[4] For the statistical year 1936 there were none.
[5] Congress in 1936 appropriated funds for the construction of three additional institutions of this type and intimated that three more might be authorized in 1937.

they provide security and opportunities for classification without the necessity of a wall. Both are surrounded by ample acreage for farming operations and include all of the structures necessary for a well rounded program so far as it is possible to accord such to prisoners serving short terms, which range from a few days to a year's duration. A small section of the cell block at Milan has been completely sealed off from the rest of the institution and contains twenty-two cells for women prisoners who cannot safely be held at Alderson or who have shown themselves unable or unwilling to profit by the advantages offered them at that place.

The difficulties which the Bureau of Prisons encounters in securing suitable accommodations for short-term prisoners were recounted in Chapter III. The purpose of the Federal jails may be said to be twofold: first, to serve as bases of negotiations, as an alternative refuge while dickering with local authorities; and, second, to demonstrate the possibility of maintaining clean, secure, economical jail care. No escapes have been engineered from within the Milan, La Tuna, or New Orleans jail, and the cost of maintenance is lower than the average daily rate (83 cents) paid to county organizations.

United States Hospital for Defective Delinquents, Springfield, Missouri

Much time and thought was put into the planning and construction of the United States Hospital for Defective Delinquents, now called the Federal Prison Medical Center, authorized by Act of Congress in May, 1930,

for the care and treatment of all persons charged with or convicted of offenses against the United States, and who are in the actual custody of its officers or agents, and who at the time of their conviction or during the time of their detention and/or confinement are or shall become insane, afflicted with an incurable or chronic degenerative disease or so defective mentally or physically as to require special medical care and treatment not available in an existing Federal institution.

Except in the case of Lewisburg and La Tuna all of the sites for the new construction were procured by the Bureau of Prisons without cost to the Government. In the case of the hospital the public-spirited citizens of Springfield, Missouri, donated to the Government free of expense an excellent site of 445 acres, and this location was selected from more than thirty similar tenders made by communities in the States of Illinois, Indiana, Iowa, and Missouri.

Conditions as to the care of the tubercular and the insane in the overcrowded Federal penitentiaries had become almost a scandal. The mentally deranged had to be held for long periods in cells or cramped quarters, and at the Atlanta Penitentiary it had been necessary to construct a tent colony in the yard of the prison for those suffering from pulmonary tuberculosis.

The Springfield hospital with a maximum capacity of 700 beds was opened in September of 1933. It is constructed somewhat along the lines of the modern neuro-psychiatric hospitals of the Veterans Administration with added features that give it greater strength. There are separate departments for the acutely deranged, those requiring long continued treatment, the tubercular patients, and the aged, infirm, and chronically sick. The institution under the joint management of the Bureau of Prisons and the United States Public Health Service has been equipped with the most modern hospital appliances. Electrotherapy and hydrotherapy rooms have been provided; sun porches, special treatment rooms, operating suites, and every facility are at the command of the distinguished group of physicians and surgeons to whom has been intrusted the conduct of this important and unique institution. Whatever may be our feeling as to the treatment of the normal or healthy convict, humanity demands that every effort be made to provide suitable care for the mentally and physically disabled.

There is a distinct purpose behind this Federal Hospital for Defective Delinquents. The trained staff is presented with an unusual opportunity to study the important question of the relation of physical and mental defects to crime, and it is the hope of the Bureau of Prisons that valuable contributions may be made to the world as a result of clinical and research activities carried on at this institution.

This brief survey of the structural development of the United States prison system is necessarily incomplete, but perhaps enough has been said to indicate its significance. The manner of its administration will be explained in later chapters. If it is possible to carry out the difficult task of administering prisons along lines which conform to the present-day standards, this group of institutions should be of material assistance. At least, we can say that into their planning and erection, we have put the best thought and wisdom that we could command.

Upon the completion of the entire building program authorized by Congress there was still an important link in the chain of institutions to be provided for. Something drastic needed to be done with the new type of gangster and gunman, the kidnaper and interstate racketeer, that was being brought into the Federal penal system under the new crime laws passed by Congress in 1934 at the request of Attorney General Homer S. Cummings. Nothing but stern discipline and a securely built institution would be appropriate for the punishment of such individuals. There were in the existing penitentiaries a small but dangerous group of prisoners, all guilty of serious crimes, who would not accommodate themselves to the ordinary discipline, and who made it difficult to apply the routine measures of education, rehabilitation, etc., to the larger proportion of inmates. Some prisoners just cannot get over the temptation to escape, and continually plot to accomplish this end. Others are known as agitators, "Big shots" and disturbers, and still others by an incurable disposition to disobey the rules make frequent trips to the solitary.

The Bureau of Prisons had for a long time felt the need of an institution with maximum security defenses where this group could be safely quartered.

To Attorney General Cummings goes the credit which has

Aerial view of U. S. Hospital for Defective Delinquents,
Springfield, Missouri.

Public Health Service Personnel at the United States Hospital for
Defective Delinquents, Springfield, Missouri.

been so freely accorded by press and public for the conception and establishment of the new Federal Penitentiary on Alcatraz Island.

Alcatraz Island is said to have been first discovered by the Spanish Lieutenant Bartolemé Ferrelo in 1545. It has been known at different times as "White Island" and "Bird Island" and was referred to as early as 1797 as "Isla del Alcatraz." This word is said to have been applied by Mexicans to the pelican or albatross. However, other authorities tell us that the word "Alcatraz" is of Arabic origin and was used by the ancient alchemists in the sense "the recovery of valuables from a retort."

The Island of the Pelican and the Island of the Angels, now known respectively as Alcatraz and Angel islands, are the only two islands in the Bay district to retain the original names given them by the earlier explorers.

Alcatraz was granted by the territorial Governor of California in 1846 to one Julian Workman, whose heirs conveyed it to the United States Government before California became a State in 1850.

Those who have seen the beautiful San Francisco Bay and the location of this little island midway in the opening known throughout the world as the Golden Gate can readily appreciate its strategic importance in the early fortifications around San Francisco. It remained a highly fortified spot from 1854 down to the end of the century, when it became an Army prison, known as the Pacific Branch of the United States Military Prison, later to be known as the Disciplinary Barracks. During the Indian wars many famous Indian chiefs were confined on this island redoubt, the most interesting of whom was Kaete-na, an Apache chief and a friend of the great Geronimo. He was tried by a jury of his tribe for fomenting a disturbance on the San Carlos Reservation and was sentenced by them to confinement for three years.

It was natural, therefore, that the Attorney General should see its possibilities in 1933 when the War Department notified the Department of Justice that it had no immediate use for this historic little island. In the latter part of that year, the Department of Justice took over by transfer this twelve acres of rock in San Francisco Bay. Plans were immediately laid to construct, for the dual purpose above described, a prison as nearly escape-proof as possible.

The 600 old soft-steel cell fronts of the Army disciplinary barracks were removed, and tool-proof steel with automatic locking devices replaced them. Tool-proof steel bars were installed in the windows. Tear-gas outlets were provided, and a special group of trained, experienced guards were recruited from the other Federal penitentiaries. A zone in the water was marked out with buoys into which boats are forbidden to enter. Automatic gun detectors were placed at the dock and in the doorways to the cell blocks, which record the presence of any secreted metal on the persons who pass through these openings. New guard towers were erected, flood lights put into place, and additional barriers built around the seventy-five-foot cliffs of the little island. Maintenance shops and the laundry provide work opportunities. Gun galleries at each end of the cell block control the interior of the building, while the island is controlled by a system of towers connected by overhead walks. The Alcatraz Island Penitentiary is intended as a place of maximum security for the incarceration of the worst type of Federal prisoner.

The Department was fortunate in being able to enlist the services of James A. Johnston of San Francisco as Warden of the new prison. He has had experience in both of the large California State Penitentiaries, San Quentin and Folsom, and later was a successful business man and respected civic leader in the Bay section.

The sanitation, cleanliness, and efficient administration established by the Army set a standard which it will be difficult to surpass, but which if maintained will give this institution high rank as compared with the other units in the prison service.

Great care was taken in the shipment of the first group of prisoners from Atlanta, Leavenworth, and McNeil Island.

Splendid coöperation was rendered to the Bureau of Prisons by the railroads, which provided special equipment for the purpose. A secret route was followed, and early one morning citizens of San Francisco were surprised to see a raft plying its way under the escort of the Coast Guard cutter from the rarely used docks at Tiburon to the Island of Alcatraz bearing the cars in which the transferred prisoners had been transported from the other Federal penitentiaries.

A group of anxious officials in Washington who kept in constant telegraphic touch with the "Bamboo Cosmos" (code name for the prison train) heaved a sigh of relief when word finally came of its arrival and the safe deposit of all the "furniture" without a scratch. When it appeared to Warden Johnston that one of these special trains would not arrive until after meal time, he besought us by wire to make sure that the "furniture" be well "oiled" before discharging it at Alcatraz.

Naturally the discipline at Alcatraz Penitentiary is stricter than at the other prisons in the Federal system, but Warden Johnston can be relied upon to carry out the instructions of the Bureau that no brutality or inhumanity shall be practiced. Sustaining food and adequate medical attention are supplied. The services of a chaplain have been secured, and library books will be available. The expectation is that we may continue to be able to provide steady work for those who are required to spend their days in this penitentiary. It is a hopeful sign that, of 16,500 prisoners in the Federal system, but 270 are now at Alcatraz.

Even for these few the door of hope is not to be forever closed. If any of them can demonstrate that continued detention at Alcatraz is not necessary, the Bureau of Prisons is prepared to retransfer to one of the regular penitentiaries, where in accordance with the law and regulations the way may be opened to ultimate consideration for parole.

It is hardly to be expected that an institution that places its main reliance on force should be entirely free of disturbance. It is a tribute to the skilled and courageous management of

Alcatraz that within the first two years of its operation there has been so little. A strike involving 40 per cent of the inmates was adjusted without violence or injury and the only attempt at escape was frustrated, with regrettably fatal consequences to the foolhardy inmate who attempted it.

Thus it will be seen that Alcatraz forms but one link in the development of a modern prison system, the fundamental purpose of which is the protection of society. Where such protection can be obtained only by permanent segregation, we will not flinch from that course. Where, however, a study of the personalities and possibilities of our prison population reveals the fact that they can be rehabilitated, the program of the Federal prison system demands that the attempt be made.

Structurally, then, the Federal Prisons comprise:

1. Super-maxim security f o r incorrigible and long-term offenders ....Alcatraz Penitentiary 260

2. Maximum security for prisoners seving more than one year ....Atlanta Penitentiary 2,800
   Leavenworth Penitentiary 3,000

3. Maximum security for drug offenders ....Leavenworth Annex Penitentiary . 1,600

4. Near-maximum security for long-term prisoners of a more hopeful type; special emphasis on education and training ....Northeastern Penitentiary 1,320

5. Medium security; prison-farm activities ....McNeil Island Penitentiary 1,000

6. Reformatories of medium security type ....Chillicothe, Ohio 1,500
   El Reno, Oklahoma 800

7. City jails of strong security .New York 150
   New Orleans 350

8. Detention farms for short-termers ....Milan, Michigan 550
   La Tuna, Texas 500

9. Reformatory camp, minimum security ....Camp Lee, Petersburg, Virginia .. 550

10. Reformatory for women...Alderson, W. Va. 500

11. Work camps, minimum se-
curity ....Tucson, Arizona 200
Kooskia, Idaho 100
Dupont, Washington 200
Montgomery, Alabama 250
12. Sick and insane medium
and maximum ....Springfield Hospital, Missouri 600

Any commitment to these institutions is made by a Court after investigation and with advice of the Probation Officer, in accordance with general instructions as to the function of each place. Owing to the extent of territory to be covered it has not been possible to provide a clearing-house prison to which all offenders could be sent for assignment. This object is attained, however, with the help of the classification committee at each institution, who during quarantine period continually recommend to the Bureau transfers as indicated.

Generally speaking sentences of over one year (for felonies) are served in a penitentiary and sentences of one year or under (for misdemeanors) are served in jails. The distinction between felony and misdemeanor is largely historical.

We accept the definition of a felon as one who has committed a serious crime, and we include under the category of misdemeanant that very much larger number of persons who have committed trivial offenses, without any very clear understanding as to the reason for this distinction.

Historically there were only two types of institution—the jail, to which minor offenders were sent for punishment, and the State prison. Imprisonment in the State penitentiary was referred to as infamous punishment and carried with it certain disabilities and disqualifications, which did not follow a commitment to jail. The decisions of the courts recognized the distinction between infamous and ordinary punishment. The Federal statute, instead of providing that all persons sent to the penitentiary shall be classed as felons, arrived at a similar distinction by providing that all crimes punishable by more than one year shall be considered felonies.

With the development of the reformatories, camps, training schools, and other types of penal institutions, the theoretical distinction between felonies and misdemeanors has come to have little value in penal administration. In distributing the convict population among the group of institutions herein described, the Prison Bureau is likely to have in mind the personality factors which are developed by social investigation rather than the more or less arbitrary fact whether the defendant committed a felony or misdemeanor. With the exception of the constitutional limitation which would probably prevent a person convicted of a misdemeanor from being committed or transferred to a penitentiary, the Prison Bureau is free to assign the prisoner committed by the court to the appropriate institution.

CHAPTER IX

THE PARAPHERNALIA OF REFORM

In this quest no scientific formula can be summoned to provide an answer. As some one has truly said, science may abolish disease but it cannot tell us what to do with health. It may abolish poverty but cannot tell us how to use the wealth or leisure which invention and technology afford. The answer pertains to the arts, rather than the sciences, for it is that most difficult of arts, the art of living, which we consciously or unconsciously seek to fit ourselves to follow.

WALTER LIPPMANN.

WHILE the paramount and pressing need of the expanding Federal prison system was for more and better buildings, we were all determined that the achievement of the building program just outlined was to be merely the introduction to the more important task which lay ahead. No one better qualified to undertake the development of a program of prison education and welfare could have been found than Austin H. Mac-Cormick. Trained under Thomas Mott Osborne at the Portsmouth Naval Prison, he was possessed of a rare insight into the subject. The two occasions on which he had dressed himself in a convict uniform and spent a week in a cell had given him a knowledge of the prisoner's point of view. His book "Education of Adult Prisoners" is sound and humanitarian as well as practical and is an authority on the subject.

In 1930, 11.6 per cent of the Federal prison population had never been to school; 71.2 per cent had not gone beyond the elementary grades, and only 11 per cent had the benefit of a high-school education.

No welfare policy could be adopted without a realization of the educational and vocational needs of the great majority of the prisoners, and, what is more important, a desire would have to be inculcated in the men themselves for self-improvement.

Ordinarily speaking there are three classes of prisoners: the unadjustable, the adjustable, and the self-adjusting. In the first class are those whose record and a brief examination of whose character immediately disclose the hopelessness of any attempt to induce them to mend their ways. Lawlessness has become a way of life. Their minds are warped, and what ingenuity and cunning they possess is directed towards getting through their prison term as quickly and peaceably as possible. It is a wise prison administrator who recognizes this group and sets them on one side as purely custodial cases.

For the third, considerable class of prisoners, little or nothing needs to be done. They are genuinely accidental offenders. They are full of regret and remorse. They are usually the well educated and more or less refined type of individual, and once they have finished their prison terms there is small danger they will ever relapse into crime. Members of the group prove helpful to the Warden. They act as teachers in his school, and in other ways many times are an influence for good in the prison. It is enough to protect them in their desire to do their time amicably.

But by far the largest category in the prison comprises those whose presence there is due to some maladjustment, and for whom something must be done unless they are to become chronic recidivists. It is for this group that educational and vocational training systems are devised. It is for them that libraries are built and equipped. In the Federal prison system specially trained social workers were put on the job to find out the causes of their maladjustment and search for remedies. This effort might well be called a sort of social osteopathy. What is behind a maladjusted personality? The cause may be immediate, or it may be remote. And in the same way that a skillful osteopath relieves a bodily maladjustment by manipulating to remove the pressure which causes it, so we have found there is prospect for character adjustment when we are able to discover where the pressure comes from and relieve it at its source.

It did not take us long to install educational facilities at most of the institutions. Adequately paid school supervisors with two or three civilian assistants and a large corps of the more competent inmate instructors were established in each of the penitentiaries and reformatories. Classroom instruction was supplemented by individual cell instruction on the university extension plan. Trained librarians were secured, men who not only understood books but knew how to see that the books were read. We no longer accepted donations of books from whatever source and of whatever age, merely placing them on the shelves and hoping that some day they might be read. On the contrary, we gave careful consideration to the selection of the books. In the first place volumes had to be bought that prisoners would voluntarily read, and their interest in the better class of reading stimulated by degrees.

These skilled library technicians found plenty to do. They reindexed and recatalogued the books; they conducted poster campaigns; they provided library carts to deliver the books to the cells, and in some of the institutions they were fortunate enough to have a secluded part of the building set apart as a reading room.

There was an astonishing increase in the amount of serious reading done in the institutions as a result of this intelligently planned campaign. At McNeil Island Penitentiary, for example, the amount of non-fiction reading at one time exceeded the amount of fiction distributed. The average number of books distributed per man per month rose to five volumes. For the year ending June 30, 1934, 37,500 fiction and 14,500 non-fiction books were circulated. Nowhere, it seems to us, is the reading of books a more potent influence in the lives of men than in prison.

Nor were we unmindful of the importance of proper surroundings. If the reading of a book is designed to take a man out of himself and to put him on a higher moral and intellectual plane, why may not that be done in pleasant and agreeable surroundings? I know prisons where the cell inmate must sit with his back against the barred door, holding his book close to his eyes in order to see by the dim incandescent lamp in the corridor outside. Compare this condition with that in the reading room of the prison library at the Northeastern Penitentiary.

> *Books are like an open door*
> *Out of which the mind can soar,*
> *Rove the world on mighty wing,*
> *Watch the stars and planets swing.*
> *Though the body shackled be,*
> *Books can set the spirit free.*
> E. KATHLEEN JONES.

I doubt if even now our prison wardens throughout the country have sensed the tremendous opportunity for diversion and culture that is possible from a judicious use of their libraries. The American Library Association stands ready to be of material assistance to the prisons of the country, as it has demonstrated in several of the States. Miss Kathleen Jones in Massachusetts and Miss Perrie Jones in Minnesota are shining examples of skilled library workers who appreciate the importance of good prison reading.

I interviewed a rather prepossessing hill billy at Chillicothe one day in connection with his application for parole. He was twenty-one years of age but had never gone to school. His only acquaintance with the Three R's came after he had been arrested and sent to the Chillicothe Reformatory. He frankly admitted that he felt himself completely educated at the end of his six months in the prison school. I asked him how much was nine times seven, and he thought it was fifty-six; but he also thought that eight times seven was fifty-six and then naïvely said, "I don't guess I need no larnin'." I attempted to argue with him as to the advantages of a knowledge of arithmetic and said: "Suppose you had to go to the store to make some purchases. Wouldn't you want to know that you were getting the right change?" To which he replied: "No, sir, I send my wife to the store. She's got all the larnin'."

But not all prisoners are fortunate enough to have an intellectual spouse, and while many of them undoubtedly are much

New Northeastern Penitentiary, Lewisburg, Pa. Opened for occupancy Nov. 14, 1932. Cost $3,000,000—capacity 1350 men.

Library of U. S. Northeastern Penitentiary.

more blissful in their natural state of ignorance, the task of the prison is as much to convince the prisoner of the advantages of an education as it is to teach him, once he is enrolled. Many of the officers in the average prison do not, or cannot, implant this desire among the prisoners, and they lose opportunities thereby. It is refreshing, however, to see, once the interest is elicited, the rapid progress which they make in the prison school. The experiment at Chillicothe with many of these mountain boys has shown that they progress in their school grades approximately four times as fast in prison as the average school child outside goes through the same grades. In other words, the native intelligence is there, the cultivation of it has been neglected. What a pity it was necessary to brand them as criminals in order to discover their educational possibilities! Forty per cent of Federal prison inmates avail themselves of classroom instruction, and many hundreds more do special work on university extension lessons obtained and paid for by the institution.

The prison welfare division concerns itself with many things in addition to education in the school or cell and the hours that may be spent in reading. Nothing can be much more important than the establishment of a well balanced ration. Through the Bureau of Home Economics and with the approval of the Secretary of Agriculture we early secured the services of Dr. Paul E. Howe, in charge of nutrition investigations, Bureau of Animal Industry, as nutrition adviser. There is no more prolific source of trouble than improper or poorly cooked food. With Dr. Howe's help we have set up at low cost a nourishing standard ration in which the proper proportions of food elements are present.

Perhaps the first and most important of the truly welfare projects in a prison falls to the lot of the medical service. It is difficult to find the right type of physician to employ in the average prison. One is obliged to be content either with some old, discouraged, broken-down veteran who is tired of actual practice, or some young and untrained man anxious to make his institutional experience serve as a stepping-stone to a lucrative practice. The medical director in a large penal institution is an extremely important cog in the machinery.

The Federal Prison Bureau made a ten-strike when it secured the interested coöperation of the United States Public Health Service. From the moment that this highly trained, mobile force of doctors, surgeons, nurses, dentists, and psychiatrists took over the work of supplying these services in our prisons, our own part of the problem was practically solved. The reputation of the Public Health Service under Surgeon General Hugh S. Cumming was such as to assure the assignment of competent medical men for service in the prisons and make certain that standards would be maintained through the mobility of the members thereof. Under the skillful guidance of Dr. Walter L. Treadway adequate medical, hospital, psychiatric, and dental services have been established and maintained. The hospitals at Atlanta, Leavenworth, Chillicothe, Northeastern, and Springfield have been given a Grade A rating by American College of Surgeons. A fully staffed dental clinic at each institution, and consultant services in the way of orthopedics, eye, ear, nose and throat, genito-urinary, and other special services, have been provided. In addition to the hospital and surgical services an out-patient clinic was established with a daily sick call. Thorough admission examinations are made, and routine reëxaminations before discharge. Antiluetic and other prophylactic services are regularly maintained. At our suggestion the medical director has constituted himself the sanitary inspector for each of the prisons, and monthly reports are forwarded to the United States Public Health Services and the Bureau of Prisons. Started more or less as an experiment, the use of female nurses in our male prison hospitals has proved to be a helpful and refining influence, and with one exception no untoward incidents have resulted therefrom.

No one yet knows the true extent of the relationship between physical and mental infirmity to crime. But if one is to proceed on the assumption that the first step toward reformation is to remove the source of infection and physical disabilities, then it may truly be said that if nothing more were done in the Federal prison system than the thorough and continuous remedial activities of the United States Public Health Service, we would be well on the way to the accomplishment of our major task.

W———— G———— had had a long and more or less unexplainable record of pugnacious criminality. Shortly after his commitment to the Northeastern Penitentiary he got into an unreasonable argument with a fellow inmate, hit him over the head with a piece of pipe, and seriously wounded him. All his "good time" was taken away. The medical department commenced to study his case and shortly afterward determined that he was suffering from glandular trouble and operated on his thyroid. Shortly after his discharge from the hospital he became an entirely different person. None of his former truculence developed. He was scrupulous in his obedience of the rules. A year later his good time was restored to him in recognition of his greatly improved behavior. This may sound like testimony from some revival meeting, but it is attested by the record of the United States Public Health Service and is only one of many striking instances where the removal of physical defects has resulted in a marked change in the conduct and behavior of the individual.

Among the thousands of cases where obvious disabilities have been removed—old hernias reduced, carious or abcessed teeth extracted, defective eyesight remedied, deformities repaired, artificial limbs supplied, venereal taint removed—we find many cases of change in behavioristic tendencies which entirely justify the $500,000 annually expended for medical work in the Federal prisons and reformatories.

While the psychiatric work of the United States Public Health Service is largely diagnostic, it is an extremely important part of the routine in all institutions, not only where frank mental disease is discovered but where the advice of a competent alienist is needed as a prerequisite to administrative action.

It is not difficult to see that the work of the Public Health

Service is an investment not only in individual rehabilitation but in community protection as well. Every time a prisoner is isolated for tuberculosis and his case arrested, or a man is cured of venereal disease, a source of community infection is likewise removed. We like to think that there is a parallel between this kind of medical work and the attempt at moral rehabilitation. Every unchecked criminal career is a focus of moral infection, and to the extent that we return one of these individuals with the danger of contagion removed, to that extent may we be said to be contributing to a program of crime prevention.

When a man enters the prison system with one leg and goes out with two, even though one of them is an artificial one, when he comes in diseased or enfeebled, or with his capacity for hard work at low ebb and goes out without these handicaps, or whenever he enters with a hideous deformity or a loathsome disease and emerges in condition to face a competitive industrial system with confidence, a constructive public service has been rendered.

We draw the line, however, at cosmetic surgery. We realize that beauty is only skin-deep, and the enthusiasm which some members of the Public Health Service feel over the straightening of a deviated septum is not allowed to proceed to the extent of removing warts or moles or other superficial blemishes, records of which as identifying marks appear on police blotters throughout the country, and which the cunning convict would be only too glad to have removed.

X——— Y——— recently accomplished his object, albeit in a roundabout way. He repeatedly presented himself at a Veterans Hospital and obtained treatment to which he was not legally entitled. His fraud was discovered, and he was given a sentence of ten years in a Federal penitentiary for defrauding the Government by obtaining medical treatment. It might have been cheaper to give it to him in the first place, because he has now been transferred to the prison hospital at Springfield, Missouri, for treatment for a chronic degenerative disease. He will get the treatment just the same although he had to become a convict to do so.

Prisoners can be punished in a mass, as we have said elsewhere, but they can only be reformed individually. A part of the program of individualized education and welfare for the adjustable group (and also a step in determining whom to put into the adjustable group) must be the preparation of a case history of each individual concerned. We realized that this was a job to be handled by specially trained persons. We were a little bit sensitive about calling them research assistants or social workers, but the name "warden's assistant" seemed to be reasonable enough and could not offend even the most captious critic of our penal methods. High standards were set up for these new members of the prison staff. While, as the next chapter will indicate, we insist upon a minimum training for our custodial officers, these men, holding positions more nearly as personnel workers, must be more highly qualified. The Civil Service requirements for the job therefore were graduation from a standard university with at least 118 semester hours, 20 of which must have been in sociology, economics, or psychology; and for the senior warden's assistant, at least one year's experience with a recognized social-work agency.

To these men was delegated the duty of gathering together the verified facts of the social, industrial, family, and institutional history of each inmate. The personal problems of the prisoner which did not fall under the heading of medical, educational, or disciplinary problems were to be referred to these warden's assistants. About forty trained college graduates have been put to work at this important task. They assist with the home contacts. They recover property abandoned at the time of the hurried commitment to prison. They prepare legal documents, when necessary. They act as secretary of the classification committee. They frequently appear as counsel for an accused inmate when brought before the intramural "good time" board or disciplinary court. They do not preach or strive to convert, but they are alert for opportunities to give sound counsel and advice when they can do so without intrusion. They present in their activities one of the more hopeful developments in prison work today. Many a prisoner is beset by fears as to what is happening to his wife or his children, or his property, or his chances for a job. He has few friends that he trusts and no money to employ a lawyer. The whole prospect of any successful attempt at rehabilitating him depends upon his being placed in the proper frame of mind. A social worker trained in the art of helping others out of trouble is a necessary adjunct to every prison.

It was in the big mess hall of the Atlanta Penitentiary. Sixteen hundred convicts were having their noonday meal of stew, tea, bread and butter. Waiters were going up and down the aisles with large pails of stew, ladling out second helpings if they were called for. As we walked down the center aisle we noticed the obvious immaturity of one of the prisoner waiters. But his agitation was apparently greater than ours, because he dropped the stew on the tile floor, to his own chagrin and our discomfort. I immediately said to Warden Aderhold:

"It seems to me that boy is too young to be in Atlanta. If you forward a recommendation for his transfer to Chillicothe, it will be promptly acted on."

The recommendation came through—in fact it had already been prepared—and one evening a year later, as I was passing through a class in the night school at our crack reformatory institution at Chillicothe, Ohio, a young man who had been working at a typewriter got to his feet, saluted and addressed me by name, and in a confident respectful tone said:

"You don't know me, but I am the boy who spilled the soup."

If ever an improvement or reformation had been made, it had been accomplished in the case of this shy, scared, young criminal, who at least has been taught how to support himself. But should it be necessary for a boy to spill a pail of stew in order to get the attention of the authorities?

Assembly at San Quentin Prison, California.

It is indeed no easy matter to preserve to any degree the individuality of the prisoner. In prison we take away their names and we bestow numbers. We outfit them all with uniforms. We march them in regiments. We get them up by the bell and feed them by the whistle. And yet, every one is different. Each has his own particular troubles. The outstanding task of modern prison administration is, first, the recognition or isolation and, second, the solution of the individual problem. We can provide the paraphernalia of reform (which we have done)—clean beds, adequate food, hospitals, additional schools, libraries, recreation fields, consultant services, and so on—and if a prisoner has the will to reform and if he steps out of the ranks he may avail himself of these opportunities. But stand, as I have done, in the corridor of one of our large prisons and watch the endless file of men shuffling by. Even as you and I, each one of them is to himself the center of the universe.

In the effort to become better acquainted with the characteristics and needs of each individual we have provided a classified group of institutions. It is to further this effort that the population of each institution is divided into smaller groups. The machinery for truly individualized attention was, however, set in motion through the adoption of the classification committee plan.

In 1934 our good friend Austin MacCormick moved on to accept a position as Commissioner of Correction in New York City, where he immediately obtained further fame and distinction, leaving behind him a host of friends and some splendid achievements in the Federal Prison Service. To his successor Dr. F. Lovell Bixby, whose intellectual brilliance is accompanied with sound common sense, goes the entire credit for the establishment of the prison classification program, perhaps the most progressive improvement in welfare work which we have installed. Under the enlightened leadership of Dr. William J. Ellis, Commissioner of Institutions and Agencies in the State of New Jersey, Dr. Bixby had taken a part in the development of prison classification in that state.

E——— C——— was thirty-one years old. Medical examination on his admission at the Atlanta Penitentiary to serve three years for illicit distilling showed that he was blind in the right eye and had very little sight in the left. He was of normal intelligence with eighth-grade education and good general physical health but with a marked personality inadequacy on account of his visual handicap. The classification committee realized the special character of this case, appointed a subcommittee, and a full program was worked out for him. Mental hygiene treatment was provided in the medical department, not so much to cure his defect as to reconcile him to it. The social service unit made arrangements with the local school for the blind in his home town to furnish him with a correspondence course in Braille; and the vocational rehabilitation division of the Department of Education in his own State was contacted, and agreed to accept him for rehabilitation on his release. His vocational problem was met by assigning him to the mattress factory, which is one of the common occupations for the blind. A follow-up report indicates excellent progress and that he is very much pleased at learning a trade. In his spare time he has been taken into the school and is learning typing and dictaphone operation. Can any one say that E——— C——— has not a reasonable chance of being released better fitted and less likely to become a public charge than when he entered the prison?

While this is an extreme case, it can be matched by scores of others in which, by means of the systematic work of the classification committee, the special needs of the individual are discovered and supplied.

Every inmate on arrival at a Federal penal institution is placed in quarantine for thirty days. His record is obtained. His case history is completed and verified. He is inoculated and examined by the medical department. Psychometric tests are administered. The educational director, the superintendent of industries, and the chaplain all interview him, and the secretary of the classification committee receives the nine reports from the members of the committee, digests and compiles them into what is known as an admission summary. Each week, or oftener if necessary, the members of the classification committee [1] meet. Each has his own report and a copy of the complete admission summary. The prisoner is called before the committee. The plan which has been devised for his individual guidance and improvement is submitted to him. He may make any suggestions or protests that he desires. At his withdrawal the committee agrees upon his status and recommendation for treatment. This includes degree of custody, health program, educational recommendations, kind of labor to be undertaken, religious needs, recreational activities, and whatever psychiatric services he requires.

By this means we are enabled to give that measure of individual attention to each case without which no reform is possible. Frequent changes in the plan may be necessary, and as a preparation for parole a further reclassification may be indicated.

The outstanding advantages of the classification scheme are these:

(1) It permits individualized work in a large institution. While physical classification may not always be possible, we aim to separate the old and the young, the well intentioned and the evilly disposed, and through groups of institutions to carry out some of the major classifications. But there are limits beyond which the division into groups cannot be undertaken. There are industrial, religious, educational, racial, and many other kinds of classifications which cut across one another. If men are to live again in normal existence they must school themselves to get along with all kinds of people and still be masters of their own destinies. According to their individual needs the classification plan seeks to prepare them to this end.

(2) It brings to bear the varied and combined judgments of all of the members of the staff in each case.

[1] The classification committee consists of warden, deputy, director of the social service unit, chief medical officer, psychiatrist, psychologist, supervisor of education, chaplain, superintendent of industries, chief of mechanical service, and parole officer.

The cornerstone of coöperative enterprise is mutual understanding and a common objective. Workers in penal institutions tend to confine their activities to their respective specialties. Each department head jealously guards his own prerogatives and almost dares anyone else to claim any knowledge of his field. Each confuses the other by a polite barrage of technical terminology. Each is inclined to attach more importance to his own findings than to those of his associates. There often seems to be a lack of mutual understanding as to the ultimate objectives which is essential to a proper balancing of values and the development of an integrated program.[3]

(3) It eliminates favoritism. Neither the warden, deputy warden, nor any other influential member of the prison staff can dictate an assignment for a prisoner.

(4) It keeps all members of the staff constantly in touch with the real goal of prison administration; namely, the reformation of the individual inmates.

(5) It provides a reliable basis on which transfers between institutions can be made.

(6) It affords the Board of Parole an impartial and accurate mass of data as to the character and possibilities of every prisoner.

(7) It induces a clarity and a comprehensiveness of judgment. Every member of the staff is brought face to face with the attitude and judgment of every other member.

(8) It assures the inmate that he is not subject to the despotic control of one individual, but that the combined resources and the reflection of all viewpoints of the institution are brought to bear for his assistance.

On one occasion I sat in with the classification committee at the Northeastern Penitentiary. We heard several actual cases, and one could not help being impressed with the earnestness and devotion of this group of men of varied minds who were bringing their talents to bear upon the question at hand. This particular individual had a schizophrenic trend. Some careful work would have to be done to adjust him to his surroundings.

[2] R. A. McGee, Former Supervisor of Education, U. S. Northeastern Penitentiary.

Classification Committee in session at Chillicothe Industrial Reformatory.

This task was awarded to the psychiatrist. Another individual had never been trained to work. Patently the first thing to do was to give him a job which would not only prepare him for a life of industry but teach him the value and necessity of daily toil. A third individual had a bad family situation. His wife had been unfaithful. His children were running wild, and the prisoner was distressed on that account. Obviously, a challenge to the social worker.

And then came along a case where all seemed to be normal. This prisoner's intelligence quotient was high. He had had a good education, possessed a knowledge of a trade, was brought up in reasonably good family surroundings. The classification committee were in a fair way to be stumped.

At this point I asked the question, "What do you do with a man who is a plain crook with no evident reason for it?"

With one accord, they all turned to the chaplain.

The traditional job of chaplain in a prison was best described by calling him a "man of all work." He preached and prayed on Sunday. He comforted widows on Monday. He taught Bible class on Tuesday evening. He tried to get some free films out of the moving picture people on Wednesday. He interceded with the Governor for a pardon for à man on Thursday. He officiated at the last rites of a prisoner on Friday, and on Saturday he tried to think up something new to say to the men on Sunday.

With the separation of duties it appeared to us that the ministry of the chaplain in a penal institution had entirely changed. The prison school had been taken over by trained educationalists. Family contacts were handled by the social workers, and the libraries staffed by trained librarians. Apparently there was nothing but religion left for the chaplain to busy himself about, and that could be done on Sunday in an hour or two. But just there we made a mistake. We have now realized that the chaplain's job, rightly construed, is an extremely important job in any institution. But he must be a new type of "sky pilot." He must know something about the social sciences. He must be a man of strong and attractive personality. He must not depend too much upon homiletics. He must know something of psychiatry, and he must be able to talk the language of the man he would befriend.

We have convinced the Federal Council of the Churches of Christ in America of this fact, and we have discussed it with representatives of prominent Catholic organizations who have expressed interest in the matter. They have agreed with us to select specially qualified men for this distinctive service. The preaching of a sermon on Sunday is not the most vital part of a chaplain's duties. In fact, the more frequent the changes in the pulpit, the better the prisoners will like it and the more often they will come to church. But unless we are to neglect one of the most important elements in the individual reformation of the prisoner some man not too closely identified with the organization, who yet understands the pitfalls and the dangers of being attached to a prison, must secure and maintain the confidence and friendship of the individual and thus exert upon him a truly religious influence.

Again, I say, we have supplied the paraphernalia of reform. The chaplain of the newer order will have to be relied upon to stimulate the will to reform.

CHAPTER X

GUARDS OR LEADERS

The more vicious, the more base, the more abandoned the class of society, on which any department of justice acts, the more and the weightier is the reason, that those who administer it should be elevated above all interest, and all fear, and all suspicion, and all reproach. Everywhere the robe of Justice should be spotless; but in that part, where it is destined to touch the ground, where from its use, it must mix with the soil, there its texture should contain and preserve whatever there is of celestial quality in human life and conduct, there, if possible, its ermine should dazzle, by exceeding whiteness; and be steeped, not only with the deep fountains of human learning, but be purified in those heavenly dews which descend alone from the source of divine and eternal justice.

Josiah Quincy, Judge of the town of Boston, 1822.

In a prison, perhaps to a greater degree than elsewhere, the most important element for success is the human element in its management. The most carefully devised system can be rendered useless or even harmful through careless or unintelligent or uninspired leadership. In a prison, likewise to a considerable extent, the men in the ranks hold the key to the situation. Too long have we permitted inexperienced and unqualified men to fill the positions of guards in our penal institutions.

In many States appointment to the office of warden has been considered to be a special gift to be conferred by the Governor himself, and too often the practice still obtains of selecting the warden on the basis of political prestige rather than fitness for the peculiar and onerous work of administering a prison. With this situation at the top, one could hardly expect to find any considerable groups of competent men in the ranks of prison officers who had special aptitude for such duties.

On a visit to a Missouri penal institution I was told that

within the last two years there had been a recent turnover in the guard force at that institution on account of the fact that each member of the Assembly had been permitted to select one prison officer. Within the last three or four years wholesale changes in the personnel of the prisons have taken place in Oklahoma, Illinois, Maryland, Michigan, Indiana, Pennsylvania, Missouri, Kansas, and probably other States. In many cases such changes were followed inevitably by disturbances and disorganization in the service. There are many States in which prison employees are not under Civil Service. There are others in which Civil Service only partially applies.

We have elsewhere called attention to the fact that no permanent improvement of the prison system can be expected until, once and for all, it has been taken out from the operation of the political spoils system.

Fortunately all of the prison employees in the Federal Prison Service are under the classified Civil Service. With the exception of the warden and deputy warden in the older institutions and the chaplains in all, no appointment can be made except after competitive Civil Service examination.

There are those who will point out the disadvantages and restrictions of Civil Service as they apply to the management of penal institutions; but experience in the Federal department demonstrates that its advantages and protections far outweigh its handicaps and disadvantages.

But we came to a realization of the fact that a Civil Service test alone, even as amended and modified at the suggestion of the Prison Bureau, was not sufficient to secure the highest type of prison officers. In the early days in Massachusetts prison officers were selected from the same register which furnished candidates for bridge tender and deck hands on the municipal ferryboats.[1] It did not take much argument to convince the Federal Civil Service Commission, however, that there were several requirements of the prison service which justified an attempt to select men who were qualified for that service alone. New sets of standards were devised, and special ques-

[1] This situation has now been changed.

tions inserted in the Civil Service examinations designed to discover the attitude of applicants and to give them an opportunity to express their philosophy in the matter of prison and punishment.

Early in 1930 the Federal Bureau established its first school for prison officers in New York City. Jesse O. Stutsman, now deceased, author of a standard textbook, "Curing the Criminal," and a man of wide experience in penal institutions, was placed at the head.

At that time, it will be recalled, the Bureau of Prisons was making extensive additions to its prison system, and it was of double importance that the large number of new employees taken into the system should have some training and experience. The general purpose of this school was to qualify officers to think intelligently on the practical problems of the prison of today, to give them an adequate comprehension of the historic and sociological background of modern corrective service so that they might understand the human material with which they would have to deal.

Physical education, instruction in first aid and mental hygiene and in the art of self-defense were given in order that the officer might be able to meet all emergencies. Throughout the course the emphasis was placed on the methods of controlling men by intelligence and leadership rather than by force. All candidates were recruited from the regular Civil Service register, were detailed to the Federal jail in New York, and there took part in the study course which extended over a period of four months.

The class was taught something as to the causes of crime and the methods for its control. They discussed the nature of the criminal and his background and were given lectures by members of the United States Public Health Service upon psychopathic and psychotic behavior problems. They visited penal institutions and had as lecturers superintendents and wardens thereof. They were also drilled on the functions of the various departments of the prison, including sanitation and diets, employment of prisoners, questions of discipline, recreation, etc. As a means of instilling confidence in each officer they were taught boxing, wrestling, jujitsu, and proper use of firearms and gas. Good use was made of the physical training portion of the course. Later one of the graduates of this course, doing guard duty in a prison camp, was sent without a gun or club into open country to hunt for two prisoners who had escaped. He came upon them suddenly after dark. He held out his hand as though he had a revolver and the prisoners put up their hands. When he had approached near enough for the prisoners to see that he was unarmed they rushed upon him, one of them with a dangerous knife. The guard met the attack of the prisoners in approved jujitsu fashion and sent the knife of one of them whirling to the ground at the side of the road, captured this man with the left hammer lock, and, when the other prisoner struck at him, took possession of him also with the right hammer lock and led them both back into the camp.

It is impossible to discover the inherent characteristics of a man as to courage, dependability, and alertness by a written examination, or even after a four months' course of preparation; but much can be done to stimulate judgment, common sense, initiative, and resourcefulness by such means, and at the end of the period it will become apparent that certain individuals are entirely unsuited for service in a prison. They lack the indispensable qualities or characteristics necessary for success.

Through the school in New York passed 500 candidates for the Federal prison service. About seventy of this number failed to meet the requirements for graduation or resigned during the course. The remainder were given a chance to demonstrate their fitness.

We have previously pointed out the singular difficulties inherent in the prison service. The prison officer of the future must be resourceful, courageous, confident of his ability to meet any emergency. He must know something of the purpose of a modern prison. He must be able to see the problem in its larger implications. He must be a teacher, monitor,

Custodial force of Lewisburg Penitentiary.

Custodial force of Alcatraz Penitentiary.

disciplinarian, and exemplar. Some of the requisite qualities can be acquired, but the necessary attributes of patience, tolerance, and a humanitarian outlook on life must be more or less inborn in the individual.

The guards in our prison service are still somewhat underpaid, and while the great majority of them rise above the temptations which daily beset them, there are occasionally those who succumb. Occasionally, likewise, a guard faced with the choice between being a hero and saving his skin, accepts the latter alternative. In such instances, although we may sympathize with the individual employee and his family, we have been obliged to keep before us constantly our duty to the institution and to the public. The maintenance of high standards in the prison service is of supreme importance. It is, of course, not uncommon for a guard or employee presented with notice of his suspension immediately to appeal to a Member of Congress to intercede for him. It may as well be set down here that this practice does not occasion us any particular embarrassment. With one or two exceptions we have found Senators and Representatives anxious only to determine what the facts are in a given case; and when we explain to them the circumstances surrounding the suspension of the employee and the paramount importance of maintaining the standards of our service, it is extremely rare to find any lack of coöperation from members of Congress. The employees of the Federal Prison Service know today that if the lamp of experience shows them anything it is that they hold their positions as members of that service through devotion to duty and not through political influence.

Because of the death of Mr. Stutsman, because of a cessation in the building program of the Bureau which made further large increments of prison guards unnecessary, and in no small measure because of the fact that the Committee on Appropriations thought that its maintenance was an unnecessary expense, the New York school was abandoned in April, 1933. In order to secure the necessary instruction for those members of the guard force in the service who had not gone through the New York school and to provide suitable instruction for replacements constantly coming into the service, we then set about devising a scheme of in-service training for all members of our custodial force.

The new project, which is almost entirely the product of the energy, initiative, and intelligence of W. T. Hammack, LL.B., D.C.L., Assistant Director of the Bureau of Prisons, became an established fact on January 1, 1936. It was based upon an administrative order issued by the Attorney General, which provided in brief that hereafter guards in the prison service should be called junior and senior officers; that all appointments to the prison service should be to the grade of junior officer and for a probationary period of twelve months, and that thereafter juniors should be promoted to the grade of senior officer, lieutenant, or captain only on the basis of merit as determined by written examination and by service record. No enlistments can now be made to the Federal prison service above the grade of junior officer. No appointments of higher custodial officers can be made through favoritism, politics, or influence. Nor, on the other hand, can any prison officer obtain promotion to a higher rank except on the basis of his own qualifications. Thus, once and for all, has the merit promotion system been made secure.

During the first year after his appointment the new officer—and the older officer if he desires promotion—is permitted to take the United States Prison Service Study Course. This constitutes of ten assignments as follows:

1. Outline of Course.
2. Protection as a Penal Policy, with the History and Scope of Federal Penal Administration.
3. Description of Federal Prison System.
4. The Classification Program.
5. Medical and Hospital Service.
6. Prison Industries.
7. Parole and Probation.
8. Our Jail Problem.
9. Everyday Problems in Prison Administration.
10. Some Special Features of Prison Administration.

The following textbooks are provided, and certain excerpts therefrom must be read:

Barnes: *The Story of Punishment.*
Osborne: *Prisons and Common Sense.*
De Schweinitz: *The Art of Helping People Out of Trouble.*
Morris: *Criminology.*
Robinson: *Should Prisoners Work?*
MacCormick: *The Education of Adult Prisoners.*
Osborne Association: *The Handbook of American Prisons and Reformatories.*
Queen: *The Passing of the County Jail.*
Cooley: *Probation and Delinquency.*
Sutherland: *Principles of Criminology.*
Wines: *Punishment and Reformation.*

When the lessons have been completed, written tests will be given and the actual service record of each individual reviewed. An oral examination will be held by the committee on which both the Civil Service Commission and the Bureau of Prisons will be represented. The written examination based upon the study course will count 40 per cent towards the final standing. The service record will be weighted at 60 per cent.

Thus, we shall secure not only a measure of the prison officer's mental attainments and ambitions but also a closer estimate of his actual value as demonstrated by his record of service. Twenty-five per cent of the guards may be promoted in pay and responsibility to the classification of senior officer, and from there take similar promotional examinations to the grade of lieutenant and captain.

No attempt is to be made to interfere in any way with the responsibility of the warden for the control of his custodial force. But assurance is given by means of the assistance of the examining board that each and every officer's rating is to be determined strictly on the basis of his examination and the record of his service.

The ten assignments listed above comprise in somewhat more logical form the subjects which were included in the curriculum of the New York school together with a more extended instruction in physical training, defense tactics, and the handling of weapons and gas equipment, in accordance with the standards adopted for use in Federal penal institutions.

Arrangements are made during the probationary period to test the officer who is taking the in-service course in the several capacities in the institution to determine the general or peculiar fitness for the various kinds of positions to be filled by the custodial force. Starting out with the more simple duties which fall in Class D, he may, as he demonstrates his aptitude for more complicated duties, be assigned to training in Class C or B. The jobs in Class A are, generally speaking, those having supervisory activities and would hardly be available to the newer prison officer engaged in the training course.

If during this testing period an officer, by the way in which he discharges his duties in Class D, makes it necessary to drop him from the service, the institution may give any one of the following reasons in support of its recommendation for termination of services:

(1) He does not possess the personality necessary for prison work.

(2) He manifests such inattention to duties as to indicate that he would be careless or negligent in carrying out instructions or obeying rules.

(3) He is unable to accommodate himself to institutional life —which, in short, means fraternizing with prisoners, unjustly criticizing institutional administration of officials, or discussing institutional affairs with outsiders in a manner calculated to bring reproach upon the service.

(4) He shows character defects such as timidity, insolence, overaggressiveness, bad habits, intemperance, use of profane and indecent language, or untruthfulness.

(5) Some other good and sufficient reason.

The plan briefly outlined above has received the approval of the Civil Service Commission, of the American Federation of Government Employees, and of the National Federation of Federal Employees.

It will be seen that not only does this proposed scheme offer an opportunity for developing the best and highest qualities in candidates for the position of prison officer, but it also guarantees to them something in the nature of a career service and should have a far-reaching effect on that account. Many a young college man would be willing to serve as prison officer if he could be assured of promotion in accordance with merit. The reason perhaps why so many men do not accept service in prisons today is that they see no hope of promotion to the higher and more lucrative positions. Thus there has been an endless circle of discouragement, despair, and inefficiency. We do not get good men because we do not promote them to the higher positions, and we cannot promote them to higher positions because they are usually not qualified.

The Federal Bureau of Prisons tenders a new opportunity to the ambitious young college man who has a penchant for useful social service. I ought, I suppose, to insert a word of caution at this point and say to these "ambitious young college men" that it will do no good to write me asking for a job unless they first secure standing on the Federal Civil Service register. Work in the penal and correctional institutions should be just as much a service as is the Army or Navy or such an activity as the United States Public Health Service. Nothing can stimulate loyalty and devotion to the work more than a realization that one is part of a corps or service, and nothing can destroy initiative and morale any quicker than the feeling that one's work is of the dead-end variety.

The Prison Bureau not only has insisted on the full application of Civil Service throughout all of its divisions and the organization of its custodial force on a career basis, but has repeatedly demonstrated that it believes that the heads of the various institutions should be men who have grown up in the work and earned their right to administer the institutions. In the legislation of 1930, authorizing the establishment of two new large institutions, it was provided that even the warden and deputy should be chosen in accordance with Civil Service rules and regulations, and in the other institutions where such provision is not mandatory the principle of promotion has governed the appointments. Warden Zerbst at Leavenworth began as a prison guard in the Federal service in 1895. Warden Aderhold at Atlanta entered the service as a clerk twenty-nine years ago. Warden Hudspeth at the Leavenworth Annex was promoted from the position of deputy and has been a prison officer for twenty-two years. Warden Hill at Northeastern and Mr. Merry at the Southwestern Reformatory were No. 1 on the Civil Service lists respectively for warden and for assistant superintendent. Superintendent Joseph W. Sanford at Chillicothe has been successively probation officer, member of the Bureau of Efficiency staff on a Civil Service status, superintendent of a prison camp, assistant superintendent at Chillicothe, and now superintendent. Warden Johnston at Alcatraz is one of the most experienced and best known prison men in California. Warden Swope of McNeil Island brought to his job many years of experience as warden of a State penitentiary. Without exception the other men at the heads of jails and camps have been either promoted from the ranks or appointed by reason of long experience in their particular field of work.

If we are to get better results in prison management we not only must provide opportunities for qualifying officers and employees, but must whole-heartedly accept the Civil Service principles both in the selection of personnel and in their protection from arbitrary or political removal. This will do much to restore and maintain the esprit de corps which has been so badly shattered in many of our State institutions.

In a speech on June 7, 1935, Attorney General Cummings in vigorous fashion called attention to the great need for training and educational facilities in all departments of law enforcement. After stating, "The importance of such training cannot be overestimated," he offered the coöperative services of the Department of Justice. With reference to the Federal Bureau of Prisons he said:

This Bureau now maintains a training course for Federal prison officials, the facilities of which will be made available under proper conditions to selected State and other officers in this field. Here will be studied the development of scientific information on which to base comprehensive modern methods of parole, probation, and pardon, modern methods of jail and prison construction; modern methods for the classification, segregation and treatment of criminals; the effects of various forms of punishment, advanced penological technique in prisons, jails, and work camps, and a host of similar matters.

Our Bureau is looking forward to the time when this hope may be a country-wide reality, and when it will be considered just as necessary to qualify men for service in a prison as it is for service in school or college. I regard this matter of personnel as one of transcendent importance.

The insistence of Attorney General Mitchell and Attorney General Cummings that the Federal prison service be professionalized is a position from which no retreat will now be possible. If it results in the standardization of prison service as a career service and the improvement of the human element in the conduct of our prisons, it will be the most outstanding contribution in a generation to be made to prison work in America. A prison officer can be a leader as well as a guard.[2]

[2] See generally report of the Commission of Inquiry on Public Service Personnel, *Better Government Personnel*. See also *Crime and Justice*, by Sheldon Glueck, p. 253 *et seq.*

CHAPTER XI

AND HIM SAFELY KEEP

We are all subject to some discipline. The law-abiding man recognizes the necessity, accepts it cheerfully and coöperates to attain the degree of discipline necessary to group welfare. . . . Justice and fairness are essential for exercising control of prisoners. They may grumble about rules but they generally know when they are enforced fairly and each in his heart of hearts knows when justice is done. . . . In the enforcement of rules and the application of penalties, we consider the individual, his degree of accountability and the effect of his infraction and the punishment on the group. . . . Discipline in prisons is frequently confounded with punishment. Punishment or deprivations are necessary to hold some men in line but the measures taken to avoid trouble are more important. Individual examinations; good medical attention, especial care of eyes, teeth and feet; wholesome food with frequent changes of menus to secure variety; ample bathing facilities; changes of clothing and shoes; cleanliness in quarters; good library with aid to formation of reading habits; thoughtful regard for the bodily welfare of prisoners—all contribute to the ends sought by discipline.

JAMES A. JOHNSTON
Warden, U. S. Penitentiary, Alcatraz Island.

Prison Discipline

Many wardens have been heard to remark that the first requirement of a well conducted prison is discipline. Everything must be subordinated to that end, and unless they are able to discipline their inmates they cannot control the prison. The first dictionary definition of "discipline" is: "To train to obedience, subjection or effectiveness; drill; educate." The second meaning, "To punish or chastise."

Fortunate is the warden who can maintain his institution through the imposition of the educational type of discipline rather than the punitive. When we are able to define prison discipline as punishment for the sake of training, and when

we are clever enough to instill into the minds of the inmates
some realization of this purpose of a prison, we shall have
solved some of the most troublesome of the practical problems
of prison management.

The deputy warden in most prisons is an absolute monarch.
It is his duty to pass upon the reported infractions of the rules
by inmates, to decide as justly as he can as to guilt or innocence and to mete out punishment. He must be neither too
soft nor too harsh. He must be able to penetrate the subter-
fuges and artifices with which a thousand clever inmates cloak
their peccadillos. He must not allow himself to be surprised.
He must let the inmates know that he is always the master
of the ship, and he cannot permit insolence, insubordination,
or defiance. On the other hand, he must be fair. He must be
just. He must understand the failings and the shortcomings
not only of his prisoners but of his officers. Some officers have
a knack of getting along with prisoners and never have to
make a report, others are in trouble a great deal of the time.
Sometimes it pays to overlook an infraction of the rules, provided doing so will not break down the morale of the institution.

Purpose of Privileges

The warden and his deputy in a modern penal institution
must therefore rely on something more than brute force and
punitive discipline. The days of the lash, the water cure, the
paddle, the rack, and the torture chamber have gone from
our American prisons. But the necessity for corrective discipline has not. One of the practical reasons why more privileges are given in the prisons of today is the possibility of
depriving prisoners of these same privileges, as part of the
imposition of punishment. When prisoners have no privileges,
when their existence in prison is nothing more than keeping
the breath of life in their bodies, then the prison warden has
no alternative to more bodily punishment or further torture
to enforce his regulations.

Let those who decry the permitting of simple privileges in

prison ponder this. If all inmates are at the dead level of misery and deprivation all the time, how can we differentiate between those who conform and those who do not? Consider the plight of the old-time warden. Early prison tyrants found to their dismay that, after they had whipped a man's back until the flesh hung in ribbons, the victim finally appeared to lose all feeling. What recourse was there when he had beaten and lashed a prisoner into insensibility or reduced him to a snarling and calloused brute?

J———— M———— was found guilty of taking an automobile over the State line in one of the districts of Texas. The judge gave him four years but stated that he would recommend parole at the end of one-third of this time. The State, however, wanted J———— M ———— for prosecution on the same charge for which he was sentenced by the Federal Court and placed a detainer against him. This made it impossible to consider him for parole. J———— M———— wrote to the judge and told him that it looked as though he were going to have to do his whole four years, and the judge attempted to reduce the sentence from four years to one year and a half. J———— M———— then found out that the law did not permit the judge to do this. This was too much for him to understand, and he proceeded to break every rule of the prison that he could. At the time I saw him he had been punished twenty-two times with a total residence in solitary of about 180 days. All of his "good time" had been taken away. This was discipline. Nor could one blame the deputy warden. No sooner would this young hombre get out of the "hole" (however light and airy a solitary may be, it is always referred to as the "hole") than he would openly defy the warden to put him in again.

The warden and the deputy and I talked it over. We tried to see the matter from the prisoner's point of view. The warden realized that as long as this man stayed in prison he would be defiant and they would be obliged to continue to punish him. That treatment had not seemed to work, so we finally decided—somewhat tardily, it is true—to try another.

We might recommend that the Attorney General restore the forfeited good time, which would permit the prisoner's release, and as an excuse for this revolutionary procedure point out to the Attorney General the injustice which the young man had suffered in being obliged to serve two or three times the sentence intended by the judge when it was imposed.

We called the boy in and explained to him what we proposed to do. He was somewhat taken aback. This was a new kind of approach but he agreed that if his release could be arranged he would attempt to lead a law-abiding life. The Attorney General accepted our recommendation, and the boy was discharged. This was several years ago and he has never come back to us. I hope the disciplinary treatment which he received in our penitentiary was not too much for him.

In the Federal system, realizing the underlying importance of prison discipline, we have adopted certain regulations governing it:

1. No "good time" can be taken from a prisoner—that is, his term cannot be lengthened—except after a formal hearing at which the charges of misconduct are presented. Three members of the staff of the prison compose the board. The prisoner is confronted with the charges and given the privilege of replying. He is also allowed to choose from the staff or custodial service any officer to represent him as counsel. The members of the board file their recommendations for action, and the warden administers the punishment, whatever it may be.

2. In many of our institutions, instead of the deputy warden handling all minor infractions of the rules a disciplinary board is provided which looks into each case and adjusts the penalties. This is a wholesome check upon arbitrary or hasty action and has worked well wherever it has been tried.

3. Corporal punishment is not permitted in Federal institutions. No chains, shackles, or stringing up is allowed. While a prisoner may be deprived of everything except a board and a blanket, the solitary cells are not totally dark, and sufficient ventilation is provided. All punishments must be reported

monthly to the Bureau, and wherever the solid door is closed special report must be made of that fact.

4. No inmate may be placed in solitary except after a medical and psychiatric examination by the United States Public Health Service.

On one occasion some years ago I was taken into the solitary corridor at one of our Federal institutions. A young man of twenty-one or -two staggered to his feet and, on the stern invitation of the deputy, came to the grated door of his cell. In a stentorian voice, said the deputy:

"Tell the director why you are here."

The boy didn't appear to know.

"Come, come, come. Speak up, and tell us what it is all about."

Still a look of blank amazement on the part of the prisoner.

I remarked to the deputy that this boy didn't seem to be normal mentally.

"Well, well," said the deputy, "perhaps he isn't. If, after forty-eight hours in solitary they don't respond, we have the doctor look them over."

Somehow, it just didn't seem to be my idea that prisoners should be restored to sanity by forty-eight hours in the solitary. So from then on we reversed the process, and now we attempt to discover first the mental condition of the transgressor and adjust his punishment in accordance with that finding.

5. Federal Prison Bureau rules require that every prisoner in solitary be visited twice daily by a member of the medical staff—in the morning by the chief medical officer and in the afternoon by the psychiatrist. Although claims of beatings and mistreatment while in solitary had been more or less common in the older days, since the establishment of this rule four years ago not a single complaint of cruelty or mistreatment while in solitary has been received at this Bureau office. The punishments permitted in Federal prisons as aids to discipline are: loss of privileges, such as yard time, letter writing, permission to listen to the radio or attend the occasional moving picture; reduction in grade, which postpones parole eligibil-

ity; segregation with full or reduced meals; solitary confinement with bread and water and loss of good time. Since the abolition of the more severe forms of intramural punishment no particularly bad effects have been noticed. As a matter of fact, the most orderly and well behaved institutions are those in which the disciplinary measures are most humanely administered.

All prisons distinguish between the use of solitary as punishment, where for a few days men may be placed on reduced diet and allowed to come to their senses, and the more or less permanent segregation of unruly or dangerous prisoners in a removed and protected part of the prison. This latter measure is adopted as much for the safety and welfare of the whole institution as it is to prevent infractions of the rules. An inmate in this kind of segregation is given full rations, exercise in a small yard apart from other prisoners, books, writing materials and has his privileges reduced only so far as it is necessary to keep him separate from the mass. One prisoner, who has been in segregation for several years, is even allowed to raise canary birds and has become more or less of an authority on the care and breeding of these "feathered songsters." Prisoners occasionally request to be isolated. Some have fits of uncontrollable temper in which their truculence is directed against an officer or other inmate. These prisoners have to be segregated, but reports of such action are made monthly to the supervisory authorities.

The effectiveness of the constructive type of discipline is shown in the case of R—— G——, one of the most notorious and desperate train robbers in the Northwest, with a record of several escapes from prison and from the custody of the arresting officers. He came to Atlanta and immediately proceeded to make himself a thorn in the flesh of the authorities. He was connected with a desperate plot to escape, which was foiled. He went on a hunger strike. He visited solitary often, and finally in desperation he was declared to be insane and sent to St. Elizabeth's Hospital in Washington. At the hospital the doctors stopped fighting with him and tried to understand him. It seemed apparent to them eventually that he was not insane, and he was transferred to another prison in the Federal system. There he was put to work under the guidance of one of the most humane men in the prison system. His inventive genius was allowed to operate. In the brush shop it was soon discovered that R———— G———— was a valuable assistant, and for four years this prisoner got along without any disciplinary trouble, showing no evidences of rebellion and, in fact, on more than one occasion going out of his way to help maintain order among other prisoners. What he may do when his term is finished, we cannot predict, but many of us think that the case of R———— G———— is the most striking demonstration of the difference in effect between punitive discipline and the discipline of understanding.

Of equal importance with the maintenance of discipline in a penal institution is the necessity for insisting upon equal treatment for all prisoners. Nothing is more demoralizing, more conducive to unrest and dissatisfaction, and less likely to bring about any permanent reformation among the prisoners than toleration in a prison of unearned privileges, preferences, or immunities for some of the inmates. One might say that this rule should apply in the world at large. But it is even more important in the restricted and abnormal environment of a penal institution, and by the same token equality of treatment the hardest condition to obtain.

We have read about the gangster chief with his lackeys and his minions, his bondsman and his political errand boys, his immunities from arrest and his contemptuous disregard of the law. When such an individual is finally caught and comes to the door of the prison, it is doubly hard for him to realize that he is now just a number. It is a good deal further for the gangster chief to fall to the level of everyday prison routine than it is for the man who has had to fight on the outside daily for his bread and butter.

The presence of any much advertised "big shot," especially if he is suspected of being rich, presents special difficulties for any warden to reckon with. The hundreds of self-constituted publicity agents who seem intent upon keeping before the public every little detail of the gangster's life, both in and out of prison, do not make this problem any easier. Newspaper writers and ex-prisoners seem to take extra satisfaction in regaling the public with stories, some of them pure fabrication, others with a grain of truth hidden in them about how the "big shot" wears silk underwear, how he plays tennis to the exclusion of the lesser criminals, how he can eat whatever he wants, etc. Such reports come out of many prisons whenever prominent people are incarcerated therein, and it is doubtful if anything irritates the public to a greater extent than to be told that there is one kind of prison treatment for the poor and lowly and another for the high and mighty.

It is oftentimes impossible to directly implicate the "big shot" in the prison intrigues, but wherever he goes he is likely to be surrounded with a group of disciples and sycophants hoping to get something from him. On more than one occasion a prison guard has allowed himself to get too friendly with a "politician" to his ultimate sorrow and disaster.

Governors get committed to prison occasionally; so do Congressmen, judges, bankers, and lawyers, as well as teamsters, laborers, coal miners, and those who have never had a job. The task of maintaining equality of treatment in a prison among all of these groups is an extraordinarily difficult one. Some one must shovel the coal. Some one must do the hard dirty work. But also, some one must act as interne in the hospital. Some one must teach school, and some few may be employed in the front office as clerks. So long as these favored jobs in a prison are passed out by one man, charges of favoritism (sometimes justified, alas) and the purchase of the good jobs will be prevalent. Those who work in the dining room will be accused of having extra food. Prisoners who are employed in the laundry will be given a clandestine package of cigarettes to have special work done on the shirt of one of the inmates. The deputy's clerk or the warden's stenographer will be constantly importuned to intercede for a fellow convict, and high prices have been paid in some instances for confidential information which appeared in the private records of the parole or social welfare sections.

Some years ago a scandal broke out at a Federal prison when the warden discovered a plot to obtain hospital treatment through a shifting of cultures, and one prisoner smeared some invisible paint upon his chest in order to cast a shadow upon the X-ray print and prove that he had tuberculosis. The inventiveness and ingenuity and resourcefulness of many of the convicts is inexhaustible.

Of course the elimination of special privileges and the establishment of a system of equal treatment is largely dependent upon the will and intelligence of the warden and his staff, but much can be done in the improvement of our penal system which will help bring such a condition about.

The Federal Prison Bureau has taken the following steps to improve conditions in this respect.

1. The "range line" has been forever abolished. Orders are that all prisoners now eat the same food and at the same mess. For years many prisons maintained a distinction in this regard. The clerks, the "big shots," "the politicians" of the prison, so called, reveled in steaks and chops which were cooked on the range and thereby got the name of "range line," whereas the great mass of the prisoners were on the main line and were served with the regular stews or soups or whatever the contents of the steam kettles happened to be. Every one recognized that there was no good excuse for the maintenance of this division, but it took courage and tenacity of purpose on the part of our wardens to abolish it.

2. No inmates of Federal penitentiaries now sleep outside the prison building, except where they have been formally transferred to camp status, and with very few exceptions the prevalent practice of sleeping in the hospital has been discontinued. Men may work in the warden's house or in the chicken coop but they come back into the fold at night.

3. The establishment of the prison commissary eliminated the most prolific source of privilege and discrimination which existed in the institutions. Formerly prisoners were permitted

to bring money into the institution and deposit it to their credit for the purchase of any number of extra articles. Fried chicken, ice cream, pie, and other delicacies could be purchased through the town tradespeople, and money could be dispensed as largess from the rich baron to the poor of his parish.

On September 1, 1931, the order went forward that no money was to be brought into the prison, that no purchases might be made except through the institution commissary, and then only to the limit of ten dollars per month (this has since been reduced to five dollars in some institutions), and only such articles might be purchased as were listed in the commissary. There was naturally a howl of protest from some of the storekeepers in the towns where the institutions were located who had been enjoying a very lucrative business of furnishing extras to the Federal prisoners at fancy prices. Warden Aderhold of Atlanta in a recent discussion of the evils of special privileges for prisoners makes this significant statement:

So far as this institution is concerned the commissary experiment is entirely satisfactory. Both officers and inmates are gratified with the results. I would not under any consideration go back to the old plan.

As fast as they can be manufactured, a uniform type of steel locker is being provided for each inmate, and no personal property is permitted beyond the capacity of the locker.

One can never eliminate inequality either in or out of prison, but it is my firm conviction that no warden is likely to have an institution free of riots or discontent nor will he make the most of his opportunities until he sets out to accomplish this difficult purpose.

Recently at one of our penitentiaries two men were admitted, both of whom had been more or less in the public eye. One was a wealthy banker who had been accustomed to luxury and good living all his life. The other was a high official in the Communist Party of America who had lifted his voice on many an occasion on behalf of the downtrodden masses. As soon as the banker was released from the prison hospital, where he went for treatment of a well recognized ailment, he made it a point to say to the warden that he asked but one favor, and that was that he be treated so far as possible like any other prisoner. He wanted to work. He wanted to be of such help as he could, and he did not wish to be singled out for any preference over any other prisoner. He was quickly assured that he need give himself no concern on that point, there was no "gold coast" in the Federal prisons.

On the other hand, the high official of the Communist Party, although duly convicted of a Federal crime by a jury, immediately demanded special concessions because he was a "political prisoner." Every prisoner is permitted to subscribe to one of the standard daily newspapers and, if hailing from a small town, to the local sheet published in his neighborhood. These papers are furnished regularly through the commissary. The friend of the masses, however, wanted to subscribe to all the newspapers and periodicals to which he could have had access on the outside, and he and his remarkably large number of friends and supporters outside the prison endeavored to establish the fact that he was discriminated against because he was not permitted to have as many of the radical and somewhat incendiary publications sent to him as he wished. He not only wanted to read them himself but wanted to pass them around among his fellow prisoners and take subscriptions for some of them.

Here was a tough spot for the warden. He could not very well say that one newspaper was incendiary while another was soporific. Nor could he deny this particular prisoner the right that every other prisoner had to choose his newspaper. The warden, however, could prevent the circulation of such literature among other prisoners, and this he did. He could hold the Communist down to the regulations to which every other prisoner was subjected, and this he did. When the Communist really understands the nature and purpose of the regulations, that they are meant to be enforced, that they are to bring about an approach to equality of treatment, and that after all they are more consistent with the principles for which he stands than the attitude expressed by himself and his friends, he will readily acquiesce in their application to himself.

The contrast between these two prisoners, however, not only is striking but affords a good illustration of the ticklish problems which arise in the administration of a modern prison.

4. No officer in the prison is now permitted to request the assignment of a given individual to any particular job in the prison. Thus, the assignment to work is one of the matters which come before the classification committee; and purchasing of jobs or bringing influence to bear is done away with, and the work to be done by inmates is apportioned among those who are best fitted to perform it.

5. Formerly the fortunate members of the prison fraternity could buy their own radios and use them in accordance with their own predilections. Several years ago central radio distributing systems were installed in all of the large institutions, subject to censorship and regulation. Every man was permitted to buy a head phone through the commissary. There was thus afforded a ready means of communication between the warden and the whole inmate population through the broadcasting system. It was possible to hold the use of the radio down within reasonable bounds and to regulate to some extent the kind of program which was offered. The usual limit of radio time in most of the Federal prisons (except Alcatraz and Lewisburg, where there is none) is two hours daily with some extra time on Sundays and holidays.

The immediate effect of this privilege in maintaining quiet and order in the cell blocks has been remarked by all of those in charge of the institutions. But it is a privilege that can be revoked and is not allowed to interfere with the work, study, or classroom activities of the inmates.

The large penitentiary of today is in reality a small town. It has its factories, its power plant, its farms, etc. Unavoidably there is much passing in and out. The danger of smuggling contraband articles in, or taking uncensored letters out, constitutes a constant anxiety, and here again the devilish ingenuity of some inmates has free range. Careful search has to be made of all articles which enter the prison. Files have been secreted between the soles of a shoe. A knife may be sewed into the lapel of a coat. On one occasion the wife of a prisoner in a Massachusetts jail sent in a pistol hidden in a cooked chicken. Morphine and heroin come in under the flap of an envelope or under the postage stamp, and handkerchiefs may be soaked in a solution of some powerful drug.

Every article which enters the prison sally port has to be carefully inspected. All mail coming in and going out must be read to prevent improper communications between inmates and their friends outside. The tremendous amount of work entailed in the censorship of all letters and packages is increased every time the mail privilege is extended. Letter writing, however, makes possible the prisoner's one contact with his family; and, on the theory that he must later resume his relationship with them, it is generally considered wise to permit him to correspond frequently. Here, as almost everywhere else, in the conduct of a modern prison, eternal vigilance is the price of security.

We have emphasized the need for trained and understanding prison employees who will assist in the difficult task of reforming our inmate population. We require that they shall treat the prisoners with patience, firmness, and understanding; but we must go farther and insist that they shall not lower themselves to the prisoners' level, that they shall be careful not to adopt the vulgar jargon of the underworld and shall not attempt to impress prisoners with the fact that they are good fellows. To know exactly where to draw the line requires intelligence and discrimination. Perhaps we express the idea best when we say that the guard must not fraternize with the prisoners. Results serious for him and dangerous for the prisoner may follow if a convict or a group of convicts once get the idea that an officer can be reached.

H. L. Merry, Superintendent of the United States Southwestern Reformatory, is responsible for the following story:

A probationary officer expressed admiration for a wrist watch worn by one of his fellows and remarked, "I am saving up for one myself."

A little later an inmate approached the officer, his demeanor most humble. "I beg pardon, sir, but I overheard you say something about a wrist watch. I hope you will excuse me, sir, but a friend of mine is in that business. His name is John Doe and his store is at 100 Main Street. I feel quite sure that if you will mention my name to him when you are next in town, he will sell you a watch at wholesale."

On the occasion of his next visit to town, the student officer called at the address given. The man behind the desk was suave of manner and very anxious to please the prospective customer. A large number of watches was shown, and finally the young man became satisfied with one and it was placed on his wrist. Upon being asked the price, the salesman (who, by the way, was an employee of the prisoner in question) stated, "Never mind that now, sir. What we want to do is to number you among our satisfied customers. You know it takes some time before a wrist watch becomes regulated to the wearer. Won't you wear this watch for a few weeks, calling here every time that you are in the neighborhood, in order that we may regulate the watch for you? Should the watch prove unsatisfactory, we will let you try another." The officer, well satisfied with this explanation, returned, proudly showing the new watch.

On successive visits to the city, the officer called at the jewelry store, each time making an effort to obtain a price on the watch but being put off by one clever excuse or another. Shortly he was transferred to an institution several hundred miles from the location of the jewelry store; it was some time before he became settled in his new station and thought of the watch again; so much time had elapsed that he took no action toward paying for it.

One day he reported to his superior officer that a certain inmate had offered him one hundred dollars to put a telephone call out. Many such calls were to follow, with forthcoming "centuries" as well, to the officer who would accommodate him. An investigation followed; proof was established of the attempt at bribery; the officer was praised, the inmate lost eight months' good time.

A little later another inmate offered money to the same officer for another favor. During the investigation concerning this second attempt at bribery, the prisoner charged that the officer had been successfully bribed at his former station. He cited the watch episode, with which he was evidently familiar. Called before the director and quizzed about the watch, the officer stated it was a birthday gift from his sister. Investigation resulted in the sister's denial. The officer was dismissed from the service. He was a college graduate of excellent appearance, interested and efficient. Notwithstanding his good points, he did that of which many another officer has been guilty; put himself on an equal footing with an inmate.

There are instances where a slight and perhaps unintentional favor bestowed by a guard on an inmate has led to the undoing of an otherwise good officer. It doesn't take long for the word to be passed that Guard So-and-so is a man who can be dealt with. There can be no apology or reprieve for the faithless officer, and where the evidence points to the fact that a certain employee is controlled by or under obligation to inmates, even though the legal proof may not be sufficient to convict him of wrongdoing, he must be immediately dismissed.

On one occasion a guard so far forgot his oath of office and his duty to society as to take small sums of money from outside to certain prisoners. He was prosecuted and received a sentence of eighteen months to the very prison in which he was formerly employed.

Fortunately these cases are rare, and if officers would constantly bear in mind the difference between maintaining a dignified, humane, and understanding attitude towards the prisoners and fraternizing with an individual or a group of individuals, even fewer of these incidents would occur.

Naturally, the warden's constant anxiety is to prevent escapes and disturbances of one kind or another, such as a hunger strike, or a riot in the dining room or a refusal to work. When the court commits a man to the care of the warden he is specifically enjoined to "him safely keep." Much of the modern effort at the rehabilitation of the individual prisoner has of necessity to be controlled by the ever present anxiety as to escape. The public does not readily excuse a warden who permits a dangerous criminal to force his way out of a penitentiary in which he was supposed to be safely and more or less permanently lodged.

For twenty-three months the Southwestern Reformatory at El Reno, Oklahoma, had not had an escape, in spite of the fact that three-fourths of its men were living in more or less open surroundings. The institution was building up a reputation as a place where men could be brought back to normal life. In fact, one lady was heard to remark as the Rock Island train made its way past the reformatory reservation, "There is a prison which is not a prison." She probably intended to be complimentary, but within a few days the grim significance of this remark was borne in upon us when five young convicts captured two guards, forced them to open the door to the cell block, accompany them across the brightly lighted yard, and walk past the guard tower to temporary freedom.

Whatever else it aims to be, a prison must be enough of a prison to keep men from running away. In this instance one at least of the guards was lacking in courage, and the man in the tower apparently lost his head. What does a guard do when he sees a fellow officer used as a shield by several escaping inmates? Does he shoot in the dirt at their feet? Does he aim to wound them in the leg? Under what circumstances, if any, is he justified in shooting to kill? Except for the Leavenworth incident elsewhere recounted, in six years of operation of the nineteen institutions under the Prison Bureau but one escaping prisoner has lost his life. That happened at Alcatraz, when a reckless convict had gotten over the fence in spite of warnings and nothing but the guard's rifle stood between him and a plunge into the sea. Some of the institution superintendents have given definite instructions that whenever they, or other officers who might be expected to give orders, give such an order while under the control of inmates, they are to be disobeyed.

With the right kind of vigilance, neither of the officers above referred to need have been hostaged. Arrangements might easily have been made that under no circumstances should the guard who was subject to capture have access to the keys to the door. There were several ways in which the man in the tower could have circumvented the escape without injuring or disabling his fellow officer. Emergencies such as this test the resourcefulness, courage, and quick-wittedness of a guard. There are many tricks which can be learned for disarming a prisoner, whether he has a knife or a gun. I venture to say that the officers of the Southwestern Reformatory will have a much clearer idea as to their duties the next time a situation such as this confronts them.

The warden may have 3,000 convicts, and a considerable number of them may be continually plotting, always on the lookout to find a vulnerable spot. In the case of many an escape or demonstration it is easy to see *after* the thing has happened where some simple little act of precaution might have prevented the whole thing. Many an insurrection or jail delivery has been prevented by the quick thinking or the resourcefulness of a guard, and the public hears little about it.

This tendency of guards to get careless or overconfident is well illustrated by certain circumstances which led up to and made possible the escape from Leavenworth in December of 1931. That was the occasion on which seven desperate criminals obtained possession of firearms which had been purchased by a confederate at a pawnshop in Illinois, immersed in a barrel of shoe paste, consigned in a regular order to the prison shoe factory and smuggled into the institution. The gun detector described in Chapter VII, had it been in use, might have forestalled such an event. The prisoners forced their way out of the front door of the prison with the warden and others as hostages; after a running battle with the guards and a posse hastily collected from the neighborhood, three of the escapers were killed and the others recaptured and given additional sentences. The outside man was apprehended through the clever work of agents of the Federal Bureau of Investigation and received a sentence of twenty-five years in the penitentiary for his part in the affair.

The prison at Leavenworth was probably as well guarded as the average penitentiary, but the prisoners proved to be just clever enough to circumvent the guards and outwit the officials.

While hindsight is always easier than foresight it is now plain:

First, if the storekeeper had been more alive to possibilities the innocent-looking barrel of shoe paste in which the revolvers were secreted would never have been allowed to stand most of the day on the platform outside the warehouse, later to be taken possession of by the scheming convicts.

Second, if the men in the hospital or the yard detail had been more alert, they never would have permitted one of the chief conspirators to go from his station in the clothing room to the hospital on three successive days, for no purpose whatever except to consult with some of the other conspirators.

Third, if the guard in the lower corridor had been as suspicious as he should have been, he would have stopped the man with the long overcoat who was walking toward the front end of the main corridor. If he had stopped him, he would have discovered the shotgun concealed beneath the overcoat.

Fourth, if there had been the adequate control of passes which is now provided in all Federal institutions, the prisoners who later made their escape through the front gate would never have been allowed to get within striking distance of that exit.

All these things, of course, have been rectified. Probably they never would have been regarded as omissions if the escape had not disclosed them. Every time an incident of this sort occurs, the administrators of the prison attempt to make sure that the defects thereby exposed are corrected. But the next time the attack will be made on a different line, at another place, and the warden and his staff have no more important task than to outwit and circumvent continual efforts of this kind, to anticipate all contingencies, and to carefully rehearse in advance a defense against them.

Naturally the warden or deputy warden, or even the officers who come in daily contact with the prisoners, cannot find out all that is going on. One of the most practical problems has to do with the eliciting of information from inmates. This presents some very difficult and fundamental questions.

To what extent is the deputy warden or assistant superin-

tendent justified in making stool pigeons out of certain of his
charges? Undoubtedly ways can be found to tip off the
deputy in advance and enable him on many occasions to avert
trouble. He will invariably protect the anonymity of his informers and consider himself fortunate if he has built up confidence in himself which encourages inmates to this extent.
How far can the warden go in promising an inmate that, if he
will reveal certain facts about a plot that is being hatched,
he will intercede with the parole board or recommend him for
camp or for a better job in the prison? All those who
know anything about prisons know of the existence of the so-
called "code of honor" among prisoners. Not only is there a
conscientious loyalty among convicts, but in many instances
there is a well grounded fear that it would not be good for
a prisoner to tell what he hears and knows about his fellow
convicts. Perhaps there is no more discouraging feature in
the management of a prison than this utter inability to get at
the truth of what is in the minds of the men and what is
going on behind the officers' backs.

Forty men are asleep in a dormitory. The officer has just
walked in and found that everything is quiet. He resumes his
rounds. All of a sudden a crash and a scream are heard. The
officer turns back, switches on all the lights, and finds one of
the prisoners on the floor writhing in pain with a deep wound
in his neck. There is, of course, latent excitement throughout
the whole dormitory. The officer calls the night captain, and
they immediately start to interrogate each of the other thirty-
nine men. The chances are ten to one that they will find out
from them absolutely nothing as to who committed the assault.
Even the man himself, wounded and perhaps dying, will possibly not tell who his assailant was. The next day each of the
men will be brought separately before the deputy warden.
But from one motive or another all will decline to give evidence. Fortunately, a resourceful deputy may build up a
"prima facie" case which will enable him to prove who did
the cutting. He may know about some previous difficulties
between the man who was cut and his assailant, and probably

his best chance will be that the attacker himself will admit his guilt.

Many times have I pondered over the inherent difficulties in such a situation. Why is it that men in prison have so much greater loyalty to their own kind than they do to society at large? Why do we not more frequently find conscientious and public-spirited prisoners who feel that murder or assault in a prison is just as wrong as it is outside, and who are willing to help authorities place the responsibility for such an act?

The fact remains that even in our best penitentiaries the warden and deputy have many times been obliged to see a cutting scrape go unpunished for the simple reason that they were unable to get reliable evidence to prove the guilt.

On a certain September afternoon H—— F—— was seen to step out of the long line of prisoners marching to the mess hall at the Atlanta penitentiary, to run ahead fifteen or twenty paces, and then a metallic object was heard to drop upon the concrete walk. Immediately a convict named S—— was seen to double over and walk rapidly to the hospital. There was discovered to be a small wound in his groin which did not seem to have a fatal aspect. After eight days in the hospital, however, during which certain disquieting symptoms had developed, S—— was operated upon. It was then disclosed that the dagger, or whatever instrument had been used, had penetrated the diaphragm. S—— died under the anesthetic.

One civilian at least and probably fifty prisoners actually saw the attack. There is no possible doubt of the fact that F—— assaulted S——; but S—— refused to name his assailant, and one after another the prisoners found excuses for not testifying. Eventually, however, two or three gave evidence which seemed to point to the fact of a deliberate assault, and some of them were transferred to other institutions at their own request. In the meantime F—— admitted to the deputy that he cut the prisoner and intimated that he did so to settle an old score. Later on at the official investigation F—— again signed a "confession." At the trial in court the judge ruled that the latter confession was made under such circumstances that it could not legally be admitted, and, to the surprise of every one, including no doubt F—— himself, the jury found him not guilty even of manslaughter.

So confident had F—— been of his ultimate fate that while the jury was out deliberating he inquired of one of the guards as to where the hanging would probably take place.

How much the necessity for complying with strict rules of legal evidence had to do with the unexpected termination of this case, no one can say; but at least it is a striking illustration of some of the troublesome situations which confront the warden in his efforts to keep order among a large number of more or less desperate men restive under the abnormal restraint of a prison.

But the sequel to the story is even more dramatic. On the very next working day after this verdict became known throughout the prison another stabbing occurred which might well have had a fatal termination, but for the efficient care of the victim by the officers of the United States Public Health Service. The two men involved in this second affair were not known to have had any previous altercations, nor were they regarded as members of a gang or treated as particularly dangerous individuals. One of them plunged a crudely fashioned dagger four times into the chest of a fellow convict and then, calmly turning the knife over to the officer who came immediately on the scene, casually admitted that he had done the cutting.

I have never believed that punishment had the deterrent effect which some people think it has. But here was a man who had no doubt been nursing a grudge to the point of desperation. He knew, as possibly did every convict in the institution, that F—— had plunged the knife into S——, had confessed that he had done it, and yet with the help of an able lawyer and a sympathetic jury had "beaten the rap." Perhaps he could hardly be blamed for assuming that in that penitentiary one could "get away with murder."

It is well enough for the layman to ask why convicts are

allowed to have knives in a penitentiary, to demand that men who have a tendency to assault each other be kept separated, and to call for greater and closer supervision of every inmate. To some of those who think that this is a simple task, I recommend that they accept the responsibility of being a prison warden over 3,000 men in a prison originally planned for 1,800.

Another poignant problem which confronts the custodial force of any prison is the prevention of abnormal sex relations between the inmates. This matter quite properly is not often publicly discussed, but it weighs upon the mind of every prison administrator. Some foreign countries have frankly met the issue by permitting furloughs or visits between married people one of whom is serving a sentence. Every known precaution is taken in the Federal penitentiaries to circumvent and prevent abnormal practices. Everything considered, degeneracy is not so prevalent as some people believe. Most men have a natural repugnance towards homosexuality, and celibacy in prison for them is no different than it would be outside. But it is inevitable that an occasional individual who has not practiced self-control and who is temporarily overccme by his emotional reactions should act unnaturally in this respect.

Here, perhaps, is one of the chief arguments against the overcrowded prison. The classification committee and the custodial force can be ever so alert to keep suspicious characters under supervision, and yet the staff of any prison will occasionally be outwitted. On some overdeveloped personalities intramural punishment has little effect, and every prison warden quite naturally hesitates to take a case of this kind into court. The orders given to Federal institutions are definite, however: this practice cannot be tolerated, and, if sufficient punishment cannot be meted out in the form of forfeited "good time," an additional penalty must be sought in court. We can try to keep such misconduct at a minimum, but under the present prison system it is safe to say it will never be entirely eliminated.

The same code of honor which leads one prisoner never to

inform on another even applies to covering up all such incidents, although in noteworthy instances the abhorrence of an inmate has overcome his discretion; such was the case recently in one of our institutions, and the result was the meting out of substantial sentences to several inmates. Many times illicit relationships of this kind engender particularly high feeling, and in not a few of the stabbings which occur in all prisons homosexual aberration is at the bottom of the trouble. The recent killing of Loeb in the Illinois State Prison at Joliet, while it was highly publicized on account of the former prominence of the inmate, is not by any means the only incident of this kind. It takes extraordinarily courageous, clever, and intelligent work by the warden and his staff to handle such situations.

How can these things be prevented or minimized?

First, by scrupulously good housekeeping, by being constantly on the watch to see that suspicious alliances are broken up, that inmates' cells are frequently searched for suspicious letters, weapons, etc.

Second, by the careful work of the classification committee to determine the presence of degenerate tendencies in individuals, and the dissemination of such information among those who have such inmates in custody.

Third, by the prompt punishment of proven offenders.

Fourth, by the attempt to build up a new kind of morale or conscience among the inmate body which will not tolerate such relationships and the sometimes bloody consequences.

In the effort to solve these last two problems and in despair of ever being able to control the large number of inmates by force or intimidation, some of the more progressive prison wardens have appealed to the men themselves. Some form of inmate self-government is necessary if prisons are to become instrumentalities for reform. One need not go to the extent that Osborne did, or turn the management of the prison over to its inmates, to recognize the practical help that comes from utilizing this method of obtaining the confidence and coöperation of prisoners.

If the warden wishes to find out what is really going on in certain parts of his prison, he cannot appeal to individual inmates for assistance. They become branded as stool pigeons or favorites of the warden, and even the best prisoners hesitate to ally themselves with the management even though they may really desire to do so. If there is in the prison, however, a duly elected inmate committee chosen for the purpose, they may consult the warden without suspicion.

When the reformatory at Chillicothe, Ohio, was in its early stages, and before the permanent buildings had been occupied, a disturbance took place one morning at breakfast time. There was dissatisfaction with the food, and an outbreak of plate throwing ensued. A considerable portion of the inmate population had to be returned to quarters. At that time there was no duly appointed committee, and the superintendent and assistant director, who happened to be at the institution, experienced the usual difficulty in getting any inmate to talk or to explain the grievances of the inmates as a whole.

Shortly after this episode a change in management took place. One of the first things was to provide for the selection, by ballot of the inmates, of a representative from each group to serve as an advisory committee. This provided a normal channel for the presentation of grievances on behalf of the inmates, and a ready means of consulting with representative prisoners was always open to the superintendent. This inmate committee was divided into subcommittees, and it did not take long for the whole inmate body to realize that the continuation of certain privileges depended upon their own observance of the rules; and a new and more lasting morale was soon built up. The pressure for conformity to the rules comes from the men themselves and not from those in authority over them, of whom they were always suspicious and against whom they seemed to be allied from the very nature of things.

Evidence soon began to accumulate that this plan was working. Men who had been paroled, who had gone out and failed and had come back again were soon ostracized by the inmate body. It was realized that such renegades had hurt the chances for parole, of other prisoners.

An inmate escaped from Chillicothe and hastened to the home of an ex-inmate near by. Under all usual circumstances he would have been fed and clothed and assisted on his way. But this ex-inmate had sense enough to see that, if this escape was made possible through his assistance, he not only might be guilty of a crime but might cause some of the inmates' privileges to be cut off; and he prevailed upon the escaping prisoner to accompany him back to the institution.

Let the warden of any institution learn that there is a gun or knife secreted in the institution, and then let him endeavor to find it. In at least one instance that has been recorded, a wise warden called to him the inmate committee and said: "Now, boys, we have tried to be fair with you. We have given privileges to those who have earned them, and if you wish these privileges continued it is for your benefit to keep this place clean and orderly. I am told that there is a gun hidden in this institution. I am not looking for culprits, but I want the gun." The next morning the gun was found upon the superintendent's desk.

On a visit to the United States Industrial Reformatory at Chillicothe, not long ago, I was invited to attend a meeting of the inmates' advisory council. There were forty prisoners chosen by ballot, five from each of the eight units of the institution. The method of election was interesting. Without any previous announcement [3] the executive committee of the council called an election, and the inmates were free to suggest the names of as many candidates for the council from their dormitory or cell block as they desired. These preliminary nominations were sorted, and the fifteen men in that unit having the highest number of votes were placed upon the ballot; at the second election the five receiving the highest number of votes were declared members of the council. The five men, constituting the unit committee, held frequent meetings in

[3] This was explained as their method of eliminating "political campaigns." Who says prisoners do not have progressive ideas!

each dormitory, and every other week the forty members of the whole council met to discuss questions of general interest to the inmate body. The meeting that I attended was conducted entirely by the inmates, and the discussion at that time centered upon ways and means whereby the idea of the inmate council could be "sold" to the incoming inmates. Several reports were offered, indicating that progress in this line was being made. One delegate from the committee which was in charge of school meetings reported that, since the prisoner committee had undertaken to assist in the control of discipline in the school building, not a single "shot," or conduct report, had been received from that department of the reformatory.

The discussion then rather naïvely turned upon the question of obtaining the interest and coöperation of the prison officers. The chairman reported that Mr. B——— in Dormitory C thoroughly understood the aims and objects of the inmate committee and was very helpful in his attitude; also that Mr. K——— in Cell Block No. 1 was thoroughly in sympathy with their objects. Then he reported that Mr. R——— in Dormitory E had not yet been convinced of the merits of the idea, but they hoped to bring him around before long. A member of the Dormitory E committee rose, and with obvious sincerity reported that he had had a little talk the day before with Mr. R———, and he was pleased to report that Mr. R——— was "coming round." This announcement was received with approval, and the chairman admonished the members of the council to continue in their efforts to interpret the work of the council to the officers and obtain their continued coöperation.

I could not bring myself to doubt that this movement was genuine. Nor have I ever seen a more complete demonstration of the value of inmate participation in the management of a penal or reformatory institution.

One other example of the wisdom of the superintendent of this remarkable institution, Joseph W. Sanford,[4] was exhibited

---

[4] No relation whatever to the writer—in spite of newspaper asseverations to that effect.

at this same meeting. The deputy superintendent remarked to the inmate group that the classification committee was finding difficulty in getting enough inmates to man the kitchen detail, and he wanted to know if the representatives of the inmate body present could tell him why the prisoners fought shy of an assignment in the kitchen; if matters didn't improve they might be called upon to draft ten or a dozen more men arbitrarily to do that work.

The superintendent then briefly and logically explained the advantages of a kitchen assignment. He said that many inmates were going back to the environment of a large city, such as New York, Cleveland, or Philadelphia; that, while they might like a farm assignment, it would not help them much in New York to have learned how to take care of pigs; that he could also understand the desire to go into one of the fine new vocational shops, but, after all, there were not many openings in the mechanical trades. On the other hand, people always had to eat; there were thousands of restaurants and cafés in New York City which were always looking for experienced help, and it might be for the benefit of the men themselves to ask for an assignment to the kitchen. He also stated that he would give them the benefits of the study course in either cooking or baking. He then said that, even though the detail to the kitchen was short, he was not going to peremptorily assign men to work there but would leave it to the classification committee to convince the newcomers that it was for their own interest to accept this kind of assignment; that they would recruit their details through the regular procedure of the classification committee and in no other way, but if any of the older inmates cared to apply for this work, the classification committee would consider a change in their detail.

One has to know something of the traditional method of prison management to appreciate the farsightedness and cleverness of this method of approach. It is safe to say that there will be no sabotage or lack of discipline in the kitchen in Chillicothe so long as the system is adhered to. A reformatory that helps men to reform themselves and to improve their own

Lines of prisoners marching out of dormitories at U. S. Industrial Reformatory, Chillicothe, Ohio.

Prisoners marching to cell block at U. S. Industrial Reformatory, Chillicothe, Ohio.

prospects will be infinitely more successful than one which attempts to jam reformation down their throats.

With a certain class of prisoners it is psychologically true that to surround them with walls and fences and guards is to invite them to attempt to escape. When you put them in a sense upon their own honor, when you point out that any "sap" can escape from an honor dormitory, then you build up the attitude among the prisoners that such things are just not done and, if done, they react against the general welfare. You can erect a more effective defense against temptation and, in addition to that, build a new kind of stamina into the characters of the inmates themselves.

There are 122 men in the honor dormitory at Chillicothe. There is no officer present, night or day. There are no locks upon the doors. The men form themselves into line on three occasions during the twenty-four hours to attend meals and permit the count to be taken. From my own observation, while there is order and discipline all through the Chillicothe institution, there is a higher degree of order and control in the honor dormitory than in any other part of the institution.

The warden or superintendent who builds up a reputation as being fair and playing no favorites, but who is not afraid to meet an issue, will find unexpected and gratifying support in the prisoners if he makes the proper approach to them. If he has his own spies and stools, he may get along for a while; but sooner or later he will have trouble. If he can put across the idea that he wants to treat everybody alike but that he insists that the inmate body help him to help themselves, he will have a much larger measure of success.

The practical problems of prison administration are many and varied, and perplexing in the extreme. They will be solved, not by brute force and by the administration of more and more punishment, but by the newer type of intelligence, knowledge of human nature, courage, and willingness to take the inmate body into partnership in their solution.

CHAPTER XII

SUPERVISION AND CENTRAL CONTROL

Oftentimes have I heard you speak of one who commits a wrong as though he were not one of you, but a stranger unto you and an intruder upon your world.

But I say that even as the holy and the righteous cannot rise beyond the highest which is in each of you,

So the wicked and the weak cannot fall lower than the lowest which is in you also.

And as a single leaf turns not yellow but with the silent knowledge of the whole tree,

So the wrong-doer cannot do wrong without the hidden will of you all.

.   .   .   .   .   .

And when one of you falls down he falls for those behind him, a caution against the stumbling stone.

Ay, and he falls for those ahead of him, who though faster and surer of foot, yet removed not the stumbling stone.

Kahlil Gibran, "The Prophet."

THE time has gone by when a prison can be managed autonomously. During the last twenty-five years penal systems have been rapidly evolving, and the prison, instead of being the one penal institution in the State, has developed into a link in a larger and more comprehensive institutional program. Many questions in administration of this larger penal organization have arisen which cannot be dealt with by insularized institutional management.

In the place of one institution caring for all kinds of prisoners, we have a group of classified institutions—prisons, reformatories, training schools, farms, camps, defective colonies, etc. This group of institutions will not function properly without some supervising agency. The question, for example, of transferring individuals from one institution to another in order to secure the best working of the system must be handled by some central administrative body.

Many phases of the problem will be common to all institutions and can be dealt with to greater advantage by a central supervising agency—purchase of supplies and equipment, Civil Service Regulations, standards of farm management, architectural advice, are but a few directions in which the controlling body has been of assistance in the development of our individual institutions.

Supervisory control obviously should guide or restrain institution management but not so far as to relieve the institution of responsibility for working out its own destiny. How to get the institution heads and their staffs to comply with suggestions which the control department feels are for the better management of the institution and still not to take from them the sense of accountability for their own acts is a rather delicate problem. The possibility of realizing this ideal, of course, depends on tolerant, intelligent, and persevering men in both positions.

In the Federal Bureau of Prisons, when the importance of organized social service departments in the prisons was first discussed, there were those who felt that all this work should be organized from Washington and be carried on in the institutions more or less independently of the direct custodial work of the warden and his staff. Fortunately, such advice did not prevail. There can be but one supreme authority in any penal institution, and that is the warden. There can be no divided allegiance, and until the warden has become convinced of the wisdom of the new methods it is best to postpone their establishment.

The wise executive officer will not load up the warden with too many suggestions. On the other hand, it must be remembered that most wardens today are sincerely anxious to fulfill the higher ideals of prison management. An official who supervises by the snooping method, who seeks publicity to force his judgment on the officials in the institutions, who places upon them the burden of carrying out impossible ideals which they are equipped with neither money nor personnel to accomplish, will have little success. It seems to me that the cardinal principle of penal administration is to take the warden or superintendent into your confidence, to work out important problems of prison administration with him and not against him so long as he is warden, giving him the credit for his institution, and thus to hold him strictly answerable for its derelictions and deficiencies.

I remember one occasion when a new warden of a large institution was appointed by the Federal Bureau. None of us had any particular confidence in the man who held the position of deputy warden. But it was made clear to the new chief of that institution that he was to have the right to retain the deputy or appoint one of his own choosing. He preferred to retain the then incumbent as deputy, and we all felt it was better to concentrate responsibility in the new warden than to force upon him our own opinions as to the suitability of his deputy. If his first assistant was incompetent, he would have to be the one to find it out. We could not afford to give him any excuse to say that a man whom he himself did not trust had been forced upon him.

It has been my great good fortune in eighteen years of experience to work with prison wardens and superintendents who not only are experienced, efficient, and honest men but have never hesitated to state their disagreement with or qualification of our policies. Only in such manner can the worth of any proposition be tested. When the matter has thus been decided, the administrator and the warden will present a united front to the legislative committee, to the public, or to whoever needs to be convinced of the soundness of such policy. Thus an administrative officer will leave the details of institution administration to the warden or superintendent, and until he has lost confidence in him will ask him for a report on what takes place in his institution. If the time comes when he has lost confidence in him, he will ask for his resignation and will no doubt receive it promptly. Until that time he will realize that the warden is on the bridge, and that responsibility for the management of his institution must repose in him.

As stated above, in the proper utilization of such a classified institutional system the transfer of inmates from one institution to another is of significant importance. It is easy to allow the removals of prisoners to be dictated by the wishes or convenience of the inmates or their friends. The only safe method, of course, is to base the transfer of inmates upon a careful schedule of the facts in each individual case, to the end that the classified penal system may be of the greatest benefit to the individuals treated thereunder.

Of course, there are times when an ambitious superintendent or warden becomes impatient and feels that his freedom of action is impeded by too much supervision, too many restrictions, and that he is unable to carry on to the best advantage. It may be that whatever disadvantage flows from having to appeal to a higher authority for permission to take certain action is more than outweighed by the obvious advantage of having progressive, sympathetic oversight. There will be many times when it will be a real comfort and refuge to a warden to be able to say, "Well, of course, I should like to do this for you, but the rules of the Bureau forbid."

There is strength in uniformity. There is a certain security in feeling that one is part of a larger system. One cannot get the best results from maintaining a single institution. It is only when standards can be compared, when the experience of each man can be made available for the guidance of the others, that progress is possible.

In the Federal system, for example, before the establishment of the Bureau the average daily per capita cost was 68 cents. With the establishment of a supervisory cost control plan and a monthly check-back on the amounts of money spent by each institution, the per capita cost per day per man, exclusive of salaries, for all institutions was reduced to 47 cents.

It is well that institutions have some one to report to. A monthly report of punishments imposed is in itself an effective check upon the too frequent or indiscriminate resort to punitive measures. The weekly list of the assignments of all prisoners to labor helps the warden to analyze his own labor problem, and thus in many instances the mere making of reports has an advantageous effect on the administration of the institution itself.

In addition to the direct oversight of institution management the supervisory body will find itself concerned with many of the larger aspects of the problem. During the Congressional season the Washington members of the Bureau are constantly in touch with Senators and Representatives. The annual appropriation bill must be prepared with care, and the expenditures of each of the nineteen institutions discussed with the committee on appropriations. Legislation which is proposed must be carefully scrutinized to see whether or not it will affect the operation of the Government penal institutions. Many Congressmen have friends who inquire as to the status of the 2,000 employees and of the 16,000 inmates. None of these Congressmen would have time to consult each of the nineteen institutions to get answers to their questions. The maintenance of all case records and an adequate statistical Bureau in Washington is for the convenience of the public and the public's representatives.

Perhaps my experience has been more fortunate than many others, but I have come to the conclusion that the average Congressman or legislator has a very real and sympathetic interest in the problems of the public's penal institutions. He is the representative of a certain community in the National or State capital and, as such, must make frequent inquiries of administrative boards and officials. Generally speaking, what the members of our legislative bodies desire is facts rather than favors, and if an administrator has the facts at his command they are no more unreasonable than any other individuals.

There may be exceptions, it is true. Some years ago an influential member of Congress called on the Bureau for the names and addresses of all persons who had been appointed by us to positions in Washington, a list of all other positions that had not been filled, and at the end of his letter, remarked rather significantly: "I would like to have this information at once as your appropriation is coming before Congress in a few days and I wish to be able to discuss it intelligently."

On one other occasion a certain Congressman requested the transfer of an inmate from one institution to another. We patiently and thoroughly explained to him why this could not be done. The Congressman did not take "No" for an answer, and after inducing several of his fellow legislators to call us up about the same matter hinted that his friend in the institution who desired the transfer had given him a great deal of information to the discredit of the prison and he might be obliged to make a speech about it on the floor. We told him the only thing it was possible to tell him, that if complaints had been made against the institution and he did not feel as though he could report them to us in order that we might remedy them, he had better go right ahead and report them to Congress. He did not do so, and the man was not transferred.

Just now these are the only two instances that I can recall, of unfair pressure brought to bear upon the supervisory authority.

I realize that this is not the place for an extended disquisition on the mysteries of representative government, but there is another phase of legislative activity which is worth mentioning. For reasons easily understandable, it is noticed that certain Congressmen feel it to be their duty to represent special interests (particularly if they have votes in their districts) as against the interests of the people as a whole.

A member of Congress often urges the release of a criminal on parole, but rarely stresses the necessity of keeping one in, that the rest of his constituents may be safer. Another will plead that a manufacturer in his city be allowed to sell shoes to the government at a higher price and therefore with greater expense to his tax-paying constituents than they can be furnished by prison industries. We had a long argument with a member from the hard-coal district who refused to listen to any statements that soft coal cost the government less—that made small odds to him; his district should profit from these prisons even at the taxpayer's expense. And what a battle we went through over the prison bus! The railroads had refused to give us any reduced rates in transporting prisoners in lots; so, with the approval of the Committee on Appropriations, we purchased a bus and moved over 5,000 prisoners safely, conveniently, and privately without the loss of a man. In one and one-half years we saved money enough to pay for it and now have several thousand dollars' clear profit. Bus movements cost us less than one cent a mile including salaries, where railroad fares ranged from two cents to three and six-tenths.

But the most bitter criticism I ever had was from a Congressman who claimed repeatedly from the platform that I had not only put the railroads into bankruptcy but also defeated Hoover for reëlection by this misguided effort for economy and efficiency in Government operation! It has occurred to me to ask, Whom do we work for anyway? "We" meaning the Congressmen as well as the Prison Bureau.

The public should remember, in connection with the criticism so often made to the effect that our public institutions are controlled by politics, that the politician is an agent, and that he acts in accordance with what he considers to be the desire of his constituents. When the general public makes it plain that the institutions should be conducted impartially, intelligently, and fearlessly, the members of Congress and the State Legislatures will be the first to join in carrying out this demand. Considering the number of requests made of them and their natural tendency to respond, most public administrators may congratulate themselves upon the intelligent, coöperative and farsighted attitude of the average American politician.

Two examples of effective oversight may be mentioned. Following the holocaust in the Columbus Penitentiary in 1931, when over 300 prisoners lost their lives, a systematic campaign of fire prevention was undertaken from the Federal Prison Bureau. An experienced corps of fire prevention engineers was sent to each institution. The interest and coöperation of the National Fire Protection Association was secured. Estimates were secured for the necessary equipment and structural changes, and the central bureau was instrumental in securing the necessary funds for the carrying out of all the engineer's suggestions. Installation of fire mains, standpipes, fire doors, sprinklers, enlarged water supply, etc., were all undertaken. A fire chief was appointed in each institution, and a systematic report of all existing fire hazards was demanded. Inmates were trained in what to do in emergencies, and renewed vigilance was secured from all of the members of the staff and the custodial force.

In a similar manner accident prevention campaigns have been inaugurated in all of the institutions through the oversight of the National Safety Council. Poster campaigns urging more care on the part of the inmates have been undertaken. Careful check-up has been made on all existing hazards, and a considerable amount of money spent to remove dangers and install safety devices on all machinery.

Of course this work could have been done by the institutions separately, but the answer is that they would not have done it. Both fire prevention and accident prevention work requires scientific and professional assistance and supervision. The nineteen institutions under the direction of the Federal Bureau are very much safer places because these efforts have been undertaken.

Care must of course be taken to see that supervision does not become intermeddling. Neither employees nor inmates should be encouraged to take matters up with the bureau which can and should be taken up with the warden. Complaints against the management of the institution are referred to the warden himself for investigation.

I remember one historic incident in which the superintendent of one of our institutions felt called upon to suspend both the president and the secretary of the employees' union. Undoubtedly they both deserved it. They had been extremely disloyal and their disloyalty was known throughout the institution. We had many anxious moments over this particular case, but we took the national leaders of the government employees' union to the institution and they proved to be reasonable and helpful men. The superintendent convinced us and convinced them that the welfare of his institution required that he should indicate who was in command there, and that he could not tolerate the kind of disloyalty that these two men had practiced and still retain the respect and coöperation of his men. This was the courageous and farseeing thing to do, and we backed the superintendent to the limit, with the result that today he heads one of the most successfully administered institutions in the system.

While it might seem that the principal function of the supervisory authority is to criticize and correct and object, it will be advisable to take advantage of the many opportunities that are presented for a word of praise or commendation. It is just as important that recognition be given to meritorious acts as that lapses or derelictions should be reprehended. Frequent conferences between not only the heads of the institutions but groups in charge of special activities, such as the clerks, vocational teachers, chaplains, social workers, medical directors, are exceedingly helpful in maintaining morale and improving the service.

In the Federal Bureau we try to keep somebody in the field most of the time. The chief financial officer, the mechanical inspector, the parole executive, the assistant director in charge of classification and welfare, and the Commissioner of Federal Prison Industries as well as the Director himself make frequent visits to the institutions.

I have presented several of the more important aspects of penal work as applied to a supervising administrative body, sufficient to show, no doubt, that there are substantial tasks to be done outside the walls of the institution. In addition to these definite undertakings it is more or less to be expected that the policy governing the work as a whole shall be determined by the board of control or the supervising executive. Here, perhaps, is the most significant duty of all. These policies should be modern but not fantastic; they should be scientifically devised but not sentimental; they should keep in mind the fundamental objectives in penal work.

One of the delicate problems of supervision has to do **with** news and other publicity. Is it possible to run a prison in a goldfish bowl? Probably not, but it is equally impossible to keep it out of the papers indefinitely. Newspapers want news, not hand-outs. Unfortunately more people read scandal than homiletics, and while newspaper editors should lead rather than follow public opinion, they are human, and they like to sell papers. I have found a few general rules helpful.

1. Treat all news men and news services equally.

2. If one gets a scoop on you, let him have the benefit of it—the rest will expect it of you.

3. Don't try to cover up important news. If you have anything to tell which you think might react unfavorably on the institution, it is much better to give it out formally than to let it "come to light." It will do less harm and will preserve the news men's confidence in your candor. Besides, the public are entitled to know the bad news as well as the good.

When, on rare occasions, we encounter a news hawk who seems bent on getting us into a verbal battle with some one, or who quotes to us a story that might have happened but didn't, and asks us to confirm or deny it, or who shows an uncanny ability to turn a perfectly straightforward and routine statement into a sensational "exposé of prison life" or who plays any other of the well worn tricks on us, we feel like including the irrepressible reporter in the list of life's little irritations, and we are apt to recall Kipling's lines:

> *If you can bear to hear the truth you've spoken*
> *Twisted by knaves to make a trap for fools . . .*

We have to bear in mind, however, that the only way in which the general public can learn about our institutions is through the newspapers. By and large it has been my experience that newspaper men are honest, truthful, and reliable, and that, if you tell them anything in confidence, they respect it.

An invariable rule in the Federal Prison Bureau is that inmates shall never be interviewed by reporters or mentioned by name, except in case of death, escape, discharge, or other unusual event. That it is strictly maintained at Alcatraz can well be appreciated. The public generally and most newspapers editorially commend this rule. Too long have the inmates of some of our prisons enjoyed front-page prominence. An indispensable part of prison discipline, at Alcatraz particularly, is to deflate the "big shot" who feeds his ego on publicity and to protect, as well, the really penitent convict who wants to be forgotten if not forgiven.

The prison administrator will find it hard not to be sensitive to public criticism. It is well that he should be sensitive to it, responsive to it, but not that he should be swerved thereby from a determination to accomplish carefully thought-out projects. He will be tempted to turn aside to interest himself in specific cases of individual prisoners who will enlist his sympathy. He may find it unwise to do this in that it gives him an improper perspective of the whole job. It may turn out that his interest in individual cases will not be for the benefit of the individuals and will interfere with the impartial administration of the larger job. He will, nevertheless, want to be close enough to the real work to permit occasional interviews with prisoners and their families.

He will find no difficulty in his attitude towards his associates in the work if they are competent and loyal people. They will differ from him on occasion, but he will draw many of his inspirations and stimulations from them and will spend not a few profitable hours accepting or rejecting their suggestions, as seems to him wise. He will perhaps have moments of difficulty with those in positions superior to his. Fortunate is the man who can secure and retain the support of those higher officers who are more directly responsible to the constituency for whom all public officers work. Having made his argument clear and temperate and without apology or genuflection on some important matter of penal policy, he will accept the final conclusion with gratitude, if it is his way, and with philosophical resignation, if it is not, hoping that in a more favorable moment events may prove that his judgment was the correct one.

The administrator will have many routine duties to perform, but, after all, the creative side of the job is the most important. Always to have a list of goals towards which to work is a necessary part of his equipment. Having determined upon these goals and the policies to be adopted in reaching them, shall he rigidly adhere to them, or shall the earnestness with which he adheres to the policies vary with the public mood?

Many prison administrators have pondered on this question. If the general policy of protection through rehabilitation is sound, is it not as sound in hard times as in good? Must it not be adhered to in the days of crime waves as in times of comparative freedom from such manifestations? It cannot be denied that, for one reason or another, public ideas change, and at certain times it will be more difficult to establish these desired ends than at others, and the sagacious administrator will realize that he can make better progress towards the realization of his ideals in certain years rather than in others. "Don't forget to specify when time and place shall serve."

There will always be a defensive and an offensive side to prison administrative work. Investigations will have to be made, criticism answered, faithless employees removed, nasty situations cleared up, and the institutional work put before the public in its true and proper light. But between times the administrator will find the opportunity now and then to take the offensive, to make an occasional assault upon the citadels of prejudice and ignorance and to push a little higher the general level of intelligence, understanding, and devotion in the attempted solution of an important social problem.

Defensively, he must do what he can to keep the institutions clean, honestly administered, and free from scandal. Offensively, he must, without neglecting these major duties, progress constantly toward the realization of the higher ideals of penology.

CHAPTER XIII

THE PRISONER SPEAKS

LAST VERSE

How strange is Life that takes our trust
And turns it, sometimes, into dust,
That takes the spirit's high desire
And tramples it into the mire,
That keeps us toiling on and on
Long after faith and hope are gone—

    How strange is Life
    That leads us still
    Against our dreams,
    Against our will,
    Against the hopes
    That once were ours
    As bright as springtime's garden,
    And then reveals in whimsy's mood
    The purpose else misunderstood—

    How strange is Life
    That brings us cares,
    Defiances, regrets, despairs,
    But is so sweet
    That we must cling
    Despite the hurt, the loss, the sting—
    How strange is Life—yet fashioned so
    Because the soul has need to grow.

Contributed by an inmate of the Federal Reformatory for Women to "The Eagle," the inmate publication.

RARELY do I visit an institution without availing myself of the opportunity of interviewing as many of the prisoners as care to talk to me or as I have time to see. I do not claim that an official can get any real insight into the prisoner's mind and what he thinks about by conversing with him in the front office. But one thought is constantly registering itself, and that is that many of these men as they come and go are not greatly different from other members of the body politic. Why should they not be consulted more frequently as to the conduct of the places in which they spend so large a portion of their lives. Of course, there are reasons why their suggestions cannot be accepted, and a great many of them are insincere. They will conspire to tell you something that they think you want to know, or they will repeat the most arrant hearsay of a scandalous nature. But, after all, no one is better able to tell you what the prisoner thinks about than the prisoner himself.

An elderly colored man who had sent in an interview slip at Atlanta one afternoon, ambled good-naturedly into the office where I was holding interviews, and said, "Good afternoon, Mr. Bates."

"Good afternoon, Joe."

"Yes, a nice day."

After a pause, I said, "Well, what did you want, Joe?"

"I didn't want nothing. I heard the boys talking around here about Mr. Bates, and I just thought I would like to see what he looked like."

Some visits perhaps have no more definite purpose than this one; other interviews are requested for the purpose, perhaps, of breaking the deadly monotony of a day in durance vile, or of telling about troubles which no one else would listen to.

The American Prison Association recently sponsored a prize essay contest among inmates of Federal and State penitentiaries. The following topics were chosen and prizes of fifteen dollars, ten dollars, and five dollars were awarded for the best treatment of each subject: (1) A Prisoner Looks at the Law; (2) A Prisoner's Views on Prison Reform; (3) Does the Law Prevent Reformation of the Prisoner?; (4) Criminal Law and Prison Reform. Warden Lawes of Sing Sing Prison, James V. Bennett of the Federal Bureau, and others were on the committee which selected the winners. So highly did the members of the Bureau of Prisons think of these essays that we had them bound in permanent form. They should be read by every prison administrator. Tinged with bitterness at times and undoubtedly somewhat warped in viewpoint, they contain many suggestions well worth considering.

Somewhat later I availed myself of an opportunity to talk to a prisoner who had written one of the prize-winning essays. It was one of the most stimulating and instructive afternoons that I have ever experienced. An ex-policeman from a midwestern city, convicted of bribe taking, he had written on the topic, "Criminal Law and Prison Reform." Here is his summary:

From the prisoner's standpoint, then, the following reforms are in dire need of enactment, if we are to turn out of our prisons a more social individual with a wider understanding of his relationship to society, with a greater sense of social responsibility, and to cut down not only the number of new commitments but also the wholly unwarranted percentage of recidivists:

1. A wider dissemination of legal knowledge among the masses.

2. A greater respect for the law by its enforcement agents.

3. Less disagreement on the length of sentence for the same offense.

4. Appointment for life of capable Federal prosecutors.

5. Appointment of a classification board for the classification of men before sentence is passed.

6. Classification before commitment and segregation of first offenders.

7. Employment of a better class of prison employee, with a more human attitude toward the convict.

8. The elimination of undue regimentation.

9. More liberal mail privileges.

10. Elimination of clubs in the hands of the guards.

11. Allowance of extra good time for educational attendance.

12. Industrial good time throughout the system as a reward of industry.

13. Institutional parole boards.

14. Payment of at least $100 upon his release together with a suitable outfit of clothing.

During our conversation on the afternoons referred to he mentioned the fact that four or five hundred men had reported to the hospital with common colds. He knew why this was so:

"Had anybody in the prison taken the trouble to find out why such a large number of men reported with colds? It is the invariable custom in the prison to require all inmates to sleep with their heads toward the barred door of the cell, and on very cold nights when the wind sweeps down through the corridors it is very difficult to keep from catching cold. We are obliged to sleep all night with the blanket or a pillow over our heads."

I suggested that this rule was probably made in order to facilitate the taking of the count. S——— then pertinently inquired:

"Do you run the prison for the accommodation of the guards or in such a way as to maintain the health and welfare of the inmates?"

He put his finger, of course, on one of the sensitive spots of prison management: it is easier to count the prisoners when their heads are toward the door. Once upon a time some enterprising prisoner had made up and placed a dummy in his bunk, deceiving the guard on his rounds along the gallery. Thenceforward it was easier to require every prisoner to poke his head out where it could be counted than to require a little extra effort on the part of the prison guard.

I remember a visit to a county jail in Michigan. In the cells in one corridor there were no mattresses on any of the beds, and at the end of the corridor there was a pile of mattresses which apparently had been removed from that particular part of the jail. Inquiring as to the reason for this, I was told that this was the drug-addict corridor, that once upon a time a drug addict had set fire to his mattress and thereafter an order was given that drug addicts should not be provided with mattresses.

This is the kind of tradition that the conscientious prison superintendent finds so hard to break down.

Our ex-policeman went on to tell me that we were not making the most of the educational possibilities for the prisoners. Why did we not use the radio for one hour every evening to give some kind of instruction of a practical character to men who might be otherwise idle in their cells? Why was it that certain officers of the prison encouraged men to go to school, while others practically forbade it? What was the purpose of the rule which denied to an inmate the right to spend money which he had earned for books to improve his mind?

This interview was merely one of many which have been helpful and suggestive. Of course one has to use the information acquired in such interviews tactfully and diplomatically. In many such instances the right thing to do is to send for the warden or other officer of the prison whose actions are called into question and to discuss the matter freely and frankly with him and the prisoner.

It must be said that a large proportion of interviews are merely for the purpose of conveying impossible requests; but there have been a few occasions where some obvious injustice has come to light—a careless clerk of court may have made a mistake and the prisoner's sentence may have been wrongly figured on that account. The writ of habeas corpus, while in many cases a nuisance to the warden and the district attorney of the district in which the penitentiary is located, proves sometimes to be the only means of adjusting and correcting an otherwise illegal or improperly computed sentence, and its legitimate use must not be decried.

The belief is prevalent that prisoners spend most of their time thinking up new ways to commit crime on their release, or bragging about their past exploits. Undoubtedly a considerable number of them do, and there would seem to be no way to prevent it, except to substitute newer and more constructive interests. It is impossible to forestall communication between prisoners. No one knows just how the "grapevine" operates, but it is as trustworthy a means of communication as any telephone line. Even if men were to be kept constantly in separate confinement they would communicate.

In the summer of 1935 I visited the old prison of St. Peter and St. Paul at Leningrad, which for years has been a museum. The old dungeons are empty, and the guards and inmates are wax figures. The guide, however, showed us the elaborate code whereby prisoners communicated with one another by means of tapping on the walls.

The modern method is to substitute for the all too prevalent jail-house chatter some more productive activities. This is why libraries are established, newspapers are permitted, and organized athletics are encouraged. The larger the number of wholesome engrossing activities that can be found to fill the minds and tire the bodies, the less opportunity there will be for the hatching of plots or the rehearsing of exploits.

In practically every Federal institution an inmate publication is maintained, printed, edited, and contributed to by inmates. On the title page of each number appears the following:

> The object of this paper is to interpret accurately, impartially, completely and fairly the life within the institution. It is hoped the inmates will find herein a medium of self-expression and a source of pleasurable and helpful information. The paper is published by permission of the Bureau of Prisons of the Department of Justice. The Bureau assumes no responsibility for the individual sentiments expressed, and reserves the right to prohibit only articles of a scandalous nature, or which tend to impede the proper administration of justice.

Sometimes these inmate publications are of a high order. One of the best prison editors we ever had was Dr. Cook, the would-be arctic explorer. *Good Words* at Atlanta, *The New Era* at Leavenworth, *The Island Lantern* at McNeil Island, *The Beacon* at Chillicothe, *The Periscope* at Lewisburg, *The Outlook* at El Reno, *The Eagle* at the women's reformatory, and *The Border Sentinel* at El Paso are some of the names chosen for these little periodicals.

Here is a sample from the pages of the Chillicothe *Beacon*:

WHAT PRICE PUBLICITY

Each time society reads of a prison break, riot, murder, its mind becomes more deeply impressed with its mental picture of prisoners. It becomes more and more convinced that we are correctly typified, and that we are really dangerous and ruthless, and that we should stay where we are.

Such recent occurrences as counterfeiting within a prison, a break which resulted in several deaths, a sensational murder in another prison: do not these things propagate a sentiment that is positively unfavorable to institutions all over the country? Can we not see these things throwing a cog [sic] into the wheels of penology which has thus far made commendable progress?

If we trace the steps of improved penological methods down through the years we can clearly see that a higher standard of morale among prisoners in general has given those in authority the necessary confidence to administer further advantages. We perceive that all the way back there were men serving time whose attitudes and righteous intentions proved that punishment should not be the controlling factor of a penal system and we also can see that it took penologists with insight and courage to recommend and put into effect such steps which were later to help close a large gap between society and the lawbreaker.

．　　　．　　　．　　　．　　　．　　　．　　　．

Within most institutions, there arises a man's first opportunity to demonstrate his slant on life. If he has made a mistake, and realizing it, takes every opportunity offered him to show it was a mistake, he is not only benefiting himself, but those who follow him; not only that: he is fulfilling the confidence of those who gave him the opportunity to destroy the adage that "Once a crook, always a crook."

On the other hand, when serious disturbances, escapes, and other malicious activities of the few cause public attention to be focused upon prisons which have tried to uphold the worthiness of a new deal, it is easy to see why a false conception of all prisoners is aroused.

The majority of men who are in prison today are there because of a mistaken philosophy of life. They are anxious to derive every benefit possible from a system of rehabilitation that is really and truly humane. They appreciate being treated like individuals; they have been given an opportunity for introspection, and with the encouragement that is emerging from understanding officials, they are rebuilding a courage that for too many reasons might easily have been broken entirely. They are not completely bitter or vindictive, and are only attempting to solve their problems with such assistance and understanding as society is willing to extend.

That is how the majority of men in prison feel, today.

Yet, a worthless few, who were ready to dish it out but couldn't take it, from time to time will throw every well-meaning, help-deserving prisoner into the fires of public sentiment with their contemptible contrivances to escape from a situation which they brought about themselves. A few moments of recklessness when the going gets too rough—they take a chance—escape or break for a freedom that will be haunted for the rest of their lives.

· · · · · · ·

Yes, they take a chance! And every time they take a chance, it is our chance they are taking. We are the ones left in the lurch; we are the ones who receive the invectives, and the bitter editorials, and the tightening of the reins each time these things happen.

So, it is possible, though unfortunate, that right within the walls or institution wherein thousands of men are striving to re-earn what they lost, one or two can overwhelm with bad publicity all the good that the majority of men have tried to attain. Newspapers do not publish articles of commendation for progressive prisoners; they scandalize the whole group for the actions of one.

Unfair? Yes; but until every prisoner realizes that whatever he does to cast unfavorable publicity on himself, hurts the others, too, only then will we begin to be regarded as we are endeavoring to be regarded now.

Lest there be those who assume that we are offering a treatise on prison conduct or characterizing penal institutions as desirable places to be, we hasten to dispel any such notion. There are no good prisons. Nothing that man is able to conceive will ever make any sane person trade his liberty and loved ones for a cell in a penal institution.

· · · · · · ·

Whether progress in that direction will continue depends to a large extent on the same things; whether a return to the older order of things becomes necessary also depends, in a large measure, on whether a small minority of helpless, worthless mutts will continue to cast unfavorable light on their fellow prisoners who depend on the future tolerance of society for another chance.

The subject is worthy of study.

How does this sound? Do you think if you were serving time you could write as rationally and as respectfully as this prison editor?

The Federal Bureau of Prisons maintains in each of the

institutions a locked letter box in which sealed uncensored complaints may be placed by each and every inmate to be forwarded direct to the Bureau.

While a prisoner may be somewhat restrained in his interview with the Bureau officials and while he may not always speak his mind in the prison newspaper, there is no reason why he cannot frankly and candidly state his grievances through this channel.

When this innovation was first installed at Leavenworth its value as a safety valve, allowing an unimpeded avenue of appeal, was attested by the fact that nearly one-half of the inmates availed themselves of the privilege. Now the novelty has worn off, but the mail box is still used for legitimate complaints and requests for special service. The number of letters received at the Washington office from all the institutions averages about 175 a month. The subjoined table gives an interesting summary of the context of 1,523 prisoners' letters received during a nine months' period.

Of the complaints, 87 had to do with conditions surrounding the prisoners' present confinement, 17 were protests as to certain mail regulations and only 5 objected to the kind of medical attention received. Of the 59 letters having to do with family affairs, 37 were requests for financial or other assistance. The letters with reference to the prisoners' sentence included 127 claims of innocence, 88 protests as to the length of sentence, and 55 requests that time spent in jail prior to the imposition of sentence be credited. Nearly one-half of the letters had to do with the prisoner's release; 289 were petitions for clemency; 224 were immediately referred to the Board of Parole; 118 contained petitions for restoration of good time. Under the miscellaneous group, 44 requested information; 22 offered certain information; 21 wrote asking for an interview with an official of the Bureau. There were 12 thank-you letters.

Ray Tucker wrote an article for *Collier's* recently entitled "Prep School" in which he referred, although not by name, to a long-term prisoner who seemed to be making a fine adjust-

A. PRISONERS' LETTERS, JULY 1, 1934, TO MARCH 1, 1935

			To Whom Referred							
			Department of Justice (Except Bureau of Investigation)						Investigation Agencies (including Bureau of Investigation)	Other
			Bureau of Prisons			U.S. Board of Parole	Pardon Attorney	Other		
			Social Service		Other					
	NUMBER	PER CENT	Alone	With Other Units	Other					
Complaints	126	8.3	109	4	5	—	—	1	1	6
Family and own problems	59	3.9	56	1	—	—	—	1	—	1
Sentence	283	18.6	128	23	19	95	14	—	4	—
Transfers	182	12.0	180	2	—	—	—	—	—	—
Release	701	46.0	93	55	14	298	236	2	—	3
Miscellaneous	172	11.2	126	2	11	3	3	7	16	4
Total	1,523	100.0	692	87	49	396	253	11	21	14

ment while undergoing his long sentence. Some time after-wards this letter went through the mail to Mr. Tucker:

Mr. Tucker, in justice to myself, my family, and my friends, I strenuously object to that sentence in the third paragraph of your story, to wit, "As a last hope the officials tried to distract him from his hatred of society." Mr. Tucker you are just 100% wrong, because I *do not* and *never did* hate society. The peace officers who represent society were my opponents, and we played the game according to Hoyle. When they outsmarted me we all smiled about it, and when I outsmarted them the smiles usu-ally developed into belly-laughs. Today I hold no animosity toward them, and I am sure they hold none toward me. I hope, Mr. Tucker, you will rectify that mistake in the near future.

After some personal references the letter ended, "Sincerely yours," with the following postscript: "Your statement of my hatred for society was merely a mistake. I bear you no ill will."

The prisoner is no longer inarticulate. Not only has he the right to interview persons not connected with the institution, send uncensored letters to the Bureau, but on his release often finds occasion to say what is on his mind about the prison. From Dostoievsky's "House of the Dead" to Lamson's "We Who Are About to Die," the ex-prisoner has not hesitated to express himself. A list of books of this sort is given at the end of this chapter.

It is true these accounts of prison life are too often bitter and resentful, but the public has the consolation of knowing that there are no mysteries behind the prison wall that can forever be hidden from public view.

While many convicts are unreasonable in their demands (the social service departments are kept rather busy explaining why they cannot be allowed credit for the time they spent in jail previous to the sentence, or why they should not go home and make a crop, or why the Director has no authority to overrule the Parole Board, and the thousand and one other reasons why a thing that seems perfectly plausible to the con-vict is illegal or impossible), there are other inmates who are reasonable in their requests. One unfortunate woman prisoner whose mentality had been questioned wrote urging that certain changes be made in her record and ended: "This humble convict would consider it as an estimable favor if the Honorable The Attorney General of the United States would deign to have the foregoing questions answered if possible within the next six months."

I have a friend who, like so many other convicts, rejoices in the sobriquet of "Red," and who never fails to visit with me at every opportunity. Nearly thirty of his forty-five years have been spent in institutions. Red has a long stretch yet to do, but he has developed the philosophy of submission. He is prison-wise, if any one is, and yet he can be and has been of material assistance to the warden, as he was on the occasion of a disturbance in the dining room when a serious riot was averted. He has the technical skill and the brains to make a success in life outside if he only would. His mechanical ability is valuable in any prison machine shop. One likes to talk to Red even though one feels that perhaps he is saying what the "boss" would like to hear rather than what he really thinks. Occasionally he writes me a letter. One I received when he was hoping to be transferred to the new institution at Lewisburg ends:

But my own case is much more important to myself and is more deserving. I am only hoping that one of my personal letters to you—which you perhaps never read—will catch you in the right mood to give me a break. My "two-bits" flat will be up before you folks will realize that I'll be too old to move. I beg to say that I'm in splendid writing form. Till you hear from me again,—

But Red's letter and the thousands of others all do have somebody's careful attention. A reply is made, not perhaps in such a way that the inmate can carry it around and capitalize on it; but word is transmitted to him through the warden or the director of social work in the institution.

What do we do with an anonymous letter? We do not entirely disregard such communications although some administrators feel that no unsigned communication is worthy of any credence whatever. With us, it depends upon the character of the information given. We realize that there are motives which may prevent a prisoner from signing his name. If there are circumstances which check with statements made, or if the letter suggests leads whereby more reliable evidence can be obtained, such information should not be disregarded. Some of the most significant information that I have ever received came through an anonymous letter.

One cannot help having a certain amount of admiration for the occasional inmate who confides in the warden when he thinks there is something about to be pulled off of a disorderly or lawless character. Of course if it transpires that a prisoner has given information for the express purpose of obtaining some preference or privilege the value of his evidence is thereby minimized. But it is quite common in a prison, as it is outside, to recognize and reward the giving of information. A considerable number of drug-addict prisoners who are segregated at the Leavenworth Annex Penitentiary have in the past given information to the Narcotic Bureau, and we have considered it advisable to remove some of these informers to other institutions on that account.

The wise prison warden learns not to overlook or disregard even the most trivial information that comes to him. Recently a discharged prisoner from the Springfield Hospital advised his lawyer in San Antonio (who communicated with a Bureau of Investigation agent, who took the matter up with the superintendent) that a weapon was hidden in the institution and intimated that a certain inmate would tell where it could be located. The inmate told where he had seen the gun, and it was found on a shelf of the institution storeroom wrapped in rags. It turned out that this was an antiquated shotgun which had been sawed off and had been taken from two boys who were playing in the vicinity of the old lake on the reservation a short time after the institution opened. It was later transferred to the storekeeper with some other old material for disposal. While he claimed he had the impression it was useless and simply junk, he did not dispose of it but retained it in the storehouse. He may have considered it merely a curiosity; but just the same the superintendent breathed a sigh of relief when he found that the situation was no worse, and the inmate who was decent enough to tell about it received an earlier parole.

You will conclude from the above that the rule of silence does not prevail in the prisons of America today. The prisoner thinks and also speaks for himself. He is no longer kept in solitary confinement, and if he is allowed to mingle with other prisoners at meal times, in the yard, and in the shops, it is futile to impose any prohibition against talking. After all, if men are to be returned to society, can they be best prepared for such a change by imposing upon them the abnormal rule of silence? If a man could be absolutely prevented from talking for five years, the chances are that he would not know how to talk at the end of that period.

And so through the prisoners' letter box, the occasional writing of books by discharged convicts, the passage of letters between the inmate and his family, visits with counsel and relatives and interviews with the inspecting officers, the prisoner of today not only speaks himself but has a continual outlet for the expression of his ideas.

BOOKS BY INMATES

BARTLETT, GEORGE L., Thru the Mill, by "4342"; A Prison Story That's Different. St. Paul, Minn.: G. E. Bartlett, 1915. 139 pages.

BENTON, ROGER (pseud.), Where Do I Go from Here? New York: Furman, 1936. 314 pages.

BERKMAN, ALEXANDER, Prison Memoirs of an Anarchist. New York: Mother Earth Pub. Co., 1912. 512 pages.

BLACK, JACK, You Can't Win. New York: Macmillan, 1926. 394 pages.

BOOTH, ERNEST, Stealing Through Life. New York: Knopf, 1929. 308 pages.

BRIGGS, ISAAC GEORGE, Reformatory Reform. New York: Longmans, 1924. 223 pages.

BURNS, ROBERT E., I Am a Fugitive from a Georgia Chain Gang. New York: Vanguard, 1932. 257 pages.

CALLAHAN, JACK, Man's Grim Justice: My Life Outside the Law. New York: Sears, 1928. 296 pages.

CHAPIN, CHARLES E., Charles Chapin's Story Written in Sing Sing Prison. New York: Putnam, 1920. 334 pages.

CLARK, CHARLES L., AND EUBANK, EARLE EDWARD, Lockstep and Corridor: Thirty-five Years of Prison Life. University of Cincinnati Press, 1927. 177 pages.

DEBS, EUGENE VICTOR, Walls and Bars. Chicago: Socialist Party Press, 1927. 248 pages.

DODD, WILLIAM, Thoughts in Prison, in five parts; viz., The Imprisonment, The Retrospect, Public Punishment, The Trial, Futurity. To which are added, His Last Prayer, written in the night before his death, and other miscellaneous pieces. 1782. 232 pages.

DUDDING, EARL E., The Trail of the Dead Years. Washington, D. C.: Prisoners Relief Society, 1932. 342 pages.

FORNARO, CARLO DE, A Modern Purgatory. New York: Kennerley, 1917. 178 pages.

HAMILTON, WALTER, The Legions of Purgatory and Hell. Burd & Fletcher, Kansas City, 1911. 209 pages.

In the Clutch of Circumstance: My Own Story, by a Burglar. New York: Appleton, 1922. 271 pages.

LAMSON, DAVID ALBERT, We Who Are About to Die. New York: Scribner, 1935. 338 pages.

LOWRIE, DONALD, My Life in Prison. New York: Kennerley, 1912. 422 pages.

LOWRIE, DONALD, My Life Out of Prison. New York: Kennerley, 1915. 345 pages.

LYONS, SOPHIE, Amazing Adventures of Sophie Lyons (Queen of the Burglars): or, Why Crime Does Not Pay. New York: Ogilvie, 1913. 268 pages.

MCGRATH, EDWARD F., I Was Condemned to the Chair. New York: Stokes, 1934. 312 pages.

NELSON, VICTOR F., Prison Days and Nights. Boston: Little, Brown, 1933. 283 pages.

NITTI, F. F., Escape: The Personal Narrative of a Political Prisoner Who Was Rescued from Lipari, the Fascist "Devil's Island." New York: Putnam, 1930. 267 pages.

O'HARE, KATE R. (sometime federal prisoner No. 21669), In Prison. New York: Knopf, 1923. 211 pages.

SPENSER, JAMES (pseud.), Limey Breaks In. New York: Longmans, 1935. 312 pages.

TANNENBAUM, FRANK, Wall Shadows: A Study in American Prisons. New York: Putnam, 1922.

TASKER, ROBERT JOYCE, Grimhaven. New York: Knopf, 1928. 241 pages.

WINNING, JAMES R., Behind These Walls. New York: Macmillan, 1933. 303 pages.

CHAPTER XIV

THEY ALSO SUFFER

Finally, we will beware of the cynicism that paints every prisoner drab and never thinks of him in any other capacity. When a man steps into the dock, he is a husband and father, a worker and taxpayer, accustomed to take care of himself and others, not requiring an order at every turn and two thousand rules to govern his daily conduct. The saying of a few words by a Judge does not transform him into an entirely different creature, who can never be trusted, who has no decent instinct or loyalty. If he is treated as a sensible and self-reliant man, he is likely to play such a part. Even when he has failed once or twice, there may well be some side of his nature to which appeal has not yet been made. The world owes much to those who failed and made a fresh start.
—ALEXANDER PATERSON, M.C., *The Prison Problem of America.*

COLONEL JULIA FORD of the State Charities Board of Kentucky, undiscouraged and inspired worker with the mountain folk of that State, told us this story:

In one of the towns in the eastern part of the State she met one day a tall, gaunt barefoot woman whom she recognized as living far up one of the creeks, which still are used to some extent as roads in the mountain country. She accosted the woman and found that she was tenderly carrying in one hand three eggs which she had brought down from her cabin in the hills to exchange for a postage stamp in order that she might send a message to her boy who was doing time at Atlanta for violation of the Prohibition Act.

On another occasion the night captain was sitting in his little temporary office at the Chillicothe Reformatory when a timid knock came upon the door. On opening it he discovered a dust-covered, travel-worn woman.

"Please, sir, I would like to see my boy."

"Well, I am sorry, madam, but it is long after visiting hours, and I am afraid you will have to wait until tomorrow."

"But, sir, I have no place to wait, and I have come a long way."

And so she had. She had walked and hitch-hiked three hundred and fifty miles from her cabin in Tennessee. This was too much even for the ordinarily unimpressionable night captain. She not only was allowed to visit her boy but was given lodging for the night, and a hat was passed to help her accomplish her return to what she called home.

Is there not something in these relationships that is worth preserving?

Can we consider that we have solved the problem of crime and delinquency and social inadequacy by merely sending the criminal himself to jail?

I recall an interview with a member of a mountain family who had come up before me on one occasion some years ago for parole. He was indignant, and he told me the cause of his wrath.

"They were six of us brought before the cou't. We was all makin' liquor, Ah guess. Ah reckon we all knew what was goin' on, Maw and Pappy and my four brothers and sisters, and the Jedge said that one of us would have to go to prison and said we could pick the one to go. My brother Joe had a chance to get a job so Ah said Ah would go to prison. But the Jedge didn't keep his word. He sent both me and Joe."

How much truth there was in this story, I never had time to ascertain; but certain it is that from time immemorial the mountaineers of Kentucky and Tennessee and West Virginia have made liquor, and they will persist in making it notwithstanding frequent jail or prison interruptions; and they will continue to fight off the law and stand by their families until we arrive at some newer and more permanent solution of the social problem of the mountain district. No doubt you have already read about the "Atlanta Special" which at the conclusion of each court term leaves one of the county seats in the hill district for the penitentiary bearing forty, sixty, or one hundred liquor violators. The scene on the platform with the mothers, sisters, sweethearts and wives to bid them good-by has been compared to that so common in the war days when a troop train left for the embarkation port.

No, the prison problem is not, and cannot be, a thing apart. Over 50 per cent of Federal prisoners are married, and another 10 per cent are separated or divorced but still have family responsibilities.

If the spectacle of men in prison deprived of their liberty and normal outlets does not move you, I am sure that your presence at the monthly visiting hour will. One need not have a particle of sympathy for the men who have broken the law (and justly merit their separation from the community) to still feel that in some instances the punishment bears hardest upon those who are left behind. The prisoner's life is ordered for him. His meals, though simple, come regularly. No landlord presses for his rent. On the first night the prisoner is lonesome; if he is young or emotional he cries into his pillow, otherwise he stares and curses, and clenches his fists—if ever he is penitent it is during this first night. Sometimes I have thought that if we could let certain prisoners out—if we dared to, that is—on the second morning, before they had a chance to speak to any one, we might have a better chance at repentance and reform. But except for a few who never get reconciled to prison until perchance they go mad, prisoners become accustomed; they meet others in the same predicament, and their neighbors, who are as badly off as themselves, extend to them that ready help and fellowship which comrades in distress always offer. But the wife and children have to carry on the battle—and many times it is a losing battle—deprived of their source of income, obliged to scrimp and economize in every way, and, worst of all, forced to face the taunts or shrugs of their neighbors.

The social workers connected with the Federal Prison Bureau perhaps rightly assume that the most hopeful way to reformation for the prisoner who retains any measure of self-respect is through his family. Naturally, unless he is completely calloused, he worries about his job and his property. Will the mortgagee foreclose, or will the landlord evict his family? He wonders about his children: Have they clothes and shoes? Are they snubbed by their playmates? He wonders about his wife: Will she break down under the strain? Will she have enough to eat? If there is an addition to the family expected, what will she do during confinement? And inevitably perhaps there enters his mind the tormenting question, Will she continue to be faithful to him during the two, three, five, or ten years that they must remain separated?

This is an actual case which confronted one of our social service units recently:

July 18, 1933.

DEAR MR. ———:

I wish that you would help B———'s children because their mother ran away to get away from the law and no one isn't home but the children and no one takes care of them they haven't got anything to eat or wear they their mother was gone about two weeks and everybody comes and steels all they got and they burnt the garage about a month ago They put the children's names in the paper so that some one will take them till their father and mother comes back We would keep them but we have eight in our family and we just can make a living We live in the third house from ——— and we try to help them as much as we can and they run away all over looking for something to eat and they all ask everybody when their father coming back because some one told them that he was come to-day and they stay up at nights waiting for him. So would you please help him to get out because he is a good man and I think that he will quit making whisky and try to get him a job They said that they weren't going to school till they father comes out you wouldnt like to see tham do that do you so please help him get out on parole will you so that they can go to school and quit running around like they do now.

Please help him get out on parrow.

Your truly

(let us know what you are going
to do please thank you)

(This refers to the case of ———
Eight children—ages, 19, 16, 12, 12, 9, 7, 3, 1)

One of the most amazing things to be noticed in working with prisoners is the loyalty shown by the women towards the men in prison. Occasionally we find a real "gun moll" who, either willingly or unwillingly, has joined her husband or lover in his criminal exploits and become his assistant and ally. But in the great majority of cases the woman either was an unwilling participant in the criminal activities or she knew nothing or was barely aware of her husband's delinquency.[1] She seldom fails to write him encouraging news, to tell him about the children and the neighbors and to urge him to look forward to that new start which they are all going to make when he is released.

Even with the unmarried prisoners a knowledge of his social environment is important and no permanent rehabilitation can be achieved unless to some extent his community relationships are adjusted.

There are queer cases that every prison man knows about where some impressionable woman forms an unaccountable and sometimes apparently sincere attachment for a particularly desperate and undeserving miscreant. Such a woman seems to derive a certain satisfaction from lavishing her affection on him who deserves it least.

A clever prisoner likes to engage in correspondence with some dear old lady and it does not take him long at times to convince her that he is a much wronged individual and that during his prison term he has had a chance to reflect upon his sins and that with the dear lady's help he would like from now on to lead a life of piety and virtue. The warden sometimes wishes that the impulse to render real service to the unfortunate prisoners could have been better directed and more sensibly applied than is often the case.

Prisoners have been known to forsake their wives, who have stood so nobly by them and agree to marry some one of these impressionable ladies whom they know only through correspondence.

A few years ago one of the more notorious prisoners of the desperado type commenced to receive, soon after his reception

---

[1] Only a little over 4 per cent of our Federal prisoners are women (*supra*, p. 133).

into the Federal penitentiary, letters of the most sympathetic and touching character. These epistles breathed the spirit of love to God and love to man. They called the bandit by his first name. God had spoken to the dear lady and had commanded her to go forth and comfort the public enemy in his hour of peril, to offset the terrible things that the wicked government had done to him, to bring cheer to his loyal and discouraged heart. Not only was he not guilty of the crime with which he was charged, but with the help of the writer he could become a great figure in the national life. One of her letters was thirty-seven pages long, of closely typewritten matter. At one point she waxed more than usually eloquent and described in allegorical fashion the escape and subsequent recapture of her bandit affinity. Listen!

He alighted from the car. . . . He stood majestically and suddenly his spirit towered above the surging masses. I then saw him glorified in his innocence. A halo began slowly to gather about his brow. The mists surrounding him cleared way in the brilliance of its light, and settled about the figures of the cheering mob. In that awful moment—awful in its solemnity, I saw ———— through the eyes only of God and felt for him through the Divine Heart, for his innocence was definitely and certainly revealed to my eyes, as well as to my heart. . . . And so it is today, I stand amid eternal rays with one hand stretched into the past to ————, and the other stretched into the future to God and I do not hesitate to declare that I stand, not on sinking sand, but on a rock that is firm with truth and love. . . . Even though Nero reigned today and I knew I would be beheaded the next moment, I would declare, . . . the innocence of ———— and my love and sympathy for him.

And so with many scriptural references the good lady pleaded for a chance to visit the prisoner; she would "even put on prison clothes" and will comply with every necessary rule.

Her pleadings fell on deaf ears. She did not desist, however; she wrote to her Congressman. She wrote to all the authorities whom she could contact. Her literary effusions not only were beautifully composed but had a ring of sincerity and conviction. One of her letters ended with the poem, "O Love that wilt not let me go, I rest my weary soul in Thee," and her final paragraph was:

And so, when the sun has left my loved one and I, and the whole world is fading from our sight, I shall have faith and never doubt that some other morn will find us together, somewhere, in love, beneath the smile of God.

No, this woman was not crazy, and so far as we could find out, had no ulterior purpose whatsoever. I suspected that she had never even seen the bandit in question, much less known him, and this suspicion turned out to be correct. The convict himself had no desire to correspond with her, and on one occasion she admitted: "No, I have not seen ———. Neither have I seen God. But in the same way that I love and admire the Almighty, so do I love ———."

Well, what are you to do with a woman like that? One might easily say that this is the most extraordinary case of misguided affection on record, and yet to a lesser degree we find quite common the existence of a devotion and loyalty which it is the business of those administering prisons to cultivate and preserve.

Here is an excerpt from a letter from another lady to a prisoner:

Being interested in the science of numerology, I understand the power of vibration. I understand what your name, which is perfectly balanced, revealed to me. Then, analyzing it through its numerals, I discovered that we have relative vibrations. You are 7–1–9, which, adding the 1 (J) to the 7, gives you 8–9. I am 1–7–4 = 8–4. You will no doubt say this is the "bunk," but I could tell you everything about yourself, the reason for your actions, and, even your innermost thoughts. Yours are two of the best numerals in the cycle—if they are positive. But there is the "reverse" and "negative" side to deal with. Until I studied your face, I was not positive of your vibration. But, judging from newspaper articles, I took it for granted you were pretty much on the reverse side. Now I find you are a combination of all three. Perhaps what I am going to tell you, will surprise you. . . .

. . . .

This may sound like madness—maybe it is. Aristotle handed these words down to posterity—"no soul is exempt from a mixture of madness."

.   .   .   .

And so, ———, I bring this to a close with the kindest of thoughts, and send it on to you with every good wish and a friendship, if you care to accept it, in every sense of its significance.

There is no question but the time "when a feller needs a friend" is when he is in prison. The English prison system has recognized this and has encouraged the respectable citizens of the neighborhood to visit with the convicts in their cells. But this "bedside visiting" must be carefully done, and the privilege cannot be entrusted to every one.

It is necessary in all penal institutions that visits be under supervision, but even where the family reunion takes place under the eye of the guard it constitutes, as may well be imagined, an event in the life of the prisoner. With his family the convict is always at his best. When we have perfected the character building activities in our penal institutions, we shall have learned better how to cultivate and develop in the prisoner the higher emotions which a family visit never fails to stimulate.

At the Southwestern Reformatory at El Reno, Oklahoma, visiting day is on Sunday. The Eastern Oklahoma District, like other mountain districts, contains large areas where quantities of illegal liquor are made, and on Sundays the convict's families come from incredibly long distances. On a particular Sunday a curious vehicle stood outside the administration building at El Reno. It was a small old-fashioned Ford truck, but it had a special body designed to meet the needs of the particular family who owned it. It looked more like a poultry truck that anything else. There was one seat in front for the driver, and there were three shelves or layers where the eleven children were laid in rows. They had all come in a body to pay their father his monthly visit. One was tempted to remark that the best thing that could have happened to the head of this family was to spend an interlude in prison. It was certainly quieter for him, and it ought to have been a welcome relief for his wife. We might well ask ourselves, however, what was to become of these eleven young ones? What kind of citizens of the future would they make?

Although it happened years ago I have never forgotten an investigation which we made in Massachusetts into the family of a French Canadian who at the age of fifty-two had been sentenced to the State prison for from fifteen to eighteen years for incest with his oldest daughter. The social worker looked up the family and found that this daughter was feeble-minded and the oldest of nine children, six of whom were also definitely feeble-minded and all of whom were likely to become State charges. The rural neighborhood which allowed this family to grow up in neglect, in ignorance, and in squalor would be the principal sufferer, and certainly no one can contend that the sentencing of this man to a long term in prison could to any extent be called a solution of the problem.

If contacts are to be maintained with the family and community while a man is serving a prison term, every effort should of course be made to see that they are constructive and wholesome contacts. The censorship of the thousands of letters coming in and going out of the prison is more than a perfunctory job and should be undertaken by a person who understands human nature and the principles of social work. Through this channel wholesome relationships may be established and dangerous ones forbidden. This is one reason why inmates in Federal penitentiaries are limited to certain approved correspondents. Changes may be made in these lists only with the consent of the warden or superintendent. The Superintendent of the Chillicothe Reformatory recently received the following note from one of his inmates:

Will you please sir be so kind to disconnect Miss ———— and reconnect Mrs. ————. Please sir. My Aunt has died since i have been here i am writing my cousin to encourage here she are young and just married i wish to encourage and i havent wrote since ben here.

This cultivation of proper family relationships is the business of the prison social worker. He must undertake not only the collection of reliable information about an inmate's past but likewise the verification of all data obtained. He must also act as liaison officer between the prisoner and his family. With the coöperation of outside agencies, he should prepare a plan not only for the temporary care of the bereft family but for the prisoner's resumption of communal life at the end of his term. The Federal Prison Bureau gratefully acknowledges the important and intelligent assistance of this kind that it has received from the social agencies of large centers of population all over the country.

Let us consider two or three cases which demonstrate the importance of constructive social work as an adjunct to prison rehabilitation.

Tony was sentenced for two years for counterfeiting. He became a model prisoner. He was active in work with the chaplain and maintained a good conduct record. He was twenty-two years old, Italian, Catholic, married, and a barber by trade. When sentenced, the field parole officer wrote the family service organization in the community which cleared the case and arranged for contact. Information was received that Tony's family did not seem to know that he was married. The organization asked to be advised more fully about the marital relations and whether or not Tony was intending to keep the marriage secret.

On inquiry by the institutional parole officer, Tony replied that he was married but he hadn't told his people and his wife had not told hers. In the first place the ceremony was performed by a civil official, and during a period of mourning. He was afraid to let his family know.

After the matter was discussed, Tony wanted his folks to be advised by the agency. He didn't want to tell them. Then the family organization worker called on Tony's wife. She had no means of support and lived with her mother in a single room in great poverty. Her mother contributed just food enough to keep her alive and was very angry with her. Tony's wife had no clothes or shoes. Her condition was aggravated by the fact that she was pregnant.

The agency worker relieved the acute situation in part by providing adequate food and making other essentials available to Tony's wife. The mother's anger was minimized in part when this relief eased her burden.

The agency worker then called on Tony's family to break the news to them. There was great indignation manifested over Tony's marriage, and considerable time and persuasion were necessary before any progress could be made. Finally Tony's sister said she would call on his wife, and this step was then taken.

The institution and Tony were advised about what had happened. The time for parole release was approaching. The current problems were discussed with all concerned.

Tony's wife was advised about her coming confinement. Prenatal care was afforded. Hospitalization and convalescent care were secured.

Just before Tony was to be paroled his wife asked the agency worker if a place could be found where Tony and she could be by themselves. Such a place was found. Provisions for relief to include Tony were made, and the time came for Tony's return. Through the official contact, employment had been secured and O.K.'d, and a parole adviser was certified. Tony went to work at the barbering job, but it was irregular and not adequate for his needs. The agency worker located better work and Tony changed jobs. The adviser was rarely active as such, but in view of the agency contact no change was made.

Some time later the sentence finally terminated with Tony and his family living together, and the bonds with the parent families were becoming reëstablished.

After the sentence had ended Tony called one day on the agency worker and stated that his landlord had offended his wife, and that he, Tony, was going to kill him. The agency worker listened to all the details of the plan which Tony had conceived and eventually persuaded him that the best thing to do was simply to move. This Tony did; later, when he called on the agency worker to report his continuing progress, he appeared to have forgotten the matter.

The outstanding points in this case are of course:

1. The early establishment of contact with the community agency, the community service made available through contact between the institution and the agency.

2. The continuity of service all through the institutional period, the parole period and after care had ended.

3. The correction of the faulty employment situation.

4. The preparation of the case based on the fact that Tony had responsibilities and problems to which he must return.

What would have been the result if nothing had been done until Tony had left the prison or if only official contacts had been made with the families?

W———— K————, twenty years old, was arrested for violation of the National Motor Vehicle Theft Act and sentenced to eighteen months. He had built up in a few years a considerable record for petty thieving and had served a term in the training school for boys. He was sent to the road camp but could not settle down. Something was obviously preying on his mind. It led him from one misconduct into another. His family encouraged his belief that he had tuberculosis, which did not add to his tranquillity. The prison restraint was too much and he finally escaped from the road camp. He was promptly reapprehended and sent to a closed institution. Still his disciplinary trouble continued and finally the superintendent arranged for the taking of X-ray pictures of his chest when it was definitely established that he did not have tuberculosis. He had to be shown the photographs himself to be convinced, but once that took place all disciplinary difficulty disappeared. For the rest of his term he gave no trouble whatever. The facts were communicated to his family, who took an entirely different attitude and coöperated with the authorities in the development of a suitable plan for his parole and after care.

Do not get the impression that all of the effective social work in our prisons is done by the social workers. Almost every day one member of the staff or another, from the warden down, is presented with an opportunity to speak or act in a way which may be of great effect in molding the future career of an inmate. By the same token, an ill considered word or action may result disastrously.

"John Rides-Three-White-Horses" was not his name although his own was equally picturesque; he had been sent to prison for eighteen months for the sale of liquor on an Indian reservation. Those in charge of the reservation felt that they must be severe in dealing with such violations. John had served part of his sentence and was eagerly expecting a parole. His squaw was expecting a baby with equal trepidation. John had been a good prisoner and had been working on the honor farm which gave him the privilege of earning a few extra days off per month. The Parole Board could not see their way clear to vote a parole, however, and the next day John wrote a letter to his wife in which he expressed his disappointment and despair. He advised her to go and get another man, that there was nothing left for him but suicide. The letter was intercepted by the censor and delivered to the warden. On being sent for, John came into the warden's office. Let this veteran warden with forty years' service in the Federal prisons tell the rest of the story.

"I did not speak or look at him at first. I told him to sit down for a moment as I was busy, and I purposely occupied myself for a short time with other matters. Finally, I looked up and saw two large tears starting down the half-breed Indian's cheeks. I passed him the letter and remarked that he did not want to send that letter to his wife. He seemed tremendously relieved to have the letter back and between us we tore it into bits. I said: 'John, I thought you didn't mean to write that letter. Now you go back onto the farm and do your work, and we'll see that your wife is taken care of; and the end of your term will be here before you realize it.' John was overcome with emotion and gratitude; he had feared that he would be brought back into the cell block and perhaps given a short term in solitary, but I felt that this was just the time to express confidence in him. He did go back on the farm, recovered his composure, and we had no further difficulty with him."

This ability to know when to discipline and when to encourage is an invaluable asset for all those who have to deal with human beings, but is infinitely more valuable in the warden of a prison who holds the present liberty and future destiny of his wards practically in his own hands.

The head of a penal institution carries the burden of many perplexities. He has to be an honest and intelligent administrator. He must oversee the purchase of supplies, the making of contracts. He must select and retain suitable subordinates. He must be a disciplinarian, a student of human nature, a farmer, a mechanic, a shop superintendent and he must be reasonably familiar with many other details of administration. But above all, he must not lose the human touch.

In other words, no matter how harassed a warden may be in the conduct of the daily affairs of the prison, he must constantly realize that his outstanding task is with the prisoner himself, with the prisoner as a social problem, as a member of a family or a community; and he will never lose sight of the fact that only as he is able, with the help of the social agencies and, through them, of the prisoner's community, to readjust him into society can he be said to be entirely successful.

CHAPTER XV

WHEN THE PRISON DOOR OPENS

"My name is Jean Valjean. I am a convict from the galleys.
I have passed nineteen years in the galleys. I was liberated four
days ago . . . I went to an inn and they turned me out . . .
I went to another inn. They said to me, 'Be off,' at both places.
No one would take me. I went to the prison. A voice replied,
'The prison is not an inn. Get yourself arrested and you will be
admitted.' I went into a dog's kennel; the dog bit me and chased
me off. One would have said he knew who I was. I went into
the fields intending to sleep—beneath the stars. There were no
stars. . . . I am very weary. I am very hungry. Are you willing
I should remain?"

"Madame," said the Bishop, "you will set another place."
                              VICTOR HUGO—*Les Misérables.*

DURING the year 1933 the prison door swung inward 66,874
times to admit a person convicted of some State or Federal
crime. Each of these occasions was the culmination of a personal tragedy for the individual concerned and his family.
The judge thanked the jury for its high sense of civic and
public duty. The district attorney received the congratula-
tions of his friends, and the public heaved a sigh of relief. But
the job was not done. Of equal importance to our communities, and fraught perhaps with equally tragic possibilities for
the ex-prisoners themselves, were the 64,840 occasions when
the prison door swung open during the year 1933 to discharge
that number of inmates.

After our efforts to reclaim him have been expended a
prisoner emerges from the abnormal environment of a penal
institution into an atmosphere of freedom and independence.
What is his mental attitude? How readily can he be assimilated into our competitive industrial life? Will he find the
friendly counsel and assistance necessary to bridge over this
difficult period in his career? Will the new resolutions that he

has made during the long days and nights in prison remain firm as he faces the unbridled temptations of our urban communities? Will he, after several futile attempts to hold his ground, gravitate to the level of the street-corner gang or of those semi-criminal types which may constitute the only friends and resources he has?

What is the duty of society toward him? If something is not done of a constructive nature, will he not become more of a threat to the peace and safety of his neighborhood than before he was sentenced?

The penological device known as parole contains the answer to these questions.

The ticket-of-leave man and the ex-convict have always been thorns in the flesh of the body politic. In the early days society was afraid to make the attempt to assimilate such hardened individuals. They were deported. They were branded. They were set apart from their fellows.

How can this small army of unfortunate, underprivileged or vicious individuals be made less of a menace? Many interesting experiments have been made. We find references to a procedure similar to our present-day parole in the record of Commander Phillip as Governor of New South Wales in 1790. To certain English convicts transported to Australia the Governor was permitted to make remission of part of their sentences as an incentive to hard work. Many conditionally released prisoners found opportunity in the sheep industry in that far continent.

Later, under the leadership of Captain Alexander Maconochie in 1840, the Australian system became the true forerunner of the system of conditional liberation, or parole, as we now know it. It was developed by Sir Walter Crofton of Ireland and originally applied only to convicts shipped to Australia; but in 1853, under the Ticket of Leave Act, it was applied to convicts on English soil.

A book entitled "Purgatory for Prisoners," by the Rev. Aubrey Shipley, published in 1857, describes the almost incredible success which attended the adoption of the indeterminate penal establishments in Ireland, to which discharged convicts were sent from prison, preparatory to their final discharge into the community.

The necessity for some kind of incentive for men in prison was early recognized, and many of the so-called "good time" laws adopted by the various States of America date from the first and second decades of the nineteenth century. These were quite different, however, from the parole laws; the latter began to be developed only with the recognition of the wisdom of the indeterminate sentence, which gained certain advocates in England during the middle of the nineteenth century and was first sponsored in the United States by Z. R. Brockway in 1869.

The establishment of the New York State Reformatory at Elmira in 1876 presented the first opportunity for the development of a real parole system in this country.

In default of a system of post-institution control, England had devised certain preventive detention institutions. These establishments were in recognition of the fact that at the end of a long term of penal servitude the convict was in no condition to be released, and that it was not safe, from the public's standpoint, to discharge him under such circumstances.

In the early days of prison administration in this country the pitiable picture of the discharged convict with his shaved head and prison pallor led to the establishment of so-called houses for discharged convicts and societies for aiding discharged prisoners. Many of these societies still function, although with the development of the parole system their need has been along somewhat different lines.

*   *   *   *

Parole as now administered in our most progressive States is the conditional liberation of a prisoner on a day to be decided by a board or commission as the time most advisable for him and the community. Instead of a definite sentence from which the prisoner may earn no deduction and toward which he must look without preparation or modification of his conduct, there is provided an adjustable date toward which he can work. This date can be advanced if his conduct and prospects justify it, or it can be delayed if his lack of progress and the interest of society warrant.

Parole must be distinguished from pardon. Pardon involves forgiveness. Parole does not. Pardon is a remission of punishment. Parole is an extension of punishment. Pardoned prisoners are free. Parolees may be arrested and reimprisoned without a trial. Pardon is an executive act of grace; parole is an administrative expedient.[1]

It is of prime importance that the discharged convict shall be provided with a suitable home and a job sufficient to keep him from want and temptation and that he be released under such circumstances as will induce his obedience to the laws. These concomitant factors to release can be insisted upon under the parole system, but not under the definite discharge plan.

Again, everything depends upon the mental attitude of the discharged prisoner. If he comes out at the end of a stated period, it is almost inevitable that he should have the feeling that he has paid his bill in full, that he and society are square. He may even feel that he has somewhat overpaid his debt and have no compunction about evening it up at the first opportunity.

An adjustable parole system, however, may be so devised that the compulsion can be placed upon the prisoner himself. He has not been handed a one-way ticket to freedom. He has been allowed to go out on his parole—on his word of honor, so to speak—and, if and when he fails, he may be returned without the delay of a formal trial by jury.

I recall the case of a paroled man in Massachusetts who had been arrested charged with selling "snow," or powdered morphine. The parole agent heard about it and attended the trial

---

[1] Clair Wilcox, "The Open Door," *The Annals of the American Academy of Political and Social Science*, Vol. 157, Sept., 1931, p. 103.

of this defendant. As establishing his innocence of the charge
the prisoner introduced evidence that it was not morphine he
was selling, merely bicarbonate of soda. The jury believed
him and he was found not guilty. The parole agent was not
so easily satisfied, however. He could not be made to see that
the activities of the parolee were particularly creditable—at
the very least he was engaged in a perpetration of a fraud
upon some wretched addict; the prisoner's parole was therefore promptly revoked, and without any necessity for trial or
the introduction of testimony he was brought back on the
strength of his own statement and required to serve the rest
of his sentence. Thus we see that the outstanding argument
for a parole system is that it constitutes a higher degree of protection to the public.

Which is the safer method of discharge for convicts of all
classes, of all degrees of criminality and all types of personalities: to be released from prison without let or hindrance, lacking
the guidance or restraint of personal or official supervision, or
to be returned to the community under close control? [1]

A young prisoner in a Federal penitentiary is approaching
the end of his sentence. Through all his term he has maintained an air of truculence and unwillingness to abide by the
rules. Much of his time he has spent in segregation. He was
asked by an official of the prison, "What do you propose to
do when you have served up until the last day which the Government can hold you on this sentence?" His answer was this:
"I propose to go out and kill every officer of the law that I
meet." Bravado, no doubt. When he breathes the free air of
the outside once again, he may change his tune. The fear of
prompt retribution may deter him. The officer of the law may
get him first. But just suppose that 60,000 men emerged from
prison each year for the next ten years with that attitude of
mind!

The transition from unusually constricted prison life to
self-supporting existence in a free community is an extraor-

---

[1] We might better understand its function if we referred to prisoners
as being *subjected* to parole rather than *granted* parole.

dinarily difficult one even in normal times. In these times of unemployment the problem becomes increasingly acute. Consider the millions of law-abiding men unable to get permanent positions, and then visualize, if you can, the almost insurmountable handicap that faces the discharged prisoner. It is out of no sentiment for the prisoner but with an eye single to the welfare of society that we have in the last decades insisted that all of our prisoners go out by the method known as parole.

Sad to say, this system has been subjected to grave abuses in some of our States. Stories are current that gangsters and desperadoes, who perhaps never should be released from prison, have been prematurely or improperly turned loose; and the public calls this parole.

We must distinguish between the exercise of clemency through the pardoning power of a governor, on the one hand, which is not parole at all, and the release of prisoners after careful examination into their individual cases by an intelligent, fearless, honest, full-time parole board, such as functions in the Department of Justice in Washington.

Much discussion has been had from time to time as to the type of person who should be released under parole: whether parole should be confined to first offenders or hopeful cases and denied to other classes of prisoners. Sound practice and the protection of the public will undoubtedly demand that some dangerous men who give no prospect of reform should never be released from an institution. With that principle most penologists have no quarrel; but 98 per cent of all prisoners must be released at some time, and when they do emerge it is much safer to have them all under parole supervision for a longer or shorter period of time than otherwise.

The arguments in favor of parole then may be summed up as follows:

1. It gives to the public the added protection of a supervised release.

2. It offers an incentive for good behavior.

3. It sends the prisoner out of prison under an obligation rather than with a score to settle.

4. It permits the time of release to be fixed at a favorable occasion.

5. It acts as a bridge between the abnormal environment of the prison and life in the community.

6. It saves expense.

7. It gives an opportunity to correct mistakes and reduce excessive sentences.

By now the story of Dr. Samuel Mudd is known to millions of Americans through the moving picture, "The Prisoner of Shark Island." Possibly some of the circumstances of this heartrending story of the unfortunate physician may have been distorted, but it does not seem possible that a community, even in the face of the tremendous resentment at the assassination of the martyred President, could have been so cruel and relentless as the accounts that we have received would indicate.

After John Wilkes Booth had leaped from the box at the Ford Theatre he fled to the Eastern Shore of Maryland, and early the next morning stopped at the house of Dr. Samuel Mudd, a country physician, who, perhaps without being too inquisitive, did what many doctors in his position would feel called up to do—set the broken leg of the fugitive and ministered to his wants. The next morning, so the story goes, he discovered that he had helped the murderer of Lincoln, and he immediately notified the authorities. He was found guilty of harboring an assassin and sentenced to life imprisonment, first in the old house of correction at Albany, New York, later at Fort Jefferson on Dry Tortugas Island, off Key West. Later, after he had attempted to escape, he was placed in an underground dungeon and chained to the wall with his negro companion. Nor were the shackles removed until in the midst of an epidemic of yellow fever which carried off one-third of the population of the little island his services as a physician were necessary. When he had finished his ministry of mercy the shackles were put back, and it was several years later before his pardon came. But it came too late. Within a short time he died of exposure making a hurried call to aid a suffering neighbor.

What we do today may not seem reasonable to us tomorrow. No judge, no legislature, no governor, is wise enough to foresee how we shall be thinking five, ten, or fifteen years from today. During the World War we imposed terrific sentences upon the hundreds of conscientious objectors and other wartime offenders but when the hostilities were over and the excitement had died down it did not take us long to release them all. In fact, largely by means of commutation of sentence not a single one of those whom we had sent to prison remained in confinement at the end of 1923.

Why is it that many criminal lawyers choose to take their cases before one judge on a certain bench rather than another? Is the amount of time which the man is supposed to stay in prison to be determined by the individual mellowness or asperity of a particular judge or by the condition of the same judge's temper and digestion on a certain morning? Is the judge, who after all is a human being, to be permitted to pronounce the word which is to be the last word for all time with reference to the fate of a given individual? [Curiously enough, most of the criticism hurled at boards of paroles is because of an alleged tendency toward leniency. The errors that they make on the side of severity are hidden from view.]

In our readiness to criticize parole boards we sometimes overlook the fact that judges too are fallible. They cannot hit it exactly right in every case. Sometimes they do not impose sufficiently long sentences, and the community may perhaps suffer therefrom. On other occasions, responding to the temper of the times, sentences completely out of line with what the defendants really deserve are imposed; and not infrequently in such case the judge whispers in the ear of defendant's counsel that he has done it for its effect upon society, and that no doubt in a year or two arrangements will be made to pardon or parole the prisoner. Undoubtedly there are times when a long sentence has to be administered for the deterrent effect that it will have upon the community, but when the community situation is changed there is no need for such an example being made of the prisoner and even the judge who imposed the sentence will join in the request that the sentence be mitigated.

That parole is an additional burden on the prisoner as well as a protection to society is oftentimes demonstrated. The Federal Government amended its parole law in 1932 to provide that even those prisoners who had received no consideration by the parole board and were released on expiration of what is known as their minimum sentence should be required to go out under supervision. This move was purely in the interest of safeguarding our communities. At first the inmates of our penitentiaries were inclined to rebel against this extra restriction. The Board indicated, however, that, so far as it could, it proposed to require all prisoners so discharged to report regularly, to get work, if that was possible, and to live up to the terms of their permits. During the first year of operation of this new system it was necessary, perhaps as a demonstration, to revoke about 25 per cent of this class of paroles. But the news spread abroad that the Federal Government meant business, and the number of revocations dropped the next year to 15 per cent. As will be later explained, this revocation rate is twice as high as that prevailing where the board remits part of the sentence.

That parole supervision really amounts to something, at least as operated by the Federal government, is indicated by the following letter received by the superintendent of one of our prison camps.

They is a man ther in your care by the name of ———— his home adres is Osborne. I am the mother of his wife. Mr. ———— they tell me that his people is trying far a pardon. I do pray you will help me to see that he dont get a pardon for we want him on parole. You see men that is sent from this mountain most haff rased and when they get pardon or make ther time in full or is in no time till they do something els and haft to go

back to prison and every man that is sent back from prison
we have plenty of them here on parole they are the best men we
have in thes mountains. They are a frade to violate the law for
they no they will be sent back. I am a woman of 50 years of
age and what few days i have to live i wood like to live them in
Peace and i no just how it will bee if ———— is pardoned or if
he makes his time in full you see Mr. ———— the county offercers
here in this county they don't care how much a man lays drunk
and they can carry guns and do almost innithing they want to
but all of the men that is on parole are afrade of the Government and that is why i am pleading to you to help me to see that
———— dont come back home free from the law of what he is
now charge with. They is old farmers here on this creek that
has told me they will furnish ———— all the land that he can find
and everything in the seeds that he can plant and also horse
power free of charge for they no what it will bee for me in the
futcher if he is in parole. Please help me all you can for you no
what a dear mother needs in her old days is Peace.

What are the elements of a good parole system? These
have never been more correctly stated than in the resolution
adopted by the Attorney General's Crime Conference in
December, 1934, as follows:

1. The minimum and maximum of indeterminate sentences
should be compatible with adequate punishment, rehabilitation
and public welfare and protection.

2. Paroles should be granted only by a full-time salaried board
of duly qualified persons.

3. Full information should be available and sought for the
use of the board as to the prisoners' records, habits, environment, family and prospects.

4. The names of all persons endorsing a prisoner for parole
should be made public on request of the press or any responsible
person or organization.

5. No parole should be granted except where adequate employment and rigid supervision are provided.

6. Adequate appropriations must be provided for obtaining
requisite data and furnishing necessary supervision.

7. One parole officer should not be expected to supervise
more than a number to whom he can give adequate attention.

8. No political or other improper influence shall be tolerated.

9. Machinery should be provided for the prompt revocation

of any parole when continuance at liberty is not in the public interest.

A notable example of a tribunal which functions intelligently and conservatively in accordance with these principles and with due regard for both the prisoner's future and the welfare of society is the parole board set up in the Department of Justice under the able leadership of Hon. Arthur D. Wood. Under the Federal statute, although a prisoner is eligible at one-third of his maximum term, the board must be satisfied that "such release is not incompatible with the welfare of society." The members of the board are thoroughly informed, trained by special aptitudes, and freed by the Attorney General from any control except that dictated by the facts.

The extent to which they have lived up to their grave responsibility is indicated by the fact that, as intimated above, although the supervision is strict[2] and parolees may be returned (and indeed are) for breach of the rules and without committing any crime, all but about 9 per cent of the prisoners so released completed their parole terms without default during 1935.

The theory of parole is sound. But, unfortunately, it is not always administered in conformity with the rules just enunciated. Parole cannot guarantee the future probity of every person released thereunder. Some boards have made mistakes —and bad ones—and from time to time will make them. Newspaper writers have called attention to the fact that a considerable number of the desperadoes who with great difficulty have been brought to justice have had at some time in their criminal careers one or more paroles. Naturally, these failures of parole are highly publicized and greatly deplored. There is no gainsaying the fact that every time a parole board releases a criminal it takes a certain risk. If he commits a new offense they are the last in line and are sure to catch the blame.

[2] The scrupulous insistence of the Federal Board on this matter of supervision is attested by the fact that no less than 20 per cent of voted parolees have not been released on account of the fact that suitable employment has not been certified.

Even though the public reads only once in two or three months the story of some ruthless bandit who has been paroled, that is sufficient to inspire the belief in the public mind that the parole system is necessarily bad.

Some newspapers go even further and proclaim from time to time that the parole system has broken down. What do we mean when we say that the parole system has broken down? If there never was to be another parole, how would the ex-convict be kept from committing new crimes? The question is not how many have been paroled, but to what extent the parole system has aided in keeping the ex-prisoner out of trouble and therefore safeguarded. There is only one way in which we can answer this question, and that is by reference to the most reliable statistics which are at hand.

An Oklahoma newspaper recently screamed a headline to the effect that 35,000 persons had been released on parole during the year. Well, there is nothing dangerous in that unless a considerable portion of them are found to have continued their criminal careers. What does the evidence show generally on this very point?

Of course it has to be remembered that parole boards are no more anxious to advertise their mistakes of judgment than the police are wont to report the occurrence of crimes which they have not been able to solve. The most reliable statistics that we have as to the percentage of successes, however, are those gathered by the Census Bureau.

Reports from eighteen selected States indicate that out of 35,327 persons on parole January 1, 1931, and taken on parole during that year, there were 2,496 violations declared during the year. During that same year and in these same districts 16,763 persons were released from prison and taken on parole and 12,620 had their paroles terminated. Roughly speaking, about 7 per cent of the total number on parole during the year were violators.

The Census tables [3] point out that, of the 2,496 persons

[3] U.S. Bureau of the Census, *Prisoners in State and Federal Prisons and Reformatories, 1931–1932*, pp. 42–43.

declared parole violators, only 980 had committed new crimes recorded in the Federal Bureau of Investigation. Other paroles were revoked for violation of parole regulations. The percentage of persons on parole during the year who were declared violators for the commission of a crime would, therefore, read as follows:

Paroles terminated	12,620
New crimes committed	980
Percentage	8
Released on parole during the year.........	16,763
New crimes committed	980
Percentage	6
Total number on parole during the year.....	35,327
New crimes committed	980
Percentage	2.8

About 50 per cent of the men discharged from prison in the reporting area were discharged on parole. These figures are as follows:

Year	Total Discharged from Prison	Discharged by Parole	% of Total Discharges Released by Parole
1926	44,964	19,917	44.4
1927	47,560	21,652	46.8
1128	52,644	23,969	45.5
1929	53,006	24,138	45.3
1930	61,653	29,509	47.5
1931	68,894	34,982	50.6
1932	72,482	37,137	50.6
1933	69,022	34,839	50.4

It will be noted here, as elsewhere, that a great many of the revocations of parole are not for the commission of new crimes but in order to prevent the possibility of lawlessness.

Take these figures for what they are worth and no more. Our present generation is interested primarily in the current crime crop, so to speak. The "Uniform Crime Reports" published by the Federal Bureau of Investigation have furnished some interesting statistics as to the number of persons currently arrested who are found to be on parole.

Its bulletin covering the first three months of 1935 [4] indi-

[4] The last quarter for which parole statistics have been published.

cates that during that period 90,504 persons were arrested for various crimes. Of this number 509, or 0.6 per cent, were arrested during the period of their parole. Of the 1,535 arrested for homicide, none were shown to be on parole.

Thus we find that less than 1 per cent of the persons arrested for crime whose fingerprints are sent to Washington for identification are found to be on parole at the time of arrest. Even admitting its inadequacies and inefficiencies, we are hardly justified in heaping the blame upon the parole system for any considerable share of responsibility for contemporaneous crime conditions. When these same "Uniform Crime Reports" disclose the fact that only one burglar out of five, only one robber out of four, and only one automobile thief out of eight is even arrested, it is impossible to contend that, because 1 per cent of those who are arrested are found to be on parole, either parole has broken down or its breakdown had any very general bearing upon the prevalence of crime.

What statistics we have, furthermore, seem to indicate that somewhere in the neighborhood of 10 per cent of the persons released on parole have to be brought back during the term of their sentence. We have seen that a very small proportion of those now being arrested are found to be on parole. But still we have a rather well defined feeling that some dangerous criminals have had their sentences unduly shortened by the board of parole or the pardoning authorities. It may be said that many of these clemency agencies have little reliable information on which to base their judgments and often act on guesswork or under improper political or other influence.

Many instances have been broadcast in the newspapers of desperate prisoners who have received long sentences and have been released after serving only a fraction thereof. In the public mind the idea of parole is inextricably confused with leniency. To the uninformed, the release of a prisoner on parole merely means that he has not been kept in confinement long enough. Now this may or many not be true. We have elsewhere noted that foreigners have claimed that sentences in the courts of America are the longest in the world. In many instances these sentences are given purely for deterrent purposes; and in other instances they are known by everybody to be merely maximum sentences, and no one, neither the court, the prosecuting attorney, nor the defendant himself, ever really expects that the prisoner is to serve anywhere near the maximum indicated. It is quite simple for the courts to adjust their sentences to prescribe the proper amount of service in the prison to be followed by a parole supervision term. A sentence of eight years, knowing in advance that perhaps only about four years will be spent in prison and the last four years under supervision, is safer than a sentence of four years every day of which must be served.

There is of course room for argument that this is a fictitious situation and that it might be better if the maximum sentence were reduced so that the court would more nearly mean what it says. We still cling to the belief, however, that a sentence of seventy-five years meted out to A will deter B from crime, even though we never intend A to serve more than ten years of it. Let us inquire now, however, as to the amount of time which the prisoner serves before being released, irrespective of the length of the term imposed. What does the evidence show as to the length of time that has elapsed prior to his release under supervision? These statistics are not only difficult to gather and compile but not particularly easy to interpret once they have been accumulated. In 1931 and 1932, however, the Census Bureau found that the average time actually served in prison by all defendants throughout the reporting area who had finished out their terms and been released by expiration was 50.2 months, and that the average term served in prison by all persons who had been released under supervision or by parole was 56.1 months.[5]

The Census Bureau again in its last published report[6] gives these results:

[5] U.S. Bureau of the Census, *Prisoners in State and Federal Prisons and Reformatories, 1931–1932*, p. 38.
[6] U.S. Bureau of the Census, *Prisoners in State and Federal Prisons and Reformatories, 1933*, p. 43, Table 40.

MEDIAN TIME SERVED, BY OFFENSE AND METHOD OF
DISCHARGE: 1933

OFFENSE	METHOD OF DISCHARGE		
	All Methods	Expiration	Parole
All offenses	Months 16.9	Months 17.0	Months 17.4
Homicide	43.5	43.4	48.8
Robbery	32.2	36.3	32.8
Aggravated assault	17.3	15.6	21.1
Other assault	13.9	8.0	18.9
Burglary	17.3	18.0	17.3
Larceny, except auto theft.............	15.7	15.6	16.1
Auto theft...........................	18.5	21.3	18.0
Embezzlement and fraud	14.6	15.3	15.6
Stolen property	15.8	16.3	16.1
Forgery	17.6	19.3	17.8
Rape	32.4	31.4	33.2
Other sex offenses	17.9	20.2	18.2
Violating drug laws	16.7	19.8	16.3
Violating liquor laws	10.1	10.0	10.4
Other offenses	12.8	9.2	15.6

If these figures mean anything, they mean that the average
time served preliminary to parole was longer than the average
time served on the definite sentence.

This evidence is not given in an attempt to justify the release of desperate criminals by parole or any other method—
only to prove that the parole system has not been used, generally speaking, to shorten sentences below what they would
otherwise have been, nor for the purpose of emptying out our
prisons. As a matter of fact, the Census Bureau figures also
show that during 1933 there were 8,548 fewer persons admitted to prison than in 1931 and that notwithstanding that
the prison population at the end of 1933 was only 899 fewer
than at end of 1931.

The Board of Indeterminate Sentence and Parole of the
District of Columbia serves without pay and has very little
financial support for its work. The report of this board dated
March 27, 1936, however, shows that of the 154 men that it

paroled during the year only 15 have had their paroles revoked, 11 for minor infractions of the law or for violation of
the parole rules. The most serious crimes committed by District of Columbia paroled men consist of one case of imper-
sonation, one of robbery and assault, and one of drinking and
attempted suicide. Out of a total of nearly 5,000 arrests for
felony in the District of Columbia during the same year, only
15 parolees from the District of Columbia were picked up.

All those who have seen men come into prison and go out
again, and have witnessed their struggles to rehabilitate themselves and to regain the respect of their fellows, have marveled
at some of the outstanding successes of the parole system.
These successes must forever remain anonymous. I have in
mind two distinguished men who recently called on me, it so
happened, on the same day. They have made names for themselves as athletes, as war veterans, and they stand high in the
esteem of their fellow men. One of them is idolized by the
youth of America. If I could mention their names, you would
agree with me that in their cases the service of the prison
sentence was rightly cut short by the bestowal of parole, and
that the expression of faith in their ability to restore themselves
has perhaps contributed to their success. But we cannot and
will not tell you who they are.

As in so many other things, politics is the curse of parole.
Fortunate, indeed, is that community which has an impartial,
thoroughly advised parole agency who can pass upon the important question of predictability with greater accuracy.

In the belief that there is a science of parole some intelligent criminologists have attempted to work out what they call
predictability tables, suggested no doubt by the actuarial tables
on mortality which prove to be an accurate guide for insur-
ance companies. These students have wondered whether or
not parole boards might be helped through the consideration
of similar experience on a large number of cases. Sheldon and
Eleanor Glueck in Boston, Burgess in Chicago and Vold in
Wisconsin have labored with this problem. Their theories run
something like this: There are a large number of factors which

bear upon the question of success or failure of parole. These factors may be hereditary, environmental, institutional, or personal. Given the existence of one or another antecedent or contemporary situation, is there any trend or tendency evident from which a parole board may predict the successful use of parole?

Sam Warner, whose study along this line preceded those of the others mentioned, felt that there were very few factors that had any marked bearing upon parole success or failure. The previous industrial record of the prisoner and accumulated prison experience he found to be important; *i.e.,* the more times a man has been in prison, the less likely was he to succeed on parole; and the more steady and consistent his employment record on the outside, the more apt was he to succeed on parole.

Burgess attempted to build up tables showing the percentage of success that might be expected when certain given situational factors were present. Scientific investigation of this kind may be of great benefit to parole boards of the future, but we must never expect that the granting of parole will become an automatic thing, or that it will be possible to put it on an actuarial basis. No two personalities ever will or ever can be exactly alike, nor do environmental influences have the same effect on any two individuals. The parole board will still have to bring to bear all of the empirical insight that it can command, but its judgment will be more accurate if it is guided by the actual results of previous experience as formulated in predictability tables rather than by the hunch method, or by looking at the prisoner, or by listening to the voice of politics.

The Federal Parole Board soon after its organization in 1930 made plans to check its own work and to be guided by its own accumulated experience. The first 5,000 cases were subjected to a careful scrutiny to determine the accuracy of the board's judgment. Later an additional 3,700 cases were similarly reviewed, and some extremely interesting results were obtained as to the bearing of antecedent and existing factors upon success or failure. The board was not slow to profit by the facts which these studies disclosed. This research was designed to test not only the accuracy of the board's judgment in awarding parole but also the effectiveness of post-institution supervision which was being provided by the Bureau of Prisons.

One of the outstanding situations that was disclosed by the first of the research studies was that the percentage of parole failures among discharged inmates who had venereal diseases was twelve times higher than the normal rate of failure.

This information was promptly heeded by the board and from then on special care was taken with this type of case. Either parole consideration was postponed or else more scrupulous attention was given to the type of supervision provided. The result was that in the next survey the situation was found to be somewhat reversed. The percentage of successes of the venereal cases was higher than the general percentage. One more interesting situation was disclosed by these researches, and that was that a high percentage of failure on parole came within the first two months after release. Again the board took the hint. It redoubled the intensity of its supervision during that period. Here is one parole board which is approaching its task professionally, availing itself of all the light there is on the matter and acting accordingly.

May we not say that in the field of parole as in all departments of law enforcement there is no substitute for intelligence?

Some of my readers will doubtless feel that this chapter gives an altogether too rosy view of the parole situation. It is quite possible that the statistics I have given do present a more favorable aspect than the real facts will warrant; but they are all the statistics we have, and I have given them to you just as they are. Attorney General Cummings has under way a million-dollar Works Progress Administration survey of release procedures throughout the country. Perhaps the result will be a heartening confirmation of our confidence in the system. More than likely it will uncover many defects and inadequacies in its administration. Neither the parole system nor our penal administrators should place any obstacles in the way of any intelligently guided endeavor to gather verified data on their work.

Let me say that I am under no illusions with respect to the effect of parole upon certain individuals, any more than I am under illusions with respect to any other phase of our efforts with prisoners. Many of the objects of our endeavors will be the first to scoff at them. They will undoubtedly sneer at "social work" or at psychiatry, without, of course, refusing its aid. The story is told of the two "guests" in a certain penitentiary who had been before the psychiatrist for examination. That night as they sat in their "twin bed cell"—with the beds arranged one above the other—Joe said to Bill:

"How didja get along with the nut doctor, Buddy?"

"Not so good. I forgot when they gave me the tap on the knee whether I should kick or not kick, and I didn't kick, and now I am crazy as hell."

Many prisoners will gloat over the way that they have deceived the parole board. They will evade the conditions imposed and betray the trust placed in them. For these no brief is held. The habit patterns formed in youth are too strong to be overcome.

Even though the prisoner is really "eager" to be reformed, there are times no doubt when the pressure of gang connections, the fear of being regarded as a renegade, an overcoming nostalgia for the old haunts and the old pals are apt to offset the good intentions; and the finest parole plans that man can devise often go astray. And thus "the native hue of resolution is sicklied o'er with the pale cast of thought."

Even, therefore, if a substantial majority of parolees failed either during their terms of parole or when this incentive to straight living was removed, it still would remain the wisest method of release. The difficulties just enumerated would exist in greater measure if the older system of complete discharge was employed. It is hardly fair to heap upon parole the blame which should be distributed among all of the other social agencies which fail to divert the prisoner from the primrose path of dalliance.

Certain sections of the press in their wholesale and undiscriminating condemnation of parole are assuming a heavy responsibility. If through their prejudiced efforts they succeed in doing away with parole or seriously curtailing its use as a means of release they will expose our communities to a much greater danger than now exists. Better to suffer at the hands of a few desperadoes—who are fortunately becoming fewer and fewer—than to make it necessary, by the abolition of the system, to turn tens of thousands of criminals annually back into the hopper of neglect, idleness, and lawlessness.

Some clearer thinking on the subject is obviously necessary. Many newspapers have insisted quite cogently that the difficulty was with the limited and misguided operation of parole rather than with any inherent defect in the system.

What's wrong with parole?

What's wrong with electricity? Nothing if we know how to use it. But let's not abolish it because it requires intelligence and courage to handle it.

What's wrong with social work?

Not a thing, if performed by trained people and not dominated by politics.

What's wrong with religion?

Nothing, if we would only use it occasionally.

One trouble with parole is that we do not use it enough. The case of Dillinger has been cited as a convincing proof of the failure of the parole system. It proves no such thing. For a crime for which his older and more experienced partner did two years, Dillinger, because of failure to conform to institution rules, was held nine years out of a possible ten. Can any thinking person contend that, if the remaining 10 per cent of his inordinately long sentence had been served, he would have been *less* of a menace on his inevitable release? As made clear by the Governor of Indiana, Dillinger became Public Enemy No. 1 not because he was paroled too soon but because he was not paroled soon enough. One among the factors responsible for his subsequent career of crime and pillage, not the least potent, was an overdose of prison.

We have gone at this point rather fully into the subject of parole, primarily because it is the point at which the prison problem touches the public, and about which our communities are therefore most sensitive. Obviously the success of the attempt at reformation in prison can be tested only after the prisoner has been discharged. Furthermore, I think it can be said that our attitude toward parole will indicate the soundness of our faith in the entire range of the possibilities of prisoner reclamation.

If we are convinced that occasionally judges make mistakes, that some prisoners are repentant and really desire another chance to rehabilitate themselves, even though there are many prisoners who are defiant and impervious to any attempt to improve them, and that a regulated release is safer than an unsupervised one, we shall demand that some form of parole be retained. We shall discontinue our criticism of it as a system and devote our energies to improving its administration.

CHAPTER XVI

THE PRISON OF THE FUTURE

COKESON: Ye-es, but I'm sorry now . . . He's got his three years to serve. I *want* things to be pleasant for him.

THE CHAPLAIN [*with a touch of impatience*]: The Law hardly shares your view, I'm afraid.

COKESON: But I can't help thinking that to shut him up there by himself'll turn him silly. And nobody wants that, I s'pose. I *don't* like to see a man cry.

THE CHAPLAIN: It's a very rare thing for them to give way like that.

COKESON [*looking at him—in a tone of sudden dogged hostility*]: I keep dogs.

THE CHAPLAIN: Indeed?

COKESON: Ye-es. And I say this: I wouldn't shut one of them up all by himself, month after month, not if he'd bit me all over.

THE CHAPLAIN: Unfortunately, the criminal is not a dog; he has a sense of right and wrong.

COKESON: But that's not the way to make him feel it.

THE CHAPLAIN: Ah! there I'm afraid we must differ.

COKESON: It's the same with dogs. If you treat 'em with kindness they'll do anything for you; but to shut 'em up alone, it only makes 'em savage.

THE CHAPLAIN: Surely you should allow those who have had a little more experience than yourself to know what is best for prisoners.

JOHN GALSWORTHY—*Justice*.

LET us read the final paragraphs of the Rules and Orders established by the Directors of the State Prison at Charlestown, Massachusetts, 2d August, 1811.

While it is melancholy to find so many of our fellow beings lost to honesty and virtue, as to be sentenced to this house of punishment, it is a solace of incalculable value to find that here they are well taken care of, sufficiently though coarsely clad and fed, that in the regular routine of labour, they acquire counter habits to their former lives of idleness and profligacy, and are favoured with a steady attention to their moral and religious conduct and conversation, and that all which human benevolence can accomplish is here industriously and anxiously applied that there may be "joy in heaven over one sinner that repenteth."

With the heartfelt desire of aiding in the honourable and Christian views of the government, the present Directors have undertaken to perform the arduous duties assigned them by the Executive. . . . They hope in . . . their regulations to receive the support of their fellow citizens and they sincerely desire that the blessing of providence may aid their humble exertions for the welfare of those unfortunate beings whose depredations on society have subjected them to the discipline of the prison; and that those who are restored to society, as well as such who are condemned to pass their miserable lives in penitence and labour, may have reason in another and better world to bless the authors of this institution.

And for one hundred and twenty-five years with the same naïve optimism we have been hoping that the result would justify our efforts.

All too often, however, the prison of the past has destroyed a man's intellect through idleness. It has mocked at his remorse. It has stifled or destroyed every vestige of self-respect or determination to succeed. It has fanned his resentment. It has extended his acquaintance with, and loyalty to, other antisocial and desperate individuals. The harvest of such a crop was inevitably more and more public enemies and criminal activity.

It is the aim of the prison of the present to release its prisoners if, as, and when it can be reasonably sure that they and society alike have profited by the instructions and rehabilitative efforts that have been offered to them. Have we any hope of being able to do this?

I have tried to give a picture of the jails and prisons of America with their shortcomings, their inadequacies, and their relationship to the problem of crime. I have endeavored to show why prisoners riot, what is the basis for the accepted conclusion that the prisons have failed, why men should work in prison, and to what extent we may call upon the new scientific discoveries to help us in our work. I have described at some length the operation of the Federal prison system, which due to provision by Congress of sufficient appropriations is becoming well equipped and adequately staffed. I have pointed out some of the well-nigh insoluble problems that face the prison warden, commented upon the difficult character of the persons with whom he has to deal and ended with a plea for a more tolerant understanding of the final problem of parole supervision.

The maintenance of a prison program which makes any sincere attempt at reforming the individual prisoner is a tremendously expensive process. A great deal more money than is being spent now will have to be expended before the investment begins to pay dividends. The rate of recidivism is still high. While progress is being made in many parts of the country, and while the prisons today are vastly improved over what they were fifty or one hundred years ago, has the improvement been permanent, and has it been proportionate with the improvement in other lines of social effort? If all the prisons of the country were to be reformed today, how long would they stay reformed? It seems to take a remarkably short time for a prison or a jail to slip back into its original condition of cruelty, graft, laxity, and uncleanliness. I can recall three distinct occasions when an enlightened prison administrator harnessed himself to the task of cleaning up the impossibly bad conditions in the penal institutions in New York City. When the present progressive Commissioner of Correction in America's largest city lays down the reins, how long will it be before the situation reverts to its former status? What is the reason that prisons do not stay reformed? We might attribute it to the apathetic attitude of the public, to the recurrent blight of partisan politics (which, we cannot too often repeat, is still a very real handicap in many of our States), a lack of the necessary appropriations, or the demand for vengeance; or perhaps the greatest reason is the fact that they are still prisons.

Why do so large a number of ex-convicts (as high as 60 per cent, probably [1]) become recidivists and return again and

[1] See Chapter 4, page 66.

again for new doses of prison punishment with all its attendant deprivation and despair?

Can we ever hope to return men to normal living conditions by treating them in an abnormal environment? It is possible, of course, that we have not analyzed our experience in penology with sufficient accuracy to be able to draw sound conclusions at this time. As has been pointed out, we have used prisons as places of punishment and reformation only for one hundred and fifty years, and during that period not many of the prisons have whole-heartedly dedicated themselves to the accomplishment of the task of restoring the prisoner to society. Have we had experience enough to form any accurate opinion as to whether we can reconcile the demand for punishment by imprisonment with the demand that we guarantee the moral probity of every man released? Do we know enough about the whole subject even to determine whether we are on the right track? I do not mean, in the paragraphs which follow, to suggest that penologists generally have become convinced of the hopelessness of this task. I merely wish to point to certain inescapable considerations which make very difficult and perhaps impossible the operation of an effective kind of prison. The prison of tomorrow, or whatever the institution or instrument may be called which will be used in the future for this purpose, might, perforce, have little similarity to the prison of today.

We have solved some of the prison problems which may have seemed very difficult to our predecessors. We have made headway in classifying and individualizing punishment. We have eliminated dirt and graft and cruelty from the larger prisons. There are, however, three outstanding obstacles to further improvement in prison management.

The first of these has to do with prison labor. As explained elsewhere the situation in this regard is getting worse rather than better. Even the State-use system is subject to attack. It is becoming increasingly difficult to justify the employment of men in prison, even in making goods for themselves, and not long ago a vigorous protest was filed by a labor organization against training programs in a non-competitive activity in order that when these men are released they might become more skillful workmen. Some prisons are solving this question in a furtive way. Others are handling it only partially, and a few have thrown up their hands and now maintain thousands of men in idleness. It is futile to talk about reform or restoration to future citizenship if men must be kept in stultifying and degenerating idleness through the whole of their terms.

The second obstacle has to do with the very nature of the prison structure itself. So long as the warden's prime responsibility is to prevent the escape of his prisoners, he must subordinate every other activity to that. He must have a high wall with its repressive and deadening influence. He must have guards pacing the wall with rifles on their shoulders, the sight of which does not stir any ennobling emotions in the hearts of the prisoners. He must control the activities, the conversation, the sleeping conditions, the exercise, and, in fact, all of the activities of the inmates to the end that none of them shall escape.

And this is perfectly proper. It is his first duty to keep safely the men who are sent to him.

The third obstacle which seems insuperable is the inevitable repression of the emotional life of men serving sentences. I have discussed this rather fully in another chapter. We need only repeat here that, as long as men are to atone for their crimes by being separated from their families and from normal emotional outlets, a certain percentage of them will always present behavior difficulties.

Is there any possibility of adjusting prison punishment in the present type of institution so that these three obstacles can be permanently overcome and a more general success assured? At the present time I frankly do not see any. If we are to devise some kind of institution or colony where men can work and yet not compete, where they may be removed from society and yet not confined, and under auspices where they can live normal family lives, the possibility of an island penal colony immediately recurs to mind.

Experience of our Federal Prison Bureau and of several States, such as California, Colorado, Michigan, and New Jersey, with prison camps on the mainland has been encouraging. Strangely enough, when certain types of prisoners are free to run they disdain to do so. Of course with us the extra penalty for escape is somewhat of a deterrent, but even so the record in Federal prison work camps is nothing short of remarkable. From 1930 through 1933, 9,000 specially selected men were transferred to camp from our different penitentiaries.

Let it be understood that these Federal prison camps are genuinely honor camps. There are no bloodhounds, no guns, no walls, and very few guards. A barbed-wire stockade forms the only obstacle. The prisoners say it is to keep stray cats and dogs out. At Maxwell Field, Alabama, where 200 convicts sleep in dormitories, even I, with my childlike faith in humanity, was somewhat disturbed to find only one guard assigned at night. The Superintendent finally agreed to put on another man, just to be handy in case the first guard should be taken sick.

During the period mentioned, 200 Federal camp prisoners walked away and 189 were returned, a net loss of eleven out of 9,000.

Let those who understand human nature better than we do explain this almost incredible result. Do fair treatment, fresh air, hard work, normal surroundings, and a reliance upon the prisoner's honor accomplish what steel and stone cannot? Is the most effective barrier that which is made of such intangible materials as self-respect, gratitude, and justice?

Other countries, it seems, have had splendid success with prison work camps. In addition to the Soviet Government, Germany, England, Holland, Belgium, and Turkey have experimented with this newer sort of penal discipline.

The British Prison Commissioner, whom I am fortunate to count as a personal friend, a man whose unflinching devotion to humanitarian ideals is making impress on world penal affairs, writes to me quite recently as follows:

Group of Swiss prison dogs in training at McNeil Island Penitentiary.

Road work by Federal prisoners near Tucson, Arizona.

NEW HALL CAMP, c/o H.M. PRISON
WAKEFIELD, YORKSHIRE
27 May 1936

My dear Sanford:

Five years ago you took me to the first prison camp[2] I ever saw and I remember telling the men I hoped they would make a success of it in order that we might be able to follow their example.

Today we have come out from Wakefield Prison with twenty men and two officers and we sleep tonight in the wooden huts in a clearing in a wood seven miles from any town. It is the beginning of the first prison camp in England. So it is only fair to write the first letter to you and your colleagues to thank you for the idea.

We move slowly in this old country and it has taken just five years to get it going. But once started I am confident it will grow. We have room for 100 men here and some day there will be other camps.

Every good wish to you all.

Yours always,

ALEX PATERSON.

The other day I received a copy of the personal report of an enlightened young Turk who was given permission to take fifty selected convicts from a prison in Istanbul to a remote and uninhabited island. Some of his paragraphs are well worth reading:

Finally the much longed for day arrived and I now find myself amidst fifty ill-fated citizens. I am alone with all their troubles and sufferings, their faults and merits. I am unable to express to what an extent the task of attaching these people to the nation as productive and sound elements uplifts me. I have to learn all about them; I have to penetrate into their most intimate life with the curiosity and compassion of brotherly benevolence with a view to finding a remedy for their physical as well as moral defects. . . . There have been times when our contact with the mainland was altogether severed. I had and still have to face a multitude of deficiencies which I would be ashamed to characterize as "privations" but I must admit that I have never before in my life experienced such moments of real happiness which derives its strength from deep sources. . . .

The health of the convicts is most satisfactory. At first I

¹ At Fort Meade, Maryland, in 1931.

was somewhat uneasy lest their constitution accustomed to un-
healthy surroundings would suffer a shock in this place which
from every point of view forms a contrast with the penal institutions they came from. In fact, a few of them did get unwell.
One day, especially, three of them fell ill at the same time.
That day I was most concerned and disconsolate. My hands
were practically tied in a place without a doctor and surrounded
by a surging sea. For a week now we do not have a single sick
person. They are getting healthier and stronger every day.

. . . .

There have been practically no falterings of any importance
to record in their new manner of living to which they are not
at all used and which they even claim "never to have dreamt
of." Those who have experienced some difficulty in adapting
themselves and who gave me some grounds for concern are convicts used to city life, such as carpenters and iron workers whom
I had to take along by force of necessity. However, I am sure
that they too will turn out all right.

. . . .

One day I also gave them the name of the person who feels
much compassion and sympathy for convicts, and who was the
first person to suggest to me this island. Promptly they named
after him a small but beautiful and fertile valley.

At these different spots I told them the necessary things and
narrated pertinent anecdotes. I also read various passages. At
other places we kindled a wood-fire. Then they played guitars
on the sea shore which was reddened by the setting sun. Why
should these people who have gone astray in social life be still
further estranged from humanity by useless restrictions. . . .
Why annihilate them behind damp and murderous walls . . .
Why do this by spending heaps of money . . . and then, years
later send them back to society physically and morally crip-
pled? It is most gratifying that this thoughtless process is near-
ing its end.

Suggestions that the United States use some of its island
possessions for this purpose have recently been made—usually
by persons who have become impatient with what they think
is an increase in crime and the tremendous expense of maintaining prisons.

There is, no doubt, a well established prejudice in this

country against penal colonies, influenced perhaps by the stories which have filtered through of cruelties alleged to have been practiced in the Devil's Islands of other nations. The tales that have come down to us of colonization in New Zealand and parts of Australia by convict immigration contain details of unbelievable barbarity. Whether the horrible conditions reported in connection with these British experiments were due to the penal character of the colonies, or whether the hardships of sickness, death, and misery would have prevailed in the case of any band of colonists under equally primitive environment is, of course, conjectural.

Margaret Wilson, brilliant novelist and wife of a British prison official, says [3] that banishment is one of the most natural of punishments and also "it is the one most difficult to foresee the extent of"; that those who have suffered from homesickness shudder at the thought of it. She quotes Romeo's answer to the Friar when he heard of his banishment:

> *There is no world without Verona walls,*
> *But purgatory, torture, hell itself.*

> . . . .

> *. . . Heaven is here,*
> *Where Juliet lives; and every cat and dog*
> *And little mouse, every unworthy thing,*
> *Live here in heaven and may look on her;*
> *But Romeo may not . . .*
> *. . . "Banished"?*
> *O Friar, the damned used that word in hell.*

When the island prison merely substitutes a sheet of water for a wall of granite and the prisoner is torn from his family or his surroundings to be sent there, it may well be described as "hell itself." It would not be necessary to make life upon the penal island one constant round of cruelty and barbarity.

The purpose of exile is to rid the neighborhood of its dan-

[3] *The Crime of Punishment* (Harcourt, Brace & Co., 1931).

gerous elements. This could be accomplished, and still life upon the penal island could be more humane and more tolerable than it ever could be made in the prison.

It might not be so easy to find suitable islands where a self-supporting existence could be carried on as it was a century ago. The Aleutian Islands[4] have been suggested, as have the Virgin Islands to the south. Could not a prison colony be maintained with ample work opportunities for all, with a chance to rear a family and to live a somewhat more normal existence, in which neither the fear of nor the incentive to escape would be the dominating factor? Not only the public enemy and the unadjustable criminal might be deported to the great relief of the law-abiding element, but the law breaker of lesser degree who finds it difficult to cope with and survive the industrial struggle might find literally a new lease of life in such an environment. These colonies might be classified in a manner similar to the way in which we have classified our prisons, one for the hardened criminal and others for the more reformable type of prisoner. It might even be that penal colonies of this sort could be developed in unsettled or sparsely populated regions of our own country.

I was greatly impressed by a visit to the Bolshevo Commune near Moscow in the summer of 1935. There I found a colony of 9,000 people, only 3,500 of whom are convicted prisoners. They live in all of the freedom of a small village community. They labor at standard wages. They marry and raise families, they provide their own discipline. In other words, they work out their own reformation and salvation, which leaves them free to develop rather than restricts them abnormally. They do not have to worry about escapes—that is impossible under the Soviet passport system, and they have no incentive to do so, because they are just as well off where they are; at least they have steady work to do. They do not have to worry about their families, since they are permitted to carry on family relations in a normal way. As their time is fully

---

[4] Col. Seone has made the suggestion and developed a plan for utilizing the Rat Islands in this group.

taken up with productive labor, they are not idle enough to get into conduct difficulties.

It will, of course, be recognized that we cannot at this time, at least, suggest duplicating such an experiment. But the Soviet Government claims complete success for this method of handling the ordinary type of criminal. It has substituted the idea of colonization for correction. We are obliged so to devise our correctional system that it will aid in the readaptation of the prisoner in normal life outside. The Soviet Union realizes the insuperable difficulty of such a process—restricting and reforming at one time. Perhaps the idea of the rural resettlement can be expanded in this country to the extent of redistributing throughout the wide-open spaces some of the victims of our improper distribution of population, that enter our penal systems.

These prison colonies or communities may succeed where prisons have failed, on the theory that no man will escape unless there is an incentive to do so. He will go or stay where productive employment is possible, and he can prosper best under the operation of influences which assist in his reformation rather than impede it.

Since the failure of the British colonial penal ventures we have discovered much about sanitation, hygiene, and protective medicine. The telegraph and the radio make even the far corners of the earth less remote. There is no inherent reason why a prison colony should be a place where cruelty abides. Perhaps it would not be an El Dorado or a City of the Sun, but at least it can be made humane and encouraging in its outlook and yet reserved for those who find it impossible to live and obey the laws laid down for our settled communities.

Will the prison of the tomorrow be simply a better prison, or will it be something conceived and constructed on an entirely different plan? Former Attorney General Mitchell stated that the prison of the future would be a place of permanent incarceration for the incorrigible, a school for those who can be reformed, and a laboratory for the study of the causes of crime.

We should not need a bastile to accomplish these purposes. But of course we must be willing to substitute the concept of protection for that of punishment very largely in the development of this ideal. If the prison of the future is to be upon the structural models of the prisons of the past, its administration will require not only intelligence and money and good will but an inexhaustible supply of optimism.

A prison hereafter, if it lives up to its ideal, will be clean and busy, will use all of the resources of science, and will give prominent place in its personnel to the psychiatrist, the sociologist, and the physician. Its employees will be under Civil Service and specially trained for the job. The sentences will be indeterminate and all releases therefrom will be under supervision only after judgment of a highly qualified parole board.

It is possible, with the support of an enlightened public opinion, that such an institution may be made into an agency for social rehabilitation and restoration. It is also possible that the obstacles referred to as being insuperable will never be overcome and that some entirely new method of handling the long-term criminal may have to be devised.

If, after an adequate trial and the frank facing of the problem—as disclosed by the pending researches into penal policies—it turns out not to be possible, at least within the limits of the public purse, we might do worse than to consider the development of a humane penal colony as the prison of the future.

CHAPTER XVII

ALTERNATIVES TO IMPRISONMENT

From the foldings of its robe, the Spirit brought two children; wretched, abject, frightful, hideous, miserable. . . .

They were a boy and girl. Yellow, meagre, ragged, scowling, wolfish; but prostrate, too, in their humility. Where graceful youth should have filled their features out, and touched them with its freshest tints, a stale, and shrivelled hand, like that of age, had pinched, and twisted them, and pulled them into shreds. Where angels might have sat enthroned, devils looked, and glared out menacing. No change, no degradation, no perversion of humanity, . . . has monsters half so horrible and dread.

Scrooge . . . tried to say they were fine children, but the words choked themselves, rather than be parties to a lie of such enormous magnitude.

"Spirit! are they yours?" Scrooge could say no more.

"They are Man's," said the Spirit, looking down upon them. "And they cling to me, appealing from their fathers. This boy is Ignorance. This girl is Want. Beware them both, and all of their degree, but most of all beware this boy, for on his brow I see that written which is Doom, unless the writing be erased. . . ."

"Have they no refuge or resource?" cried Scrooge.

"Are there no prisons?" said the Spirit, turning on him for the last time with his own words. "Are there no workhouses?"

The bell struck twelve.

DICKENS—*Christmas Carol.*

	Population	*Prison Population*
Belgium	8,159,824	4,000
England	37,354,917	11,000
France	41,834,923 (1931)	30,000
United States of America	122,775,046 (1930)	220,000

ACCORDING to the latest available figures this represents the entire prison population of the countries named. Well may Americans ask themselves, What price prison? Must we assume that because our prison population is the highest that we are the most criminally minded nation on earth?

Have we in this country been relying too heavily upon the orthodox method of imposing discipline for the commission of a crime? Have we gone too far in assuming that imprisonment is the only remedy available? Margaret Wilson, in her book earlier quoted, says that even in England three-fourths of the men in prison never should have been sent there, and she also adds that possibly the other fourth should never come out. The hero in Galsworthy's "Justice" puts it in these words:

> There were all sorts there. And what I mean, sir, is that if we'd been treated differently the first time, and put under somebody that could look after us a bit, and not put in prison, not a quarter of us would ever have got there.

There are many acts which rate as crimes, but which probably do not merit any extended term of imprisonment as punishment. An admonition by the court accompanied by the filing of a case sometimes has the desired effect in the case of slight peccadillos. The imposition of a fine sometimes hits the defendant in a tender spot and makes him realize that even trifling with crime does not pay. Hundreds of thousands of defendants have been disposed of in this manner, informal and inexact though it may be. But when the offense proves to be a serious one, when it involves some moral turpitude, or happens as a result of a preconceived plan, the average judge has very little to do in the matter but to send the defendant to jail or prison.

Unfortunately the alternatives to imprisonment are not many. We discussed the question of colonization in the last chapter. In a sense such disposition might be called an alternative to imprisonment, but as a matter of fact it is merely a different type of restraint. We cannot go on overcrowding the prisons we have and building new ones. By doing so we only add to the burdens and the perplexities of the prison warden, and we are not sure that we are offering any permanent protection to society thereby. So what?

Perhaps the best thing that can be said about the modern

penal device known as probation is that it offers the judge another alternative. He may think that the offense is too grave to warrant the dismissal of the culprit with merely a caution or a threat. On the other hand, he may not consider it to be serious enough to justify the risk of stigmatizing the offender by a sentence in prison. Probation provides the answer. It offers a method of inflicting supervised discipline, at less expense, under normal conditions, and with better hope of success. It permits an unlimited individualization of treatment, and it can be made really deterrent in its application.

Since the appointment in 1878, in the Commonwealth of Massachusetts, of the first salaried probation officer there has been a gradual but steady development of this practice. There is no particular mystery about probation. It is, in a sense, an adaptation of the methods often followed by parents in the discipline of their children, by school teachers, and others who have conduct problems to deal with. Mother Nature, herself, repeatedly puts us on probation, accompanied by a warning as to the dire consequences to follow if we do not mend our ways.

The distinguishing feature of a good probation system is an effective supervision and guidance which is suited to the specific needs of the probationer. Johnny is brought into court for playing baseball in a forbidden area. Of course, it may be true that Johnny had no other place to play. In which case the city fathers might well be indicted as *participes criminis*. But, granted that he violated a city ordinance by playing ball in this particular place and he broke the window of a complaining neighbor, an understanding judge may feel a great deal of sympathy for Johnny and yet also be of the opinion that he cannot be discharged with merely a few words of admonitory advice.

It will cost $1.50 to replace the window. The judge should not have much difficulty in making Johnny see that he is the one to pay this amount. It will be a mistake to permit Johnny's father or mother to pay it for him. But the boy has a paper route out of which he makes about fifty cents a day. So the judge proposes that Johnny be put on probation, and that he pay twenty-five cents a week to the probation officer until he has paid for the window. In the meantime, a trained probation officer will have succeeded in procuring for Johnny other places in the city where he can play ball without getting into difficulties.

Now, in such a case is not this sort of treatment infinitely superior to that which compels the boy to come into court, to be scared for the time being, to have some one pay his fine, and to go back to his gang with his prestige heightened? It is also much more constructive and helpful than to send the boy to a jail for a few days or to a training school for a year or more. It retains his self-respect and puts him under a lengthened disciplinary treatment. The chances are that the boy offender will remember it more vividly if the punishment is distributed over a period of time. Every time he sells a paper or counts his change he realizes that part of his earnings must go to pay for his carelessness or indiscretion.

Make the case as trivial or as serious as you please. The value of probation is not confined to its application to trifling instances of wrongdoing. With due regard to the effect on the community, its use should depend on the character and reformability of the defendant and not upon the name of the crime or offense with which he is charged. For this reason a reliable pre-sentence investigation is indispensable. Probation is preëminently social case work. While the character of a probation worker must be above reproach and he should possess a personality which commands respect and a desire to follow his guidance, nevertheless, training in social work technique is of prime importance.

If the probation officer has furnished the committing judge with a detailed and authenticated case history, he will be in a position to make a correct disposition of the prisoner's case with assurance, notwithstanding the enormity or triviality of the offense. At this point, as to be sure throughout the administration of a modern penal system, the idea of protection of the community will be uppermost in the court's mind.

Wherever probation can safely be imposed as a corrective discipline, its use should be given consideration.

Take the common case of the more or less despicable creature who refuses to support his wife and children. On the complaint of his long-suffering family he is brought into court. The judge imposes a sentence of three months for nonsupport. This doesn't help his wife much, and the county or State is burdened with the expense, slight though it may be, of maintaining him in jail. Suppose, instead, the court should say to the defendant:

"We will put you on probation for one year, during which time you must obtain employment and agree to turn half of your wages over to your wife; you must report weekly to the probation officer and advise him that these payments have been made, and if at any time you willfully fail to carry out the orders of the court you will be sentenced to a maximum penalty of one year in jail; the probation officer will assist you in obtaining employment, but the court will hear no excuse from you if you fail to live up to the terms of this probation agreement."

Our own opinion is that it is not to be regarded as an exhibition of leniency to put shiftless ne'er-do-well husbands to work, but that on the other hand it is a much more wholesome kind of punishment than thirty days of idleness in the county jail. As a matter of fact, judges have called our attention to many instances where defendants have preferred a short sentence to being put on probation with the requirement that they obtain and hold a steady job.

It is not my purpose here to recount the history and development of probation in this country, nor to rehearse the many sound arguments in support of the probation system. That has already been well done.[1] In some States probation has been very largely used by the courts as an alternative remedy, but in many other States there is no such thing as organized supervised probation. I venture to say there is not a prison in the

---

[1] Glueck, ed., *Probation and Criminal Justice;* Cooley, *Probation and Delinquency.*

country in which the warden could not point out dozens, or even hundreds, of inmates who, in his opinion, never should have been sentenced. It costs us, roughly speaking, one dollar a day to support a prisoner. It costs on the average ten cents a day for good probation supervision. Often a jail or prison commitment leaves a mark upon a man's character which many years do not eradicate. Good probation is a salvaging rather than a damaging process.

The Federal Government was without an official probation system until 1925, and not until 1930 was this organized on a substantial basis. Today the Bureau of Prisons supervises the work of 145 probation officers [2] and 120 probation clerks, appointed by and working in close harmony with the judges of the United States district courts. These judges, almost without exception, have testified to the assistance which they have derived from the work of these officers—not only as investigating agents, without whose services they would know little as to the real facts of the case before them, but as officers of the court in carrying out the terms and conditions of the probation sentence.

The following table will indicate not only the large growth in the utilization of probation in the Federal courts but the remarkably low percentage of probation violators, as recorded by the files of the Bureau of Prisons.

Colonel Joel R. Moore has done pioneer work in the development of Federal probation. With constantly increasing appropriations for the work we may look forward to the gradual reduction of the existing case load of 140 per officer, which is much too high. Experience is teaching us likewise that the best results in placing this service on a plane of permanent efficiency will not be achieved until all these officers are placed under the classified Civil Service.

Although there is a similarity in method to be employed both in probation supervision and in that necessary for the

[2] The annual appropriation act contains this language: "No part of any appropriation in this Act shall be used to defray the salary or expenses of any probation officer who does not comply with the official orders, regulations and probation standards promulgated by the Attorney General."

PERCENTAGE OF PROBATION VIOLATORS

Year	No. of Persons Discharged from Probation	No. Placed on Probation during Year by Courts	Total No. under Supervision during Year	No. Who Violated Their Probation	Percentage of Violators to Successful Discharges	Percentage of Violators to All Placed on Probation	Percentage of Violators to Total No. under Supervision
1931	3,300	12,340	16,621	444	13.5	3.6	2.7
1932	5,789	15,668	28,989	728	12.6	4.6	2.5
1933	10,427	18,097	41,297	1,244	11.9	6.9	3.0
1934	15,943	7,999	38,869	868	5.4	10.9	2.2
1935	14,574	8,881	31,807	726	5.0	8.2	2.3

success of any parole system, the two processes themselves are quite different. Probation offers an uncommitted offender a chance to avoid the necessity for a prison commitment and to work out his debt to society without ever being subject to a prison stigma. Parole, however, opens the door of the prison to the repentant offender and provides an intermediate status between residence in the prison and complete freedom in society.

Somehow or other probation, although it affects many times more individuals than parole, has not met the same blast of criticism. Probation is quite generally approved as affording the one more chance which we all deserve. Parole, on the other hand, seems to be begrudged by the public as something to which the prisoner was not entitled. Both are essential parts in any good prison program.

In the Federal system we are fortunate in having probation, prison administration, and parole supervision under one controlling agency, thus providing a somewhat continuing process. The probation officer's investigation into the individual's case (in the event that the probationer proves unsuitable for the extension of this privilege) is passed on to and is valuable to the prison warden, and later if the prisoner is paroled he again comes under the official supervision of the probation officer, who is already familiar with the case.

While probation is admittedly many times but a preliminary to imprisonment, or a postponement of the inevitable penalty, its use need not be discouraged on that account. At least the court will have had the satisfaction of passing on the case advisedly and in a humane manner.

In the large majority of instances, however, probation is literally an alternative to imprisonment or an avoidance of penalty. As such, it is not merely a mitigation of punishment, or, as Chief Justice Taft once termed it,[3] "an amelioration of the sentence." It becomes a disciplinary process, a successful effort at character rehabilitation and a contribution to the common welfare.

The total number of Federal prisoners at this writing is about 16,796, but there are 21,500 convicted persons undergoing probation discipline.[4]

It is hard at this point not to refer to the importance of a close alliance between the probation officer and the character building and crime prevention agencies in his district. The wisdom of the old adage that an ounce of prevention is worth a pound of cure is much more likely to prove itself through the agency of probation than in a penal institution.

An explanation of our disproportionately large penal population that may be mentioned here is that there is a large group of prisoners in the United States prisons and jails[5] which in foreign countries would not be considered subjects for penal discipline. I refer to the dipsomaniacs, drug addicts, and vagrants. These are not public enemies—they are their own worst enemies. The worst that can be said is that they are a nuisance to us. They require segregation, no doubt, but with the emphasis on cure rather than punishment. Most of them are poor; if they were not, they would be somewhere else

---

[3] *United States* v. *Murray*, 245 U.S. 347, 357.

[4] In Massachusetts, the birthplace of probation, the figures are even more striking. As against 7,500 men in all the prisons and houses of correction in Massachusetts, there are 22,000 convicted offenders under the care of the probation officers.

[5] Census Bureau figures show that out of 240,930 prisoners admitted to county and city jails for six months from January 1 to June 30, 1930, 101,487 were booked for disorderly conduct and drunkenness, and 19,493 for vagrancy, or more than one-half for these two offenses. See U.S. Bureau of the Census, *County and City Jails; Prisoners in Jails and Other Penal Institutions, etc.*, 1933.

than in prison. It is true that experiments with voluntary drug colonies and inebriate hospitals in America have not been reassuring, but it does not seem proper that our penitentiaries and houses of correction should be loaded up with unfortunates of this variety.

The enlightened community of tomorrow will discover some alternative to imprisonment for these types, as they are doing and have done for the insane, the psychotic, and the feebleminded.

Are there are any other alternative punishments by which the protracted, expensive, and debilitating experience of incarceration in a prison can be avoided? The imposition of fines, the deprivation of citizenship, the exaction of personal services, the making of restitution, the lowering in rank, the infliction of immediate pain or bodily discomfort, are measures which have from time to time been suggested and experimented with in many jurisdictions. If a defendant worships money and the things that money will buy, it may be the most excruciating kind of punishment to attack him in the pocketbook. Our old friend Shylock found it hard, you remember, to choose between his ducats and his daughter.

It is nevertheless true that the practice of administering money fines in this country has been greatly abused. One cannot imagine a much more futile process than to pick up a homeless, hungry drunk or vagrant, bring him into court, and administer the punishment which has come to be the formula in so many of our police courts, "$10 or twenty days." This is not much of an alternative in many instances, and the consequence is that our jails and workhouses throughout the country are loaded up with persons who are "serving out a fine." The question has been aptly raised, whether these men are imprisoned for crime or for their poverty.

It is also the practice even in the United States courts to administer fines in excessive amounts; under the Federal law the defendant may apply for relief at the end of thirty days of imprisonment solely on account of the fine, and if he succeeds in convincing the United States Commissioner that he has no money or property, he is released whether the fine be one dollar or ten thousand. For the year 1935 the total amount of fines imposed by the Federal Courts was $4,936,669 of which only $990,692 was collected.

If fines are to be used to punish people at a sensitive spot, it would seem as though some pre-sentence examination should be made to determine whether or not this kind of punishment would mean anything to the defendant. If the defendant has no money and no prospect of getting any, the imposition of a fine is not an alternative to imprisonment but merely another name for it. Nor is the levying of a fine always a deprivation to the defendant himself. Sometimes his father, or his wife, or his brother, pays the fine for him in order to avoid additional disgrace and publicity.

Of course fines may be much more effective when imposed in connection with probation and paid in installments than when settled by some sympathetic relative; and doubtless often such disposition of a criminal case constitutes a disciplinary measure and an adequate substitute for imprisonment.

A fine lacks meaning not only to the man too poor to pay it (except that he goes to jail if he doesn't) but also in a different sense to the man who is too rich to mind it. The practice of meting out money fines to the rich has often been condemned on this account. We sometimes hear it said, "The poor man has to go to prison. The rich man can buy immunity." No man's punishment should be lightened solely because he happens to be rich or influential.

In the case of the deliberate, cruel, scheming criminal, prison is a just reward, and the longer such a public menace is kept there the better for all concerned.

On the other hand there frequently appears a defendant—perhaps he is a merchant, a banker, small or large, a bookkeeper, or stock broker, or an unemployed artisan—who is truly an accidental offender. He has had his full dose of punishment before he marches up the granite steps to the prison. The court itself probably does not expect that a penitentiary term is necessary to reform these individuals. In fact, I have personally known men, some of them even from the so-called higher walks of life who have heaved a sigh of relief when the last hope of appeal was denied and they have entered the barred cell. Outside they have been besieged by reporters and camera men. The reproachful eyes of their families, the averted glances of their friends, and the loss of self-respect have been more bitter punishment than ever the plain gray suit and the meager fare of the prison can impose upon them. And this holds true not only in the case of the rich or influential but with men of impressionable disposition in all strata of society. The middle classes and even the very poor and their families are as sensitive to disgrace as are those more fortunately placed.[6]

If then they are not to be improved by a term in prison, and if the physical hardship or suffering connected with it is eclipsed or anticipated by their mental torment, why do we send this class of defendants there? In the first place, undoubtedly, in the conviction that we shall thus deter other men of their ilk from committing similar crimes. Have we ever definitely answered the question as to whether it is the prison sentence, or the loss of social prestige and the disgrace of exposure, which deters? In the second place, a conscientious judge believes that by imposing such a sentence he is maintaining the confidence of the populace in the impartiality of justice and proving that the law is no respecter of persons. In fact, we all take a grim and righteous satisfaction in seeing an influential sinner brought to book. We realize he has fallen further than the man of lesser estate, but we rightly say he had more advantages and a higher trust to fulfill and his penalty should be more severe.

I am not contending that prison sentences are avoidable in all this class of cases but is it a constructive process? How much real protection have we achieved?

There are many States in the country today where the conviction of a felony carries certain civil disabilities, such as

---

[6] For a discussion of the handicaps and disadvantages under which the poor have to labor to obtain justice, see Reginald H. Smith, *Justice and the Poor* and Sheldon S. Gleuck, *Crime and Justice*.

deprivation of the right to vote and hold office; but these penalties are usually in addition to imprisonment, not in substitution for it. Some day we may bring ourselves to a realization of the fact that in the case of many men the denial of their right to participate in a democratic government is a just penalty for the commission of a crime against such government, and this form of retribution need not be preceded or accompanied by a term in prison. Universal suffrage, of course, is the cornerstone of democracy with us, but there is no particular reason why we should allow ourselves to be led or our votes to be cast by men who demonstrate their utter disregard for the welfare of society as a whole.

The problem of how to employ or what to do with men who are under such disability, of course, is a serious one. There should be some method provided whereby they could earn back their civil rights by meritorious or unselfish service to the State.

Nowadays a position with the government or an honorable place in the industrial life of our cities is as high a privilege, perhaps, as liberty itself. When you take away a man's standing with his community, when his reputation for fair dealing is destroyed, when his self-respect is shattered, it is many times piling Ossa upon Pelion to add to the heavy load of shame and dishonor a term in prison.

The public does need protection, but is it entitled to this kind of revenge? If we deprive the man who has used his high office for his own profit, or has prostituted the opportunity which has been given him to serve his fellow men, his customers, or his country, forever of the chance of doing so again, we are really achieving something in the way of protection. Let the man who drives an automobile under the influence of liquor or so as to endanger lives be forever dispossessed of that privilege. Let a physician who improperly administers narcotics or assists in an illegal operation be forever denied the prerogatives of his profession, and let the lawyer who takes unfair advantage of his adversary, to conspire or connive with his criminal clients or to deceive the court, be for all time disbarred. These punishments though not so drastic can at least be made as immediate and effective as a term in prison.

A man's reputation is what his colleagues think of him. I remember a distinguished member of the Boston Bar, witty, popular, a fine after-dinner speaker and a member of several fraternal organizations. He became careless about money matters, was unable to return some of the funds that he had "borrowed" from a client and was disbarred. I have never seen a more deflated nor humiliated individual in my life. He was no longer debonair. He became a furtive ghost of his former self. No one could contend that his punishment was not crushing and complete, nor that a term in prison, no matter how long, would have added to his disgrace (it might even have relieved it) ; nor, I venture to assert, would it have materially added to the deterrent effect upon the other members of the Boston Bar.

We all know many cases such as this. It is difficult for us to observe many of these things in their proper perspective. We all need to resolve that the criminal law and our penal policies shall be shaped toward the protection of our communities rather than as channels for carrying out our private or public vengeance.

To some extent this is the philosophy behind the present penal policy of the Soviet Government. There the more orthodox crimes receive comparatively light punishment; but any luckless individual found guilty of interfering with official projects or of plotting to overthrow the present governmental structure or of conspiring against the success of the workers' state is promptly and severely dealt with. Something in the way of punishment could be devised here which would be more effective than the almost uniform system of applying the inevitable formula of "Crime plus conviction equals prison." If a man has been faithless to his trust or has stolen from his neighbor or the government, let him be compelled to work out his obligation in terms of increased service to the government. Instead of denying the right to work to men who owe the government something on account of a breach of an obligation, we could much more logically demand from them something in the way of public restitution or atonement. There is still much public work to be done. There are many public benefactions to be undertaken. If those who have done wrong and have any penitence or contrition in their make-up could be given the opportunity to repay their debt to society, society would be better off, and a culprit of the type described would himself benefit thereby.

I have known a score of men of character and culture who have gotten into prison, and whose first request of the warden has been: "Let me do something to help. Give me an opportunity to restore my standing. Let me help square myself by rendering some service to my fellow prisoners." Why should they not be permitted to be forces for good in the community?

A large part of our criminal population is composed of those who take property which belongs to others. In primitive times it was easier to distinguish between private wrongs, which seem to require a retributive or revengeful punishment, and public wrongs, which require the concerted action of the community to remove or prevent. Of course the latter are the true type of criminal action, but it is remarkable how so many of the acts which we regard today as major crimes are in effect more or less private in character.

If A steals from B, or C murders D, under the old law B could get his money back from A and the relatives of D could do to C exactly as he had been done by. We have made the avenging of these private wrongs a public concern, however, and we do not very clearly distinguish between private wrongs, such as debt, assault, deceit, and public wrongs, such as treason, graft and offenses against public order, decency and chastity. As a matter of fact, in most cases nowadays the public punishment is entirely substituted for private reparation. A criminal who has stolen money from his neighbor and who has been imprisoned for it feels that he thereby has paid the debt, and would scoff at the idea of returning the money to his victim.

Our prosecuting attorneys also look with suspicion and disfavor upon the use of the criminal law to redress private wrongs, when as a matter of fact that was its origin and purpose. It may be that, with respect to a large number of present-day crimes, we have relied too heavily upon the indiscriminate use of punishment that accompanies the redress of the more or less private wrongs. Thus there are many cases which have a criminal aspect which never come into our police courts because the defendant repays the stolen money to the complainant. I am suggesting here only that the practice of restitution as an alternative to punishment must be given a new and serious place in our penal scheme—not only restitution to the individual who is wronged but restitution to that larger society towards which the criminal has been faithless.

A prisoner who has taken the life of a child by reason of his reckless driving of an automobile might be given a chance to save the life of another or of many children as his retribution to human welfare.

A dishonest promoter who leaves a trail of disappointed and defrauded investors behind him owes them more than he will ever repay in ten years as clerk in a warden's office.

Is it not worth trying to provide the agencies to carry out some of these ideas? If it is a wholesome and regenerative process for a man who has done wrong to be given the opportunity to put himself right, there are many better ways in which we can do it other than placing him behind bars. Public-work projects, labor camps, and opportunities for individual or group service either to the government or to the neighborhood which has been wronged could be developed under much more hopeful auspices and with better chances of success than are the prisons of today.

It is evident that even with full reliance upon the utilization of these alternatives to imprisonment—(a) *probation,* for the trivial or accidental offender who can be disciplined extra-murally; (b) *money fine,* for those to whom it means a personal deprivation; (c) *disability* to pursue the calling which has been dishonored; (d) *social ostracism* or repudiation for those who have betrayed a trust; (e) *private restitution* for financial wrongs; (f) *public restitution* through service to the community whose interests and standards have been defiled—there will still be need for prisons designed for maximum security, albeit for a much smaller number of inmates.

For men of homicidal or vicious tendencies, for the incorrigible recidivist, the inveterate public enemy, the racketeer, the professional criminal, there appears to be no prospect but that of permanent segregation; for those whose personalities are warped by mental or physical disease or ravaged by drugs or alcohol, a segregation more or less permanent depending on their cure; and, for those who as a prerequisite to restoration to society need rigid training in self-control accompanied by physical, mental, and moral improvement, a reformatory regimen affording temporary segregation must be provided.

We shall doubtless always find it necessary to punish offenders who wilfully break the law. The sanction of our criminal codes must be maintained. We must never lose sight of the fact that the innocent victims of deliberate criminals should have first call on our sympathies.

A full realization of the practical value of deterrent punishment does not prevent us from predicting that to thousands of those whom down through the ages we have loaded into tumbrels and carted off to the bastile, the prison of the future may not be a prison at all. We might even go beyond that and say that the thoughtful and progressive municipality can find other and more satisfactory ways of enforcing its criminal law, which would pay substantially higher dividends in reformed manhood and public protection than can ever result from enforced incarceration.

CHAPTER XVIII

WILL IT WORK?

Guide the people by law, even them by punishment; they may shun crime, but will lack shame. Guide them by virtue, even them by *li* [mores, or equity], and they will develop a moral sense and become good.

CONFUCIUS.

WILL a prison system work which is founded on the principles we have endeavored to expound? At the last International Penal and Penitentiary Congress in Berlin in 1935, the topic which evoked more interest than all the others combined was the following:

Are the methods applied in the execution of sentences for the purpose of educating and reforming criminals (intensive humanization, extended favors, considerable relaxation, by degrees, of application of penalties) of such a nature as to produce the results intended, and are such tendencies generally expedient?

Likewise was this the only question out of twelve upon which no agreement could be reached. The majority of the countries represented felt that the answer should be in the affirmative, but the delegates were unable to come together on the exact language to express their meaning.

The difficulty in attempting to prove any thesis in connection with crime, punishment, or imprisonment is the lack of trustworthy evidence. There are too many variable factors, too many imponderable elements.

The advocates of swift and sure punishment, e.g., quote triumphantly the experience of Delaware and its whipping post and cite facts to show that thieves give the little State a wide berth (which they don't—as the figures [1] prove). But

---

[1] These figures taken from *Uniform Crime Reports,* Vol. VI, No. 4, p. 13, published by the Federal Bureau of Investigation.

they do not explain why the southern States with their chain gangs, sweat box, lash, and stocks have the highest crime and murder rates in the United States.

Most thinking people concede that there is a deterrent power in the death penalty, and yet strangely enough such statistics as we have, indicate that murder rates are lowest in the States which do not have the death penalty.

OFFENSES KNOWN TO POLICE PER 100,000, CALENDAR YEAR 1935

Eight States with Capital Punishment Four Highest		Eight States without Capital Punishment	
Alabama	30.	Maine	0.4
Tennessee	29.7	Rhode Island	1.7
Florida	23.4	Michigan	3.3
Georgia	21.9	Wisconsin	.9
Four Lowest		Minnesota	1.6
		North Dakota	1.9
Massachusetts	1.2	South Dakota	3.5
Connecticut	1.7	Kansas	5.7
Wyoming	1.9		
Oregon	2.6		

Instances are numerous where a drive on crime with a few killings and the imposition of severe sentences seems to have had a salutary effect, and yet there are times when the very publicity attendant upon a serious crime seems to stimulate further crime to an extent sufficient to offset any deterrent effect of the punishment.

When Clara Powers of California murdered her man with a hammer, the newspapers immediately christened her "The Hammer Queen." She was convicted and punished by a term in San Quentin; but a former official there is authority for the statement that, although that method of murder had been unknown in that region, three hammer murders followed closely thereafter.

I remember some years ago in Massachusetts a highly advertised case of hair snipping in the Boston subway where the culprit was caught and promptly sentenced for six months. Practically unknown at that time an epidemic of this variety of assault followed—ten or a dozen cases, as I recall it, being discovered in the next few months.

Who knows how many of the recent kidnappings and extortions were inspired and hatched in subnormal or immature minds by the tremendous publicity attending the tragic Lindbergh case? Would there have been as many if the newspapers had merely announced the event at the time and waited for the verdict to be rendered and then announced that? Would not the verdict have come far more quickly and certainly? Would not the law enforcement agencies have had an easier time? And would as many unemployed and restless boys have been tempted to try their hand at it? Who knows?

One might almost imagine the following paragraphs to have been written today. These are surely worth pondering. They were said by Judge Josiah Quincy to the Grand Jury of Suffolk County in March, 1822:

> Concerning the right of society to inflict this punishment, I can have no question. But in relation to the objects of such punishment;—terror—and the deterring of others, by the example of the victim's fate, in the forms and publicity of the execution of justice, there are strong reasons of doubt; especially with the accompaniments, which custom has established, and the law permits.
>
> A recent, and notorious instance, will explain the views on this subject, which I would bring before the consideration of the public.
>
> A villain of the baser sort, such as often escape from the gallows in Europe to find it in this country, lately paid the forfeit of his crimes in a county adjoining this metropolis. The day was appointed;—the time and place advertised. A mass of human beings, composing no inconsiderable portion of the population of this and the adjoining towns, precipitated themselves toward the spot. For what? To receive any moral, or religious, impression from the scene? To come away improved, in any feeling of the heart; instructed in any lesson of the understanding? Was there one of that vacant, gaping, thoughtless, jesting crowd, which were poised on every hill, and scrambling on every height, led by other motive than that instinctive, morbid sympathy, which in its healthy state, implanted by heaven, to make men alive, and active to relieve each other's misery, is then only

shameful, when perverted to base excitement and vulgar curiosity, in witnessing each other's sufferings?

Now, what did the scene exhibit, calculated to excite fear and deter guilt? The culprit, it is said, walked with a firm step and an undaunted air;—his confessor by his side. He surveyed the instrument of his fate unappalled, with an unconcern, expressing rather dignity than despair. He gave himself the signal for his exit. The astonished multitude surveyed him, as all crowds survey heroes; and he paid the forfeit of his crimes, it was said, with the assurance of a saint!

.   .   .   .

Learned men write the story of this hero and saint! The press scatters, in our stores, in our houses and our streets, the account of his crimes, his hardihood and his escapes; showing how slowly justice lingers; how long the wicked may enjoy a happy and hardened impunity! Now, what is there in all this to serve the end of society, in the example of his fate? On the contrary, if the love of fame be a passion common to the low as well as the high; to the base as well as the noble; if to go out of the world accompanied by the admiration of numbers, and by the promise of salvation, be one of the most natural and strongest desires in the human bosom, is not there somewhat in the scene, which I have sketched, and which is, in no part, exaggerated, of a character, almost, to invite and allure, rather than to deter?

It is possible to overdo this notion of punishment.

There are limits beyond which the conscience of a community, like the backs of the early convicts, becomes beaten into insensibility. If the victims do not mind punishment, or if they seek it in order to become martyrs, what effect can it have to control conduct?

Duranty relates the incident of three Russian communists who could easily have escaped the one-man firing squad which was leading them to death, but apparently preferred to die for a cause.

The punishment of the Christian martyrs by Rome but helped to disseminate their faith.

Can punishment overcome the inborn passions and customs of a tribe or nation? In the remote tribes of Esquimos a tribal custom prevails which permits the favored son to kill his parent. It is considered more humane in a land where there are no doctors, no hospitals, no medicines. Recently on their annual trip to this far country a Government committee found a case of "murder" of this sort. Two Esquimos are now, as a result, serving sentences of thirty years in a Federal prison—if they live that long.

Sutherland tells of a tribe in Africa where it is a crime not to have more than one wife.

Can punishment stop illicit distilling in Kentucky?

In China bigamy was permitted for the man, since it was an aid to family continuation, and to murder one's father's enemy was a vivid expression of filial piety.

Can we stop suicides? That is the swiftest and surest punishment of all.

We shudder when told that there were more than 10,000 homicides in America last year. But there were 20,000 suicides. If a man kills another, a wave of anger sweeps the neighborhood. We try him to the accompaniment of the usual courthouse hippodrome, with news reels, amplifiers, movie men, feature writers, hot-dog stands, pennants, and arm bands. We soon begin to call the murderer and his victim and the chief witnesses by their first names, and for months a large portion of the daily press and tabloids nauseate us with every harrowing detail.

But if he turns the gun on himself too, thus being a murderer *and* a suicide, the event is dismissed with half a column.

We may never be able to evaluate punishment. We may never be able to prove that any other treatment than punishment is effective.

An extremely able and thoughtful study of crime, law, and social order has been made by Michael and Adler. Their research into the subject was deep and penetrating, but this is their conclusion:

The justifiability of a mode of treatment as deterrent is, therefore, to be determined differently and separately from its justifiability as a reformative. The difficulty resulting from the separation of a deterrence and reformation in the justification of modes of treatment may be an insuperable one. Thus, for instance, it may be discovered that the infliction of pain is more effective as a deterrent than non-punitive modes of treatment and that the greater the pain inflicted the greater the deterrence. It may also be discovered that treatment is more effective in the reformation of all classes of offenders, or of most classes of offenders, to the extent that it is non-punitive. Were this known, it would be necessary to decide whether deterrence or reformation is the more effective means to the common good, or whether some compromise can be made between these opposing means. Questions of this sort may be forever unanswered and our determination of the justifiable modes of treating offenders may forever rest upon guesses or conjectures.[2]

Punishment for wrongdoing is a law of nature, you say, and needs no statistical defense. And so it is. But nature rarely overdoes it, and time after time she puts us on probation or parole. "Punishment needs no defence because it squares with our own notions of fairness and justice." To the virtuous go the rewards, and to the sinful go the penalties. This is commanded by God as revealed in the Scriptures, and after all we rather like the idea of *quid pro quo,* tooth for tooth, and eye for eye. But the defense of punishment must needs be based on one's own hunch because the statistics do not seem to prove much in its favor.

Strangely enough figures can be cited which appear to show that the less punishment a State administers, the less crime it has.

It would be foolish to claim that in Massachusetts, for instance, there is less crime *because* less punishment is inflicted, *but we can conclude that crime reduction there has been consistent with humane prison administration.*

Recent statistics from Great Britain indicate that a reduction in prison population in the last sixty years of 81 per cent was not accompanied by any increase in crime. On the other hand, we find that the prosecutions in the same period were

[2] *Crime, Law and Social Science,* by Jerome Michael and Mortimer J. Adler, p. 364.

STATES WHERE PAROLE, PROBATION, AND HUMANE PRISON
TREATMENT ARE HIGHLY DEVELOPED

	No. of Prisoners Committed 1933 per 100,000*	Offenses Known to Police for Year 1935 per 100,000†		
		Robbery	Larceny	Aggravated Assault
Massachusetts	32.1	22.8	437.2	13.7
New York	33.9	15.7	424.0	30.1
Minnesota	61.7	69.5	451.2	15.2
New Jersey	60.2	38.4	540.2	51.2
Connecticut	51.4	19.4	611.5	14.1
Wisconsin	48.6	10.4	640.6	8.6
Pennsylvania	29.8	43.2	225.6	30.8

STATES WHERE PAROLE AND PROBATION AS SYSTEMS ARE NOT
LARGELY DEVELOPED AND ORTHODOX PRISON TREATMENT
IS MAINTAINED

	No. of Prisoners Committed 1933 per 100,000*	Offenses Known to Police for Year 1935 per 100,000†		
		Robbery	Larceny	Aggravated Assault
Maryland	253.0	40.5	497.2	9.4
Virginia	114.0	82.8	1585.3	258.0
South Carolina	59.9	40.0	1905.4	152.3
Tennessee	92.3	158.0	409.7	206.6
North Carolina	64.7	65.7	813.1	523.3
Delaware (whipping post)..	—	27.2	664.2	58.2
Kentucky	132.9	139.5	1205.7	178.8

* Taken from U. S. Bureau of the Census, *Prisoners in State and Federal Prisons and Reformatories in 1933*, p. 8.

† Taken from *Uniform Crime Reports*, Federal Bureau of Investigation, Department of Justice, Vol. VI, No. 4, p. 13.

reduced 41 per cent, and crimes known to the police were reduced by 43 per cent.[3]

The London *Daily Telegraph* of April 27, 1936, under the heading "Abolition of Prisons in Britain," makes these significant statements:

Only one-third as many people go to prison each year in Britain now compared with a quarter of a century ago.

The far-reaching changes in the prison system during the twenty-five years are reviewed in the report for 1934 of Commissioners of Prisons and the Directors of Convict Prisons.

"The results so far achieved," the Commissioners declare, "justify confidence that we are advancing in the right direction."

Annual prison receptions fell from 186,398 to 56,425 between 1910 and 1934; the daily average prison population dropped from 20,826 to 12,238. This remarkable decrease in prisoners has enabled local prisons to be reduced from 56 in 1910 to 26 at the present time.

These results are attributed to important reforms in the criminal law, reduction in the number of long sentences, and a general improvement of social habits and conditions. Criminal law reforms have helped to reduce the prison population by providing for the placing of offenders on probation; giving time for the payment of fines; raising the age for committal of children; restricting the sale of intoxicants; clearing the prisons of feeble-minded prisoners who are unfit for penal discipline.

Committals for drunkenness fell from 54,452 in 1910 to 6,835 in 1934.

Following are some of the outstanding changes in prison administration during the period under review: Borstal institutions established, 1909; routine solitary confinement abolished; broad arrow removed from clothing, 1921; prisoners allowed to shave; monthly lectures and concerts; adult education introduced, 1923; women appointed to visiting committees for both women and men; conversation permitted between prisoners at work and at certain other times.

An important change was the abolition of unremunerative labor, such as the crank and treadmill, and the replacement of low-grade work, such as picking oakum and sorting wool, by industrial employment.

---

[3] E. N. Sutherland, "The Decreasing Prison Population of England," *Journal of Criminal Law and Criminology*, Vol. XXIV, No. 5, p. 884.

Not apparently by lengthening sentences, or withdrawing privileges, or denying parole, has Great Britain reduced its crime bill!

While I have expressed some doubts herein as to the ultimate possibility of establishing enough prisons that really reform, the whole thesis of this book must be seen to be a contention that constructive discipline (an absence of brutality on the one hand and sentimentality on the other); an understanding of the individual; the abolition of the county jail so hopelessly enmeshed in local politics and the substitution for it of better methods of handling prisoners awaiting trial as well as State labor camps; the increased emphasis on the duty of prisons to restore men to society less dangerous; segregation, more or less permanent, of the incorrigible criminal; a properly administered parole supervision system applying to all released prisoners; probation as a constructive discipline for minor or accidental offenders, are the component parts of a humane penal program which may succeed where swift and sure punishment unaccompanied by such effort will not.

I nourish no illusions as to the predatory criminal of the gangster type, nor the racketeer who turns to crime as to a business opportunity, nor the killer who eventually becomes in a sense his own exterminator. I share the public demand for prompt and effective retribution for the deliberate criminal. I do say, there are as many kinds of criminals as there are kinds of human beings, and that the reformable ones far outnumber the incorrigibles. While the Dillingers, the Nelsons, and the Floyds must be shot down, some one else must be laboring patiently to prevent recidivism among the occasional offenders.

Fortunately we are not compelled to rely entirely on our hopes and beliefs to prove the absolute necessity of such effort. Individual case after individual case can be cited where constructive methods have succeeded. The statistics by States (such as they are) are convincing to the effect that probation, parole, and humane prison treatment are synonymous with the public protection.

Coming back to the gangster for a moment, we may also observe that, while summary and severe punishment or extermination may serve in this generation, it will not solve the problem for the next. We shall be told that those fine-sounding principles we have enumerated above do not work in the case of the confirmed predatory criminal—and so they do not. We shall have to get at the gangster much earlier in life than we do now. If the gangster was once a neglected or unwanted child, or a mischievous uncontrolled boy, or the product of a broken home, or the worshiping satellite of some crooked politician, or the reader of a crime-soaked tabloid, or unduly influenced by the brand of sensational movie which, let us hope, is now passing away, or the victim of any other disordered social condition, we must accept our share of responsibility for his continuance.

We may control him, but we cannot cure or reform a confirmed gangster by punishment. If, however, we could get hold of him early enough, in a community that realizes the effect of heredity and environment on a growing and underprivileged boy, we could do something.

Rather than dramatize his exploits by overpublicity, or add to his prestige among his own circle by making a martyr of him, we shall remove him from the ranks of criminal recruits by furnishing him with wholesome outlets and a chance in a lawful direction to satisfy his craving for leadership or distinction.

Confronted with the early history of many of his inmates, no one realizes the need for crime prevention better than the prison warden.

We have spoken in these pages largely of our efforts with the *adult offender*. Perhaps the work with mature inmates is the most discouraging and most unpromising of all society's efforts to repress crime.

The conviction that attempts at restoring the criminal are much more likely to succeed with juveniles than with adults led twenty-five years ago to the establishment of juvenile courts throughout the country. Whether this is the right method or not is still problematical, but we are, I think, secure in the belief that young offenders are deserving of special consideration.[4]

At least we have made the effort in the Department of Justice to discriminate in the cases of the relatively few minors with which we have to deal. An Act passed by Congress on June 11, 1932, makes it possible for a United States District Attorney to waive prosecution in the case of a defendant under twenty-one years of age provided arrangements can be made with the State authorities to apply the remedy appropriate to juvenile offenders in that State. Where this cannot be done, care is taken to see to it that the juvenile, if of impressionable age and disposition, is sent on conviction to the best available industrial reformatory in his vicinity.

Thus do we obviate the necessity of installing in the Federal judicial and penal systems the separate machinery so advisable in the case of delinquents of immature years.

Much remains to be done, it may be said in passing, to bring these same State schools up to the level of the best juvenile institutions. This is not our task but rather that of the States themselves through the guidance of the Children's Bureau.

Sufficient is it for the Federal Prison Bureau to record its profound persuasion that the problem of American boyhood is in its essence the problem of America's future. We stand ready to assist in every way. A valiant effort is being made to solve it by organizations such as the Boy Scouts, Boys' Clubs of America, the American Legion, Rotary Clubs, and by Co-ordinating Councils which, as in Los Angeles, mobilize the conscience of the neighborhood.

How many mothers are finding themselves in the position of this one who writes:

I wonder what is to become of our young men? I mean the boys who are being left out while married men are given their jobs some of whom would just as soon not work, many whose wives and daughters are working. Take my own boy who was

[4] Glueck, *1,000 Juvenile Delinquents.*

laid off over two years ago to make room for a married man who worked a few days and quit.

Well, Wednesday, April 11, they are taking my boy, 23 years old, who never gave his dad and mother a minute of worry, to prison for holding up a store and getting 25 dollars. He used $1.50 to have his shoes half soled and paid $1.50 on a bill the man had sued his dad for. The boy he was with is the same type of boy. Everybody knows them both to be good, clean, normal young men. They are being taken away for from one to five years and I, his mother, don't even know which place he is being taken to, and if it is only one year what have they to come back to whether it is one year or forty. What can they do? A prison record. Their first and only mistake.

It's been hard to see that hopeless look come to my boy's face each time he came home and said, "No luck, mom," but when I told him good bye and had to see him try to smile and say, "Buck up, mom"—it was hard to take. I only hope I can still say, "Thy will be done," and mean it. Right now I can't do it.

The battle against crime is a battle on many fronts. The important thing is that there should be one master motive controlling all operations. It will not do for one division of the army to be sniping at or outflanking another, and somebody must keep the enemy from bringing up his reinforcements.

Those in charge of prisons have a duty to perform, in some ways the hardest one of all; but it is not, or should not be, inconsistent with any other effort. Police, investigative agencies, courts, probation officers, district attorneys, prison and parole officers, social agencies, and the general public all form parts of this army.

I hope I have been neither too optimistic nor too skeptical in this statement of the penal problem. I am convinced of one thing—that it cannot be solved through anger, or hatred, or oversentimentality, or prejudice, or by blinding our eyes to the facts.

Will such a system work? The experience of England, and some of our American systems, are evidence that it does work. The available statistics, a few of which have been quoted herein, prove that it works.

The prison can never solve the crime problem, however. It touches only a trifling percentage of our lawbreakers. Crime will abate only as the people as a whole resolve to set up within themselves higher and more unselfish standards of conduct. Aiding in the carrying out of this resolve will be enlisted (1) a press more devoted to leadership and less to entertainment of its readers and profit for itself; (2) an organized neighborhood movement to coördinate social betterment projects; (3) an educational system that holds instruction in character to be paramount; (4) a spirit of sportsmanship that puts civic duty above personal advantage; (5) a modernized judicial procedure which seeks only to determine truth; (6) an economic order which affords equal opportunity for all but does not remove incentive to work; (7) a wise application of the truly scientific attitude motivated by altruism rather than self-aggrandizement; (8) a reincarnated religion which relates itself to the daily life of the people. With increasing emphasis in the years that are to come, others more eloquent than I will fling the challenge of crime back to the community that tolerates it and demand its eradication at the source.

.   .   .   .

The end and aim of a penal system is the protection of society.

This is its only justification as one of our defences against crime and lawlessness.

I have tried to test all my theories by that fundamental proposition; probation, prison labor, prison camps, Alcatraz, Chillicothe, individualization of punishment, parole and prevention, and deportation, if necessary—all must contribute to that ultimate object.

Our communities are entitled to protection. They are not entitled to vengeance. If we are to achieve our portion of this object, we shall do it by a greater understanding and coöperation among all crime reduction agencies, by an intelligent and frequent use of scientific discoveries, through the enlistment in our work of loyal and devoted public servants and by never for one moment losing our faith in the ultimate worth and possibilities of redemption of the human soul.

SELECTED READINGS

BURGESS, E. C., "The Study of the Delinquent as a Person" (*American Journal of Sociology*, vol. xxviii, pp. 657–680.

GAULT, ROBERT H., Criminology. Boston: Heath, 1932.

GILLIN, JOHN L., Criminology and Penology. New York: Century, 1926.

GLUECK, SHELDON, Crime and Justice. Boston: Little, Brown, 1936.

GLUECK, SHELDON, Mental Disorder and the Criminal Law. Boston: Little, Brown, 1925.

GLUECK, SHELDON AND ELEANOR, Five Hundred Criminal Careers. New York: Knopf, 1930.

HAYNES, FRED E., Criminology. New York: McGraw-Hill, 1930.

LAWES, LEWIS S., 20,000 Years in Sing Sing. New York: R. R. Smith, 1932.

LEWIS, BURDETTE G., The Offender and His Relations to Law and Society. New York: Harper, 1921.

Reports of Proceedings of Attorney General Cummings' Crime Conference.

Reports of the American Prison Association.

ROBINSON, LOUIS N., Penology in the United States. Philadelphia: Winston, 1921.

SUTHERLAND, EDWIN H., Criminology. Philadelphia: Lippincott, 1924.

WHITE, WILLIAM A., Crimes and Criminals. New York: Farrar & Rinehart, 1932.

WINES, FREDERICK H., Punishment and Reformation. New York: Crowell, 1919.

VOLD, G. B., Prediction Methods and Parole. Hanover, N. H.: Sociological Press, 1931.

APPENDIX A

DECLARATION OF PRINCIPLES OF 1870 OF THE AMERICAN PRISON ASSOCIATION

AS REVISED AND REAFFIRMED AT THE SIXTIETH ANNUAL CONGRESS OF THE AMERICAN PRISON ASSOCIATION HELD IN LOUISVILLE, KENTUCKY, OCTOBER 10 TO 16, 1930.

I. Crime is a violation of duties imposed by law, which inflicts an injury upon others. Criminals are persons convicted of crime by competent courts. Punishment is suffering inflicted on the criminal for the wrong done by him, with a special view to secure his reformation.

II. The treatment of criminals by society is for the protection of society. But since such treatment is directed to the criminal rather than to the crime, its great object should be his moral regeneration. Hence the supreme aim of prison discipline is the reformation of criminals, not the infliction of vindictive suffering.

III. The progressive classification of prisoners, based on study of the individual, and administered on some well-adjusted system should be established in all prisons above the common jail.

IV. Since hope is a more potent agent than fear, it should be made an ever-present force in the hands of prisoners, by a well-devised and skillfully-applied system of rewards for good conduct, industry and attention to learning. Rewards, more than punishments, are essential to every good prison system.

V. The prisoner's destiny should be placed, measurably in his own hands; he must be put into circumstances where he will be able, through his own exertions, to continually better his own condition. A regulated self-interest must be brought into play, and made constantly operative.

VI. The two master forces opposed to the reform of the prison systems of our several states are political appointments, and a consequent instability of administration. Until both are eliminated, the needed reforms are impossible.

VII. Special training, as well as high qualities of head and heart, is required to make a good prison or reformatory officer. Then only will the administration of public punishment become scientific, uniform and successful, when it is raised to the dignity of a profession, and men are specially trained for it, as they are for other pursuits. The development of schools for the training of prison executives and guards, along the lines already started in this and other countries, should be promoted throughout the United States.

VII. Peremptory sentences ought to be replaced by those of indeterminate length. Sentences limited only by satisfactory proof of reformation should be substituted for those measured by mere lapse of time.

IX. Of all reformatory agencies, religion is first in importance because most potent in its action upon the human heart and life.

X. Education is a vital force in the reformation of fallen men and women. Its tendency is to quicken the intellect, inspire self-respect, excite to higher aims, and afford a healthful substitute for low and vicious amusements. Recreation is considered to be an essential part of education. It has come to be recognized that recreation is an indispensable factor of normal human life. This principle is now heartily indorsed by prison administrators. Education in its broadest sense is, therefore, a matter of primary importance in prisons.

XI. In order to the reformation of imprisoned criminals, there must be not only a sincere desire and intention to that end but a serious conviction in the minds of the prison officers, that they are capable of being reformed, since no man can heartily maintain a discipline at war with his inward beliefs; no man can earnestly strive to accomplish what in his heart he despairs of accomplishing.

XII. A system of prison discipline, to be truly reformatory must gain the will of the prisoner. He is to be amended; but how is this possible with his mind in a state of hostility? No system can hope to succeed which does not secure this harmony of wills, so that the prisoner shall choose for himself what his officer chooses for him. But to this end, the officer must really choose the good of the prisoner, and the prisoner must remain in his choice long enough for virtue to become a habit. This consent of wills is an essential condition of reformation.

XIII. The interest of society and the interest of the convicted criminal are really identical, and they should be made practically so. At present there is a combat between crime and laws. Each sets the other at defiance, and as a rule, there is little kindly feeling, and few friendly acts, on either side. It would be otherwise if criminals, on conviction, instead of being cast off, were rather made the objects of a generous parental care; that is, if they were trained to virtue, and not merely sentenced to suffering.

XIV. The prisoner's self-respect should be cultivated to the utmost, and every effort made to give back to him his manhood. There is no greater mistake in the whole compass of penal discipline, than its studied imposition of degradation as a part of punishment. Such imposition destroys every better impulse and aspiration. It crushes the weak, irritates the strong, and indisposes all to submission and reform. It is trampling where we ought to raise and is therefore as unchristian in principle as it is unwise in policy.

XV. In prison administration, moral force should be relied upon, with as little admixture of physical force as possible, and organized persuasion be made to take the place of coercive restraint, the object being to make upright and industrious freemen, rather than orderly and obedient prisoners. Brute force may make good prisoners; moral training alone will make good citizens. To the latter of these ends, the living soul must be won; to the former, only the inert and obedient body.

XVI. Industrial training should have both a higher development and a greater breadth than has heretofore been, or is now, commonly given to it in our prisons. Work is no less an auxiliary to virtue, than it is a means of support. Steady, active, honorable labor, with reasonable compensation to the prisoner, is the basis of all reformatory discipline. It not only aids reformation, but is essential to it. It was a maxim with Howard, "make men diligent, and they will be honest"—a maximum which this congress regards as eminently sound and practical.

XVII. While industrial labor in prisons is of the highest importance and utility to the prisoner, and by no means injurious to the laborer outside, we regard the contract system of prison labor as prejudicial alike to discipline, finance, and the reformation of the prisoner, and sometimes injurious to the interest of the free laborer.

XVIII. The most valuable parts of an effective prison system —the more strictly penal stage of separate imprisonment, the reformatory stage of progressive classification, and the probationary stage of training—are believed to be as applicable to one country as to another.

XIX. Prisons, as well as prisoners, should be classified or graded so that there shall be provisions for the untried, for the incorrigible, and for other degrees of depraved character, as well as separate establishments for women, and for offenders of the younger classes.

XX. It is the judgment of this congress, that repeated short sentences for minor criminals are worse than useless; that, in fact, they rather stimulate than repress transgressions. Reformation is a work of time; and a benevolent regard to the good of the criminal himself, as well as to the protection of society, requires that his sentence be long enough for reformatory processes to take effect.

XXI. Preventive measures for the care and treatment of problem children, not yet delinquent, but in danger of becoming so, constitute the true field of promise, in which to labor for the repression of crime.

XXII. More systematic and comprehensive methods should be adopted to save discharged prisoners, by providing them with work and encouraging them to redeem their character and regain their lost position in society. The state has not discharged its whole duty to the criminal when it has punished him, nor even when it has reformed him. Having raised him up, it has the further duty to aid in holding him up. And to this end it is desirable that state societies be formed which shall cooperate with each other in this work.

XXIII. The successful promotion of crime requires the combined action of promoters and operatives, just as other crafts do. There are two well-defined classes engaged in criminal operations, who may be called the criminal promoters and the operatives. It is obvious that a more effective warfare may be carried on against crime by striking at these criminal promoters as a class rather than at the operatives one by one. Certainly, this double warfare should be vigorously pushed, since from it the best results, as regards repressive justice, may be reasonably hoped for.

XXIV. Since personal liberty is the rightful inheritance of every human being, it is the sentiment of this congress that the state which has deprived an innocent citizen of this right and subjected him to penal restraint, should, on unquestionable proof of its mistake, make reasonable indemnification for such wrongful imprisonment.

XXV. Mental disorder is a question of vital interest to society; and facts show that our laws regarding mental disorder in its relation to crime need revision in order to bring them to a more complete conformity to the demands of reason, justice and humanity; so that, when mental disorder is pleaded in bar of conviction, the investigation may be conducted with greater knowledge, dignity, and fairness; criminal responsibilities be more satisfactorily determined; the punishment of the sane criminal be made more sure, and the restraint of the insane be rendered at once more certain and more humane.

XXVI. While this congress would not shield the convicted criminal from the just responsibility of his misdeeds, it arraigns society itself as in no slight degree accountable for the invasion of its rights and the warfare upon its interests, practised by the criminal classes. Does society take all the steps which it easily might, to change, or at least to improve, the circumstances in our social state that lead to crime, or when crime has been committed to cure the proclivity to it, generated by these circumstances? It cannot be pretended. Let society, then, lay the case earnestly to its conscience, and strive to mend in both particulars. Offenses, we are told by a high authority, must come; but a special woe is denounced against those through whom they came. Let us take heed that that woe fall not upon our head.

XXVII. The exercise of executive clemency in the pardon of criminals is a practical question of grave importance, and of great delicacy and difficulty. The effect of the too free use of the pardoning power is to detract from the certainty of punishment for crime, and to divert the mind of prisoners from the means supplied for their improvement. Pardons should issue for one or more of the following reasons, viz.: To release the innocent, to correct mistakes made in imposing the sentence, to relieve such suffering from ill health as requires release from imprisonment, and to facilitate or reward the real reformation of the prisoner. The final exercise of this power should be by the executive, and should be guarded by careful examination as to the character of the prisoner and his conduct in prison. Furthermore, it is the opinion of this congress that governors of states should give to their respective legislatures the reasons, in each case, for their exercise of the pardoning power.

XXVIII. The proper duration of imprisonment for a violation of the laws of society is one of the most perplexing questions in criminal jurisprudence. The present extraordinary inequality of sentences for the same or similar crimes is a source of constant irritation among prisoners, and the discipline of our prisons suffers in consequence. The evil is one for which some remedy should be devised.

XXIX. Uniform criminal statistics, gathered from every state, and skilfully digested, are essential to an exhibition of the true character and working of our correctional systems. The collection, collation, and reduction to tabulated forms, of such statistics, can best be effected through the appropriate federal bureau.

XXX. Prison architecture is a matter of grave importance. Prisons of every class should be substantial structures, affording gratification by their design and material to a pure taste, but not costly or highly ornate. We are of the opinion that those of moderate size are best, as regards both industrial and reformatory ends.

XXXI. The construction, organization, and management of all prisons should be by the state, and they should form a graduated series of reformatory establishments, being arranged with a view to the industrial employment, intellectual education and moral training of the inmates.

XXXII. As a general rule, the maintenance of penal institutions, above the county jail, should be, as far as possible, from the earnings of their inmates, and with a minimum cost to the state; nevertheless, the true standard of merit in their management is the rapidity and thoroughness of reformatory effect accomplished thereby.

XXXIII. A right application of the principles of sanitary science in the construction and arrangement of prisons is a point of vital importance. A competent and adequate medical staff is essential. The apparatus for heating and ventilating should be the best that is known; sunlight, air and water should be afforded according to the abundance with which nature has provided them; the rations and clothing should be plain but wholesome, comfortable, and in sufficient but not extravagant quantity; the bedsteads, bed and bedding, including sheets and pillow cases, not costly but decent, and kept clean, well aired and free from vermin; the hospital accommodations, medical stores and surgical instruments should be all that humanity requires and science can supply; and all needed means for personal cleanliness should be without stint.

XXXIV. Probation and parole are among the most vital factors in the rehabilitation of the delinquent and the criminal. Probation is the release of the convicted delinquent, under competent supervision, without commitment to an institution. Parole is a conditional release of the prisoner after having served a portion of his sentence. The overcrowding of our prisons, and the demoralization of young and inexperienced criminals by vicious association, can be greatly diminished by the use of these measures, but these two plans are ineffective unless efficiently organized with trained, competent, and well-paid probation and parole officers.

XXXV. It is our conviction that the most effective agency in the repression of crime is suitable education for all the children of the state. Educational training should be adapted to the mental abilities and aptitudes of each child, and should develop character, emotional stability, and the creative and productive capabilities of each individual. Education, in its broadest sense, includes more than the training provided in the classrooms and laboratories of our institutions of learning. It includes the training for citizenship which youth receives from the many environmental factors which include home life, religious training, wholesome recreation, and the example set by the civic life of the community.

XXXVI. As a principle that crowns all, and is essential to all, it is our conviction that no prison system can be perfect, or even successful to the most desirable degree, without some central authority to sit at the helm, guiding, controlling, unifying and vitalizing the whole. We ardently hope yet to see all the departments of our preventive, reformatory and penal institutions in each state moulded into one harmonious and effective system; its parts mutually answering to and supporting each other; and the whole animated by the same spirit, aiming at the same objects, and subject to the same control; yet without loss of the advantages of voluntary aid and effort, wherever they are attainable.

XXXVII. This congress is of the opinion that, both in the official administration of such a system, and in voluntary cooperation of citizens therein, the agency of women may be employed with excellent effect.

APPENDIX B

COMPACT OF FAIR COMPETITION FOR THE PRISON INDUSTRIES OF THE UNITED STATES OF AMERICA

THIS AGREEMENT made and entered into jointly and severally by and between the several States signatory hereto, as of the date of execution of each of said several States,

WITNESSETH that, whereas, under date of October 21, 1933, the President of the United States approved the Code of Fair Competition for the Retail Trade under the National Industrial Recovery Act, which said Code of Fair Competition contained, among other things, the following:

"Pending the formulation of a compact or code between the several States of the United States to insure the manufacture and sale of prison-made goods on a fair competitive basis with goods not so produced, the following provisions of this Section will be stayed for ninety (90) days, or further at the discretion of the Administrator:

(1) Where any penal, reformatory or correctional institution, either by subscribing to the code or compact hereinbefore referred to, or by a binding agreement of any other nature, satisfies the Administrator that merchandise produced in such institution or by the inmates thereof will not be sold except upon a fair competitive basis with similar merchandise not so produced, the provisions of paragraph (2) hereof shall not apply to any merchandise produced in such manner in the institutions covered by such agreement.

(2) Except as provided in the foregoing paragraph, no retailer shall knowingly buy or contract to buy any merchandise produced in whole or in part in a penal, reformatory or correctional institution. After May 31, 1934, no retailer shall knowingly sell or offer for sale such merchandise. Nothing in this Section, however, shall affect contracts, which the retailer does not have the option to cancel, made

with respect to such merchandise before the approval of this Compact by the President of the United States."

WHEREAS, prior to the presentation of the above described Retail Code to the President of the United States for his approval the several States of the United States had begun to formulate a Compact of Fair Competition for said prison industries, and

WHEREAS, it is the desire of the signatory States to continue the use of the most important instrumentality for the rehabilitation of prisoners—namely, productive labor—and to achieve this purpose in a manner which will comply with the fair methods of competition desired by modern commerce and particularly in accordance with the National Industrial Recovery Act, and whereas these States desire to apply to the prison labor problem a system of rules, uniform in principle and equitable to all, and

WHEREAS, it is equally the desire of the States signatory hereto that the provisions hereof establishing uniform principles will facilitate the maintenance of fair competition in American industry and will aid in effectuating the administration of the National Industrial Recovery Act,

NOW, THEREFORE, for and in consideration of the premises and of the mutual benefits to be derived herefrom the States signatory hereto, jointly and severally, agree as follows:

ARTICLE I

As used herein the following terms have the meaning as shown unless the contrary appears:

The term "penal or correctional institution" shall include any prison, penitentiary, reformatory, workhouse, jail or other institution wholly tax-supported and maintained for the incarceration or imprisonment of persons convicted of an offense against the laws of the United States, any State or its political subdivision, but shall not include institutions maintained under the jurisdiction of private, charitable or religious organizations.

The term "prison industry" as used herein shall mean any industry or trade in whatever manner operated for the mining, manufacture, production and/or distribution of products, in which are employed inmates of penal or correctional institutions or other persons who at the time of employment are serving a sentence imposed by a court of the United States or any State: provided, that no agricultural activities not a part of any trade or industry shall be considered a prison industry as herein defined.

"Products" shall mean all goods, wares, merchandise and minerals manufactured, produced or mined in whole or in part by prison industry for other than State use.

ARTICLE II

Hours of Labor. The hours of labor in prison industries shall be not more than those prescribed by the applicable Code adopted under the laws of the United States governing each particular industry, but in no case shall any inmate be required or permitted to work in any prison industry more than forty hours in any one week.

ARTICLE III

The hours of operation of productive machinery shall be not more than is prescribed in the code of the competing private domestic industry.

ARTICLE IV

Child Labor. No person under the age of sixteen years shall be employed in any prison industry. No person under the age of eighteen years shall be employed at operations or occupations which are hazardous in nature or dangerous to health.

ARTICLE V

Section A. Prison products, when sold by the prison or through a contractor, whether sold direct or through any agency, shall be sold not lower than the fair current price prevailing in the market in which the product is customarily sold—to wholesalers, retailers, or consumers as the case may be.

Section B. No penal or correctional institution or agency thereof shall enter into any contract for the labor of prisoners which does not insure a return from the contractor to the State or its political subdivision and/or the prisoner of an amount equal in value to the cost per unit of product for labor and overhead necessarily paid in competing domestic private industry on the comparable product provided, that the imposition or collection of such amounts or charges shall not be such as will require the sale of prison products at a higher price than specified in Section A hereof.

ARTICLE VI

State Use Products and Public Works. The restrictions in this compact shall not apply to goods, wares or merchandise manufactured, produced or mined by any penal or correctional institution which are solely for the use of tax-supported institutions, agencies, departments, or activities of any State or its political subdivision, nor shall they apply to the construction of public works or ways financed wholly from funds of the State or its political subdivision.

ARTICLE VII

Further to effectuate the policies of this compact, a committee (hereinafter called the Prison Labor Authority) is hereby constituted to coöperate with prison. industry, private industry, the several States signatory hereto, and the United States in the administration of this Compact.

(1) *Organization and Constitution of the Prison Labor Authority.* The Prison Labor Authority shall consist of nine members, six (6) of whom shall be elected annually by representatives of the States signatory hereto, and three (3) to be appointed by the President to represent labor, industry and consumers, respectively.

(2) The Prison Labor Authority shall have the following duties and powers, subject to the right of the President, on review, to disapprove or modify any action taken by the Prison Labor Authority (the President may delegate any of the functions and powers under this compact to such officers, agents and employees as he may designate or appoint):

(*a*) Generally to administer this Compact.

(*b*) To make rules and regulations for the conduct of business by the Prison Labor Authority, to appoint a secretary and/or any personnel and generally to prescribe such rules, orders and regulations as may be necessary.

(*c*) To formulate uniform cost-finding systems and require the installation of such system or some system comparable therewith.

(*d*) To determine, after conferring with the Code Authority of the industry affected and upon request of any person or firm affected, the prices, charges and amounts provided for in Article V, Sections A and B, hereof; such determination to be subject to appeal to the President of the United States. In establishing fair current prices, charges and amounts, the Prison Labor Authority shall take into consideration all factors necessary to insure the marketing of prison products on a fair competitive basis. It may consider, among other factors, the extent to which monopolistic practices exist in any trade or industry in which the prison industry operates, the degree to which prison products may be discriminated against, the ability of the prison industry to adjust its operations and production to meet changing styles, designs, and/or other conditions beyond its control, and any restrictions placed upon the marketing of prison products. The fair current price may not be such as will effectually prevent the sale of prison products or destroy existing markets, nor shall it permit the sale of prison products at such prices or in such manner or in such quantities as will depress the standards, wages or working conditions of the competing private industry or defeat the purposes sought to be obtained through adherence by a competing private industry to a code of fair competition under the National Industrial Recovery Act.

(*e*) To require such reports and statistics from States signatory hereto as may be necessary to effectuate the policies of this Compact.

(*f*) After an investigation, which shall include a consideration of economic, trade, and market conditions, and under such rules as it may prescribe: (1) formulate such regulations as may be consistent with statutory provisions and as may be necessary to assure a diversification of the output of prison industries in fair proportion to the production of the industries affected, (2) prohibit the expansion of any existing prison industry which bears a disproportionate share of competition.

(*g*) To hear and adjust complaints arising under this Compact made by affected parties: provided, however, that at the time any such complaint is made the complainant must agree to submit such facts and figures as may be necessary to the determination of the issues involved.

(*h*) To hear and adjust complaints arising under this Compact made by prison administrators or prison heads, and call to the attention of the President any unfair trade practices designed to discriminate against prison-made goods or hamper the objective sought in the preamble of this Compact.

ARTICLE VIII

Reports. All States signatory hereto agree to furnish reports to the National Recovery Administration covering data on prison industries which the laws of the United States require from competing private industries under the National Recovery Act.

ARTICLE IX

Authority for Execution. The representatives of the States signatory hereto being in some instances restricted in their action by statutes which cannot immediately be modified, enter into this agreement in their own right and subscribe to it in so far as the laws and regulations of the sovereign States they represent will permit, and they further pledge themselves to coöperate to secure the adoption of such changes in the laws and regulations by the properly constituted authorities as may be necessary to permit them to adhere fully to this compact, but nothing in this compact shall affect one way or another any Federal Act relating to prison-made products or any State Act passed or effective under any such Federal Act, if said Acts are held constitutional and valid. It is specifically understood that by signing this Compact no signatory hereto is thereby estopped from asserting the unconstitutionality or invalidity of any of said Acts.

ARTICLE X

Due to the impracticability of promptly obtaining the execution by all of the signatory States on one document, it is agreed that the signatory States hereto may execute identical copies of this Compact which execution shall be as effective as though all signatory States executed the same document.

ARTICLE XI

The effective date of this Compact shall be January 1, 1934, as to all States which have signed at that time and as to all States signing thereafter it shall take effect as of the date of such signing.

APPROVAL

............, 1933.

The foregoing Compact of Fair Competition for prison industries is hereby approved for and on behalf of the State of .... by ...., its legally constituted authority.

....
Title

APPROVED BY:

....

APPENDIX C

EXECUTIVE ORDER
ESTABLISHMENT OF THE PRISON INDUSTRIES REORGANIZATION ADMINISTRATION

By virtue of and pursuant to the authority vested in me by the Emergency Relief Appropriation Act of 1935, approved April 8, 1935 (Public Resolution No. 11, 74th Congress), I hereby establish an agency within the Government to be known as the "Prison Industries Reorganization Administration."

The governing body of said Prison Industries Reorganization Administration shall be a Prison Industries Reorganization Board consisting of five members to be hereafter appointed by the President and to hold office at his pleasure. The Prison Industries Reorganization Board is hereby authorized to prescribe such rules and regulations and to delegate to its agents and representatives such powers as, in its discretion, it shall deem necessary and proper for the performance of the duties and functions of the Prison Industries Reorganization Administration and for effectuating the purposes of this Order.

I hereby prescribe the following duties and functions of the said Prison Industries Reorganization Administration:

(1) In coöperation with the proper authorities of the several States and the political subdivisions thereof and the District of Columbia:

> (a) To conduct surveys, studies, and investigations of the industrial operations and allied activities carried on by the several penal and correctional institutions of the States and political subdivisions thereof and the District of Columbia, and the actual and potential markets for products of such industrial operations and activities.
>
> (b) To initiate, formulate, and recommend for approval of the President a program of projects with respect to replanning and reorganizing the existing prison industries systems and allied prison activities of the several States and

political subdivisions thereof and the District of Columbia to the end that the industrial operations and activities of such institutions may be so reorganized as to relieve private industry and labor of any undue burden of competition between the products of private industry with the products of such institutions; and to eliminate idleness and to provide an adequate and humane system of rehabilitation for the inmates of such institutions.

(2) To recommend for the approval of the President loans or grants, or both, to the several States and political subdivisions thereof and the District of Columbia necessary to accomplish the purposes of this Order, and to administer and supervise the program of projects approved by the President.

In the performance of such duties and functions the Prison Industries Reorganization Board is hereby authorized to employ the services and means mentioned in subdivision (*a*) of section 3 of the said Emergency Relief Appropriation Act of 1935, to the extent therein provided, and, within the limitations prescribed by said section, to exercise the authority with respect to personnel conferred by subdivision (*b*) thereof.

The acquisition of articles, materials, and supplies for use in carrying out any project authorized by this Executive Order shall be subject to the provisions of Title III of the Treasury and Post Office Appropriation Act, fiscal year 1934 (47 Stat. 1489, 1520).

For administrative expenses of the Prison Industries Reorganization Administration there is hereby allocated to the Administration from the appropriation made by the Emergency Relief Appropriation Act of 1935 the sum of $100,000. Separate allocations will be made hereafter for each of the authorized activities as may be needed.

FRANKLIN D. ROOSEVELT.

THE WHITE HOUSE,
September 26, 1935.

APPENDIX D

EXECUTIVE ORDER
CREATING A BODY CORPORATE TO BE KNOWN AS
FEDERAL PRISON INDUSTRIES, INC.

By virtue of the authority vested in me by the Act of June 23, 1934 (Public No. 461, 73rd Congress), it is hereby ordered that a corporation of the District of Columbia be and is hereby created, said corporation to be named as Federal Prison Industries, Inc.

1. The governing body of said corporation shall consist of a board of five directors to hold office at the pleasure of the President. The following persons shall constitute the first Board of Directors: Mr. Sanford Bates, Mr. Thomas A. Rickert, Hon. John B. Miller, Dr. M. L. Brittain, Mr. Sam A. Lewisohn.

2. The principal office of said corporation shall be in the City of Washington, District of Columbia, but the corporation shall have power and authority to establish such other offices or agencies as it may deem necessary or appropriate.

3. The said corporation shall have power to determine in what manner and to what extent industrial operations shall be carried on in the several penal and correctional institutions of the United States and shall, so far as practicable, so diversify prison industrial operations that no single private industry shall be forced to bear an undue burden of competition with the products of the prison workshops. It shall also have power to do all things it is authorized to do by the said Act of June 23, 1934, and all things incident to or necessary or proper in the exercise of its functions.

4. Pursuant to the provisions of Section 4 of the said Act, the Secretary of the Treasury is directed to transfer to a fund to be known as "The Prison Industries Fund" all balances standing to the credit of the Prison Industries Working Capital Fund on the books of the Treasury, and the corporation is authorized

to employ the aforesaid fund, and any earnings that may hereafter accrue to the corporation, as operating capital.

5. The Attorney General is directed to transfer to the corporation hereby created all personal property, assets, accounts receivable, and equipment of any and every kind now under the jurisdiction of the Industrial Division of the Bureau of Prisons of the Department of Justice.

6. The corporation shall assume all valid claims and obligations now payable out of the Prison Industries Working Capital Fund.

7. Said corporation shall have power to sue and be sued.

8. Any vacancies occurring in the membership of the Board of Directors shall be filled by the President of the United States.

9. The heads of the several executive departments, independent establishments and Government owned and Government controlled corporations shall coöperate with the corporation in carrying out its duties and shall purchase, at not to exceed current market prices, the products or services of said industries, to the extent required or permitted by law.

10. All powers and duties vested in the Attorney General and not specifically transferred to the corporation by said Act of June 23, 1934, or by this Executive Order and assumed by said corporation, shall remain vested in the Attorney General or his duly qualified representatives as heretofore.

FRANKLIN D. ROOSEVELT.

THE WHITE HOUSE,
December 11, 1934.

(No. 6917)

GENERAL INDEX

Administration, 214, 215
Alabama Textile Products Co., 105
Alcatraz, *See* United States Penitentiary
Alternatives to imprisonment, 280, 287
American Federation of Government Employees, 172, 211
American Federation of Labor, 90
American Library Association, 152
American Prison Association, 14, 25, 74, 217, 308
Anthropology, 121
Attorney General's Crime Conference, 1934, 254, 308
Attorney General's Survey of Release Procedures, 264
Auburn system prison architecture, 34, 134

Banishment, 275
"Big shot" in prison, 182
Board of Indeterminate Sentence and Parole for the District of Columbia, 260
Board of Parole, Federal, 254, 255, 262
Body capacity ray, 117
Bolshevo Commune, 276
Books by prisoners and ex-prisoners, 229
British penal statistics, 80, 278, 286, 300
British prison camp, 273
Bureau of the Census statistics, 30, 36, 66, 257, 259, 260, 286, 301

Capital punishment, 296
Causes of crime, 26, 29
Causes of riots, 79–84
Censorship of mail, 224
Central control, 204
Chain gangs, 35
Chaplains, 163
Charge to Grand Jury, 1822, 297

Civilian Conservation Camps, 101
Civil rights, 298
Civil service, 166, 167, 173
Classification committees, 159, 161, 187, 197
Comparative prison population here and abroad, 80, 279, 286
Colonies, penal, 280
Commissaries, prison, 184, 195
Committee on Jails, American Prison Association, 40, 51
Community responsibility for crime, 307
Conditional release, 253
Congress, relations with, 208, 210
Contraband, 188
Convict labor, lease system, 95
Cosmetic surgery, 156
Cost of crime, 26, 28
County jails, 37–62
County rings of Massachusetts, 39
Crime, 27, 30, 307
Crime and Criminals, 82
Crime and Justice, 175, 289
Crime of Punishment, 32, 275
Criminal Law and Social Science, 300
Crucibles of Crime, 37

Declaration of Principles, American Prison Congress, 25, 74, 309
Deer Island Prison, 1
Disciplinary Board, 179
Discipline, 53, 176, 179, 181, 203, 244
Discharged convicts, 247, 248
Drug farms, 287

Early prisons, 32, 33, 35
Education, 67, 68, 149, 153, 160
Elmira Reformatory, 247
Employees organizations, 172, 211
Equality of treatment, 182, 183
Escapes, 191, 192, 200, 203, 271, 272
Essays by prisoners, 191, 192, 218

NAME INDEX